100 Movie Posters

100 Movie Posters
The Essential Collection

Tony Nourmand
Introduced by Christopher Frayling

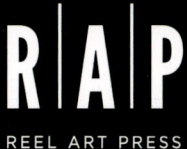

Reel Art Press

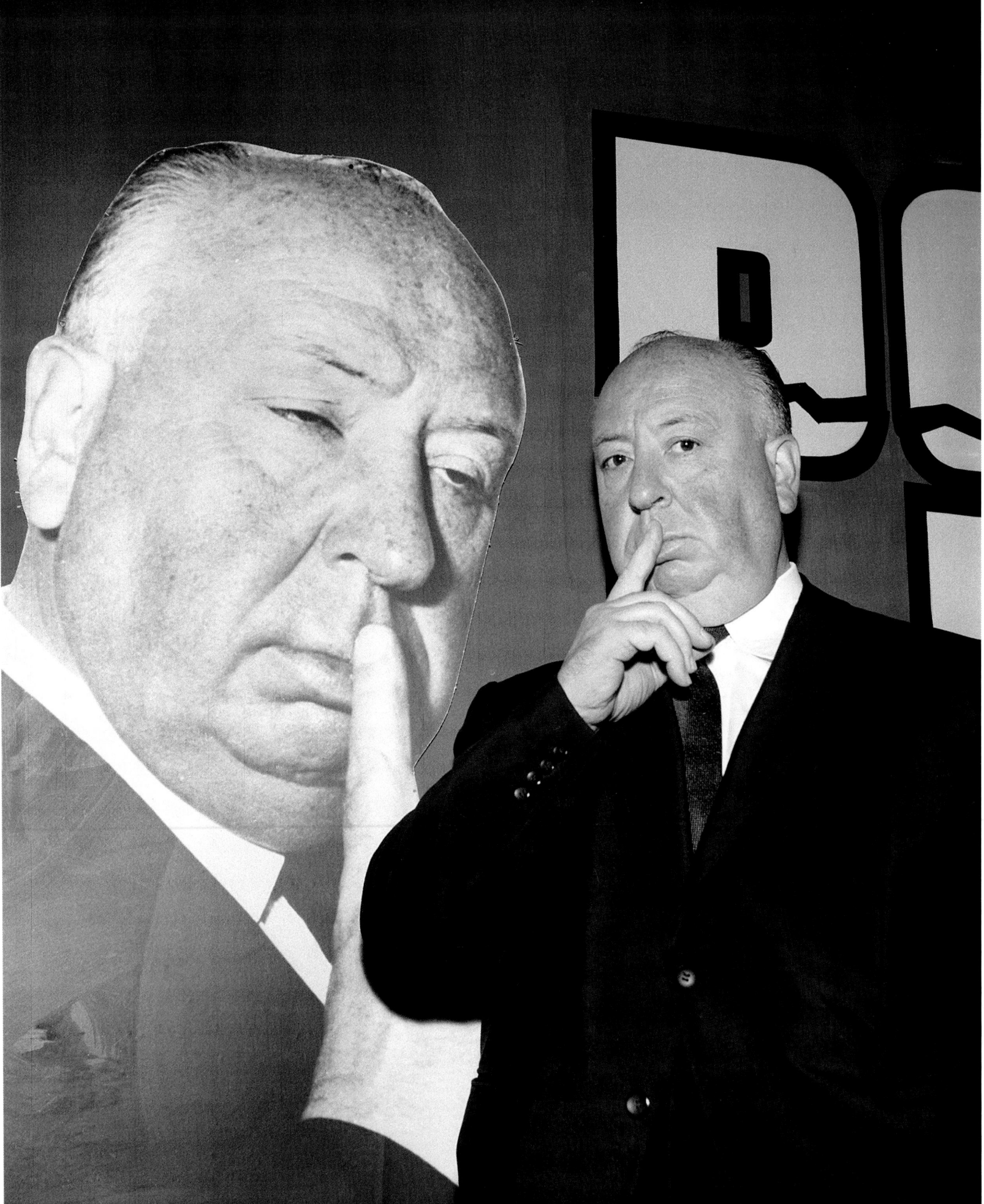

EDITED BY: **TONY NOURMAND**

INTRODUCED BY: **CHRISTOPHER FRAYLING**

TEXT BY: **TONY NOURMAND & ALISON ELANGASINGHE**

ART DIRECTION AND DESIGN BY: **GRAHAM MARSH**

LAYOUT BY: **JOAKIM OLSSON**

Contents

Introduction 9

The Essential Collection 13

100 Movie Posters 19

Appendix 218

Indexes 222

Acknowledgements 223

Bibliography 223

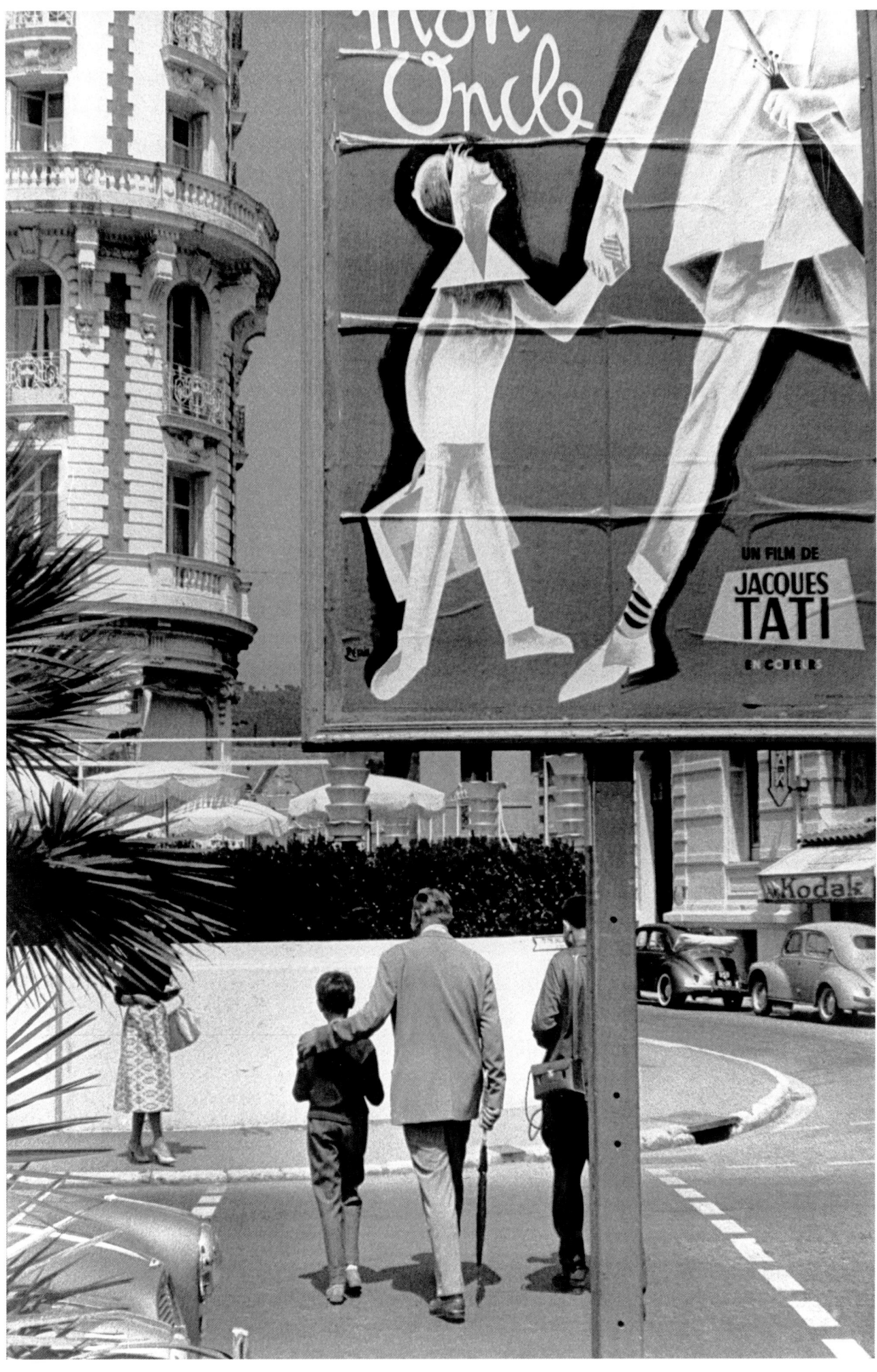

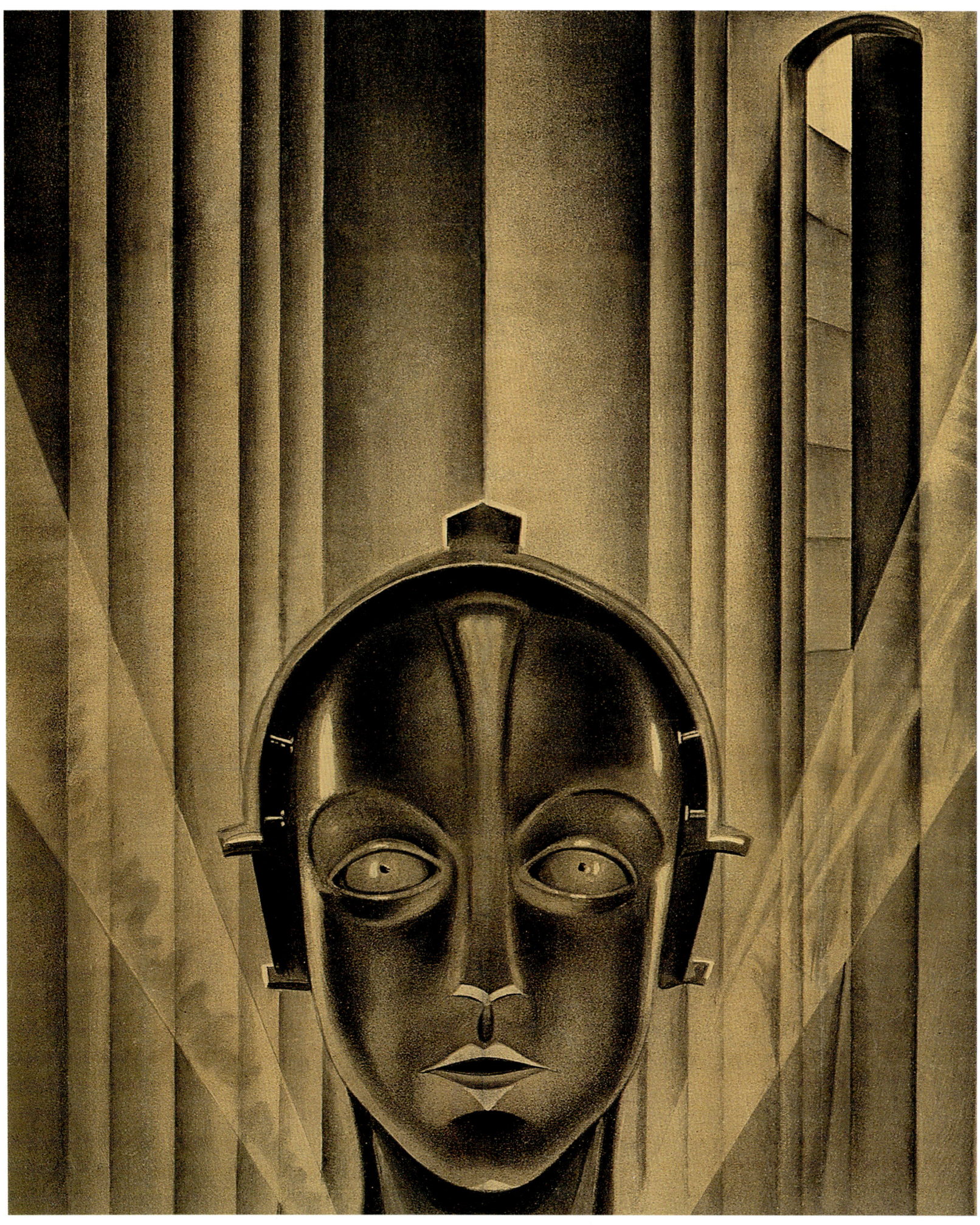

INTRODUCTION

The subtitle of *100 Movie Posters: The Essential Collection* is well chosen, because it has been *collectors* rather than historians or curators who have, since the 1960s, done most to draw public attention to the importance of this particular area of graphic design. There are many reasons for this, some of them buried deep in the culture.

First, there has been the suspicion of the word 'advertising' among specialists who write about or exhibit graphic design and typography. Graphic design, we are told, is about pure forms of communication – about *formal* elements, rather than about selling a product. And on the spectrum of 'art ... advertising', movie posters have been thought to incline too far towards the marketing end – heirs to the same carnival tradition as produced Barnum-hucksters in the nineteenth century, promising far more than they could possibly deliver. Roll up! Roll up to see the Bearded Lady! Stephen King tells the amusing story of two tough movie-producers, kings of the late-nite, low-budget market in the 1950s, who had a simple pre-production formula: think up a catchy title, trawl interest in it, then produce an even more catchy poster – with horror-comic imagery and a lot of exclamation marks – trawl interest in that, and only then – if there was enough take-up – begin to think seriously about making the movie, which might or might not resemble the publicity. Title first, poster second, movie third. Historians of graphic design have tended to think – wrongly – that all movie posters function in this way or something like it, with ad-men or rather mad-men behind them, and the thought scares them off.

Then, there's the aesthetic preference of the 'live arts' – theatre, performance, dance, music, opera – over the experience of film. This is about cultural hierarchies. Exhibitions about 'the art of the poster' at major national museums have foregrounded posters for plays, ballet and contemporary dance, concerts (classical and rock) and even zoos rather than films. Toulouse-Lautrec may have designed lithographic posters for a music hall in Montmartre from 1891 onwards – but ... *films*? And *Hollywood*? The movie posters which *have* been granted admission to the pantheon have usually been those which chime with the 'isms' of modern art history, the ones which can be placed on an already-familiar pedestal. The pedestals are called German Expressionism, Soviet Constructivism, Surrealism and American Modernism (notably Saul Bass's work for Otto Preminger and Alfred Hitchcock, with its stripped-down graphic symbols serving as a summary of the films' plots). And that's about it: so reassuring to find validation in the world of art rather than in the world of film. Of course, many movie posters *have* fed off past and present art movements; it is equally true that many have not. Historians and curators have preferred their individual design heroes and heroines (nearly always heroes) to sign their work; they have been less keen on agencies or in-house offices which bring together the talents of various creative people including illustrators, typographers, graphic designers and copy-writers under the watchful eye of an art director. As with film itself, in such a team process, who in the end is the 'author'? The preferred heroes in the design pantheon are embedded in a social milieu made up of art movements, journals, institutions, exhibitions, critics, congresses and conferences, manifestos and catalogues, and public collections. It makes them so much easier to study and to 'place'. Professional designers of movie posters on the whole belong to a very different social milieu, and in any case they are far too busy working on the next project to have time for learned discussions about the design principles embedded in the last one.

The result of all of this – and more – is that movie posters remain 'an under-appreciated thing' (in Clint Eastwood's observation about the posters of Bill Gold). Not among collectors, though. The highest record price ever achieved by a poster *for any purpose* was an original *Metropolis* piece of 1927. This was three times the highest price ever paid up until then for a Toulouse-Lautrec poster. Posters for some cult movies are worth more than your apartment. In the collector world, museum-style assumptions have morphed since the 1960s into much broader standards of value – mainly to do with design, but also with movie associations, a material relic of an emotional experience, a visual takeaway from a significant film; with street art and social history as much as cinematic imagery; and with accidental scarcity rather than deliberately limited art editions.

Where design is concerned, collectors have long since moved on from the 'isms' of art history to the kinds of criteria adopted by the *Hollywood Reporter* when judging the annual 'Key Art' awards in 'this specialised form of advertising':

DESIGN EXCELLENCE (IMAGERY / TYPOGRAPHY / LAYOUT)
EYE-APPEAL
CREATIVE APPRECIATION OF COMMERCIAL GOALS
FIDELITY TO THE FILM'S STORYLINE
ARRESTING COPY, ENHANCING THE VISUAL MESSAGE

Collectors have had no illusions about the fact that movie posters are about *selling*, part of distribution as much as – if not more than – production, and usually an element in a graphic package which may even include the film's credit titles: about marketing, as well as being an integral part of a movie's afterlife. Movie posters sell an *experience* rather than a product, by drawing attention to it, but their purpose is still to sell. In the collectors' world, the repressed has not only returned, it is *celebrated*. The art establishment has not been as quick on the uptake where this is concerned.

I once had the opportunity to discuss questions of 'high' and 'low', and in particular why movie posters tend to be under-appreciated, with Saul Bass at an Aspen Colorado design gathering, in the mid-1980s. His view was that the *only* issue which should count was whether or not the poster is an example of 'good design' – meaning not only the formal elements (though these of course play a key role), but also whether the design does its job well, is effective – interesting, challenging, questioning, involving or witty, depending on the campaign – and whether it distils the message in a direct, readable way. The kinds of poster we were discussing, he added, existed at the meeting-point of art, design and commerce, and there was no point in ignoring that. I agreed with him, and I still do.

Tony Nourmand has for the last 30 years or so been championing the importance of the movie poster – as design, as archive, as investment, as memory, as collectible, as fun. He has tracked down, like a cinematic truffle-hound, the names of designers and other visual contributors in an area beset by anonymity. He understands the importance of print quality, the size of the poster, and the edition. He has, through his numerous books and catalogues, enhanced and deepened our understanding of movie posters in ways that are appropriate to the subject. He has shown why some posters take on a life of their own, while many others do not. Who better, then, to present *100 Movie Posters* – from the silent era to *2001*; from Hollywood to Babelsberg to Cinecitta, to Pinewood, and beyond; from Saul Bass classics to Italian watercolours of the early 1960s to a woodblock for London's Academy cinema to New Wave collages and back to cult films such as *King Kong*, *Casablanca* and *A Fistful of Dollars*. Nourmand has the eye, the persistence, the enthusiasm and the experience to select a 'hundred best' that actually means something, unlike most lists of hundred bests. What is so sad, is the decline in quality from images such as the ones in this book to the digital, DVD, download era; bland movie posters are increasingly part of bland, global marketing campaigns, with graphic devices which are re-usable in a variety of formats for a variety of territories: they have in the process lost much of their distinctive identity.

All the more reason to savour this 'essential collection'.

Enjoy yourself, it's later than you think…

Christopher Frayling
February 2013

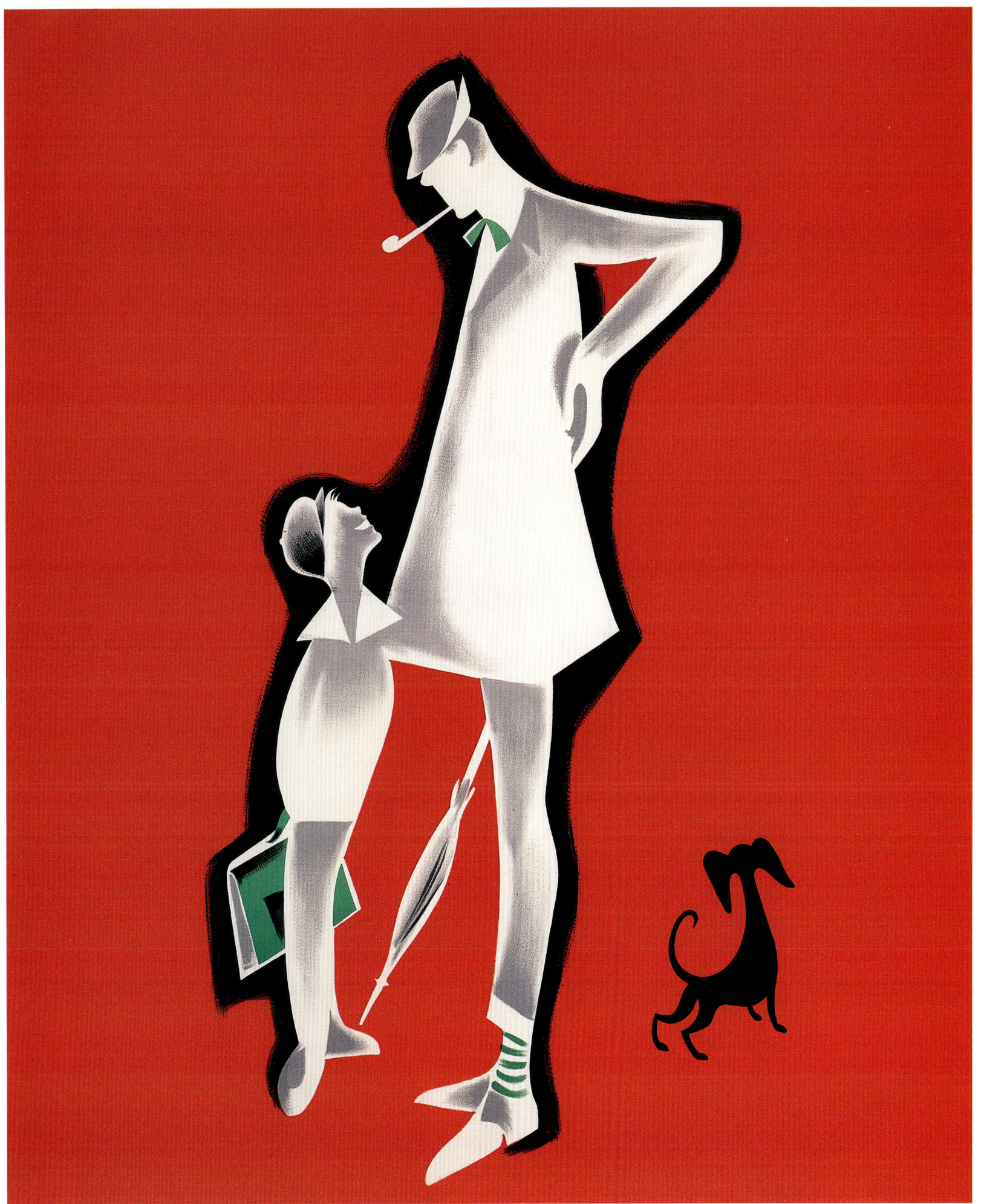

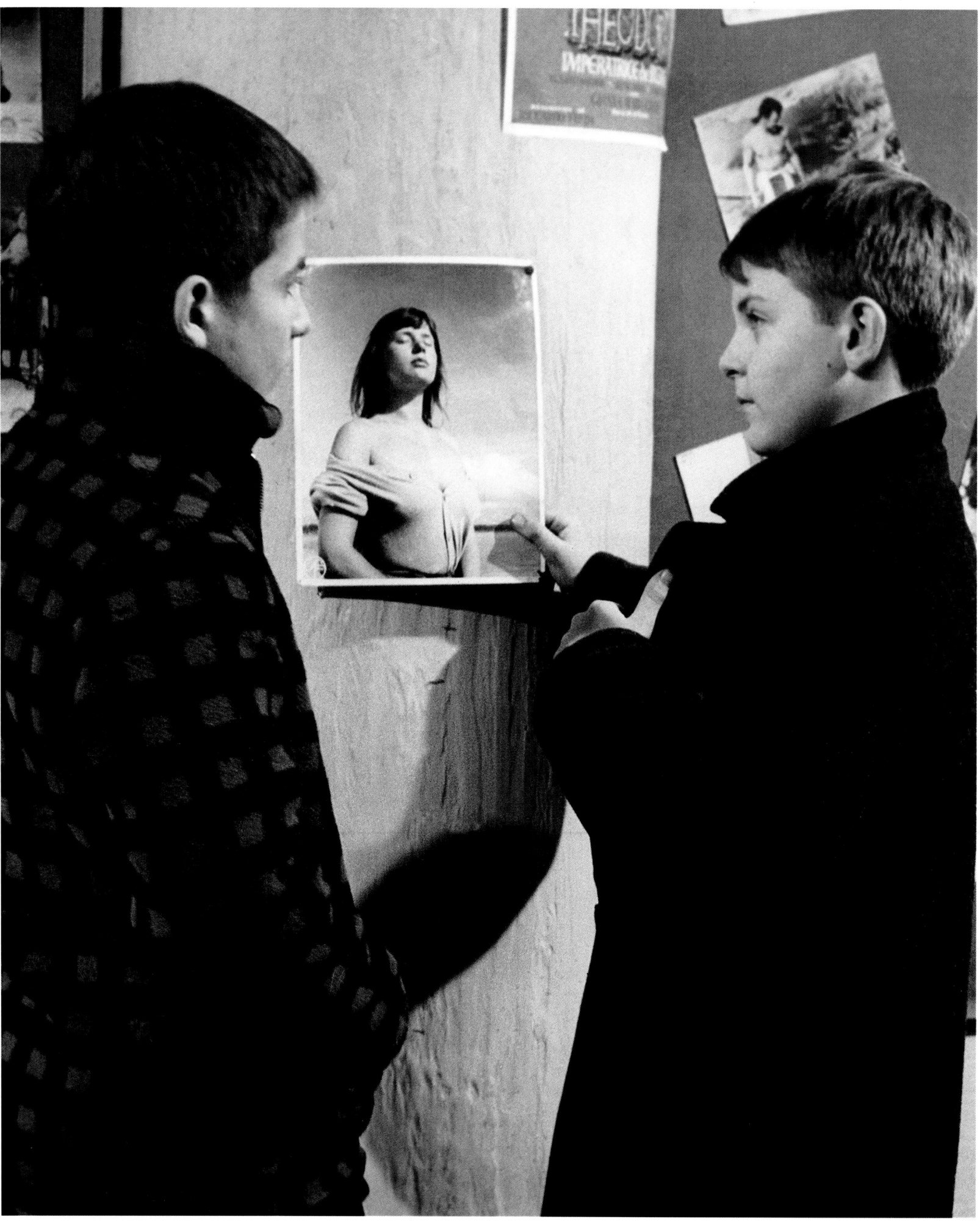

The Essential Collection

One of the things I love about movie posters is that they are so immediate. And that immediacy is an intrinsic part of their mass appeal. It is often said that music is the most immediate art and I have always felt the same about movie posters: they are all around us – in the street, on the underground – and we interact and 'listen' to them unconsciously. When we actively choose to stand in front of a poster, the average man or woman can also rarely fail to have a reaction to it. Perhaps nostalgia for our favourite film, or remembering the first time we saw *Breakfast at Tiffany's* with our partner. Perhaps an aesthetic appreciation for the creative way an artist has managed to capture the essence of a film in an abstract design. Movie posters communicate to us, and we do not need to be an art scholar or part of the cultural elite to appreciate them. Many images that are now an iconic part of the language of popular culture – Audrey Hepburn in a long black dress, King Kong on top of the Empire State Building – were introduced to the public for the very first time via the medium of the movie poster. In 1995, after the first ever Christie's, London, film poster auction, the renowned film critic Philip French wrote an article about the sale. In it, he said that movie posters were to the twentieth century what stamps were to the nineteenth century. I always loved that comparison. Both are a functional means of communication, yet also a creative vehicle for artistic expression.

Having an immediate reaction to a poster, however, is not necessarily the same thing as liking it. For me, the crucial element in a great or 'essential' movie poster is always the artwork. Sometimes the design succeeds despite the film it represents – like the poster for a lost film such as *Hollywood* (1923) or an unwatchable exploitation flick like *Acid – delirio dei sensi* (1968). Better yet is when a great design meets a great film – such as the Italian poster for *La Dolce Vita* (1960) or the American poster for *2001: A Space Odyssey* (1968).

I have loved movie posters and the cinema from a very young age. As a small boy in Tehran, my uncle used to take me to the local cinema every week. My uncle was one of those characters – or so it seemed to me then – who knew everyone, including the owner of the cinema, who would allow us to sit on the balcony to watch the weekly screenings. After the credits rolled, we would be invited into a back room that housed piles of posters. While my uncle drank tea and chatted to friends, I would be given a precious film poster of that week's release. I would carry it carefully home and lovingly tape it to my bedroom wall, only to take it down and replace it with a fresh poster the following week. For a special treat, my uncle would sometimes take me to the central repertory cinema that showed two screenings back-to-back – slightly older films like *Goldfinger*, *The Great Escape* and *Charade*. These cinema trips were always the highlight of my week, looked forward to with wide-eyed wonder.

When I moved to England in the mid-1970s, I continued to spend all my spare time at 'the flicks'. During my teens, the BBC had a season on Sunday evenings that would showcase films from the new American Brat Pack directors – movies like *Five Easy Pieces* and *Badlands*. I remember being overwhelmed at the multi-layered filmmaking and I had never seen anything like it. *Badlands* is one of those films that changed me and I was not the same person afterwards. I decided to study film at art school and would fill my evenings by going to the Everyman Cinema in Hampstead or the National Film Theatre on the Southbank and watching whole seasons of noir or other Hollywood classics, always checking out the old movie posters being displayed in the lobby to advertise the release.

The first movie poster I ever bought was in 1979 from a shop in Soho. It was the British poster for *Apocalypse Now*, which I had just seen at the cinema. I had also recently seen a picture of a great poster for *Chinatown* in an article but when I asked the shop about it, they had no idea what I was talking about. A few years later, I discovered a listing in the back of an American film magazine for companies that sold vintage movie posters. I called every one on the list, but no one had any idea about *Chinatown*. Finally I got through to Jose Ma Carpio at Cinemonde in San Francisco, which at that time was something of a mecca for movie poster collectors. Jose immediately knew the poster I was trying to describe. We started chatting and he explained that the *Chinatown* I was after featured artwork by Richard Amsel but that it was only ever used on the German and Australian posters and he could get me one if I was interested. Our conversation continued and he told me that he had original posters for *Sunset Boulevard* and *Casablanca*, which at the time were selling for a couple of hundred dollars. I had no money, yet was so excited by the idea of owning real film posters that I applied for my first ever credit card and started buying from Jose. Over the years to come, he would become a close friend and a never-ending font of knowledge. I am forever indebted to him for what I know today, and how I think about movie posters.

Around this time, I was in a sandwich shop with my friend, Philip. One of Philip's acquaintances came in and before I knew it the conversation had turned to movie posters and I had somehow sold him an original American poster for *Breakfast at Tiffany's*, which I had recently bought from Jose. Philip suggested we should do more of this, so I called Jose, bought another copy and this time managed to sell it directly to Tiffany & Co. I slowly started to develop a bit of a reputation for being able to track down posters. I began making weekly calls to Jose, maxing out my credit card and selling posters on. I was a student trying to make art films and these *ad hoc* movie poster deals are what kept me afloat.

Then, in the late-1980s, two significant events took place. In 1988, Stephen Rebello and Richard Allen published their coffee-table tome, *Reel Art: Great Posters from the Golden Age of the Silver Screen* (Abbeville, 1988). Not only did it feature hundreds of pages of movie poster imagery, it was also a source of immense, previously unpublished knowledge on the history and development of movie posters. A year later, in 1989, Christie's auction house in New York held their first ever dedicated movie poster sale with a dealer called Bruce Hershenson. Final prices realized rolled into the tens of thousands of dollars. The reappraisal of movie posters as an important twentieth century collectable – appreciated for their artwork, rarity and commercial value – had begun.

Just a few months after the Christie's sale in New York, I had a call from Carey Wallace, the head of the Rock and Pop department at Christie's in London, who had been given my name by Ira M. Resnick at the Motion Picture Arts Gallery in New York. Christie's were auctioning off film historian John Kobal's estate. Included in the inventory were around 2000 movie posters and lobby cards that needed cataloguing and valuing and Carey wondered if I could help. At this point, I was still failing to make art films and was officially unemployed, so I readily agreed. I nervously turned up at the warehouse with one of the old movie poster price guides tucked under my coat. As I began slowly going through the stock, however, I found that my extensive knowledge of film, my amateur dealings up to that point and the informal network of movie poster collectors that I could call upon for advice meant that cataloguing and valuing the collection began to make a logical kind of sense. It was such a thrill to handle such fantastic material and to adopt an appropriate cataloguing system.

The sale proved a great success and I continued to advise Christie's on a few individual items over the next few years. In 1995, Carey officially approached me again regarding an auction Christie's were holding to celebrate 100 Years of Cinema. The nucleus of the sale was singer Mel Tormé's American movie poster collection, with additional posters added by several of the collectors I knew worldwide. *Vintage Film Posters including The Mel Tormé Collection* was held at Christie's on 9 March 1995, the first dedicated film poster sale by a major European auction house. Twelve of the posters in this 'essentials' list were in that original sale, including the Italian poster for *To Have and Have Not* and the American *Cabin in the Sky*. The auction did extremely well and it was standing room only. It proved such a success that Christie's established bi-annual auctions exclusively dedicated to film posters. I also became Christie's official consultant for Vintage Film Posters from 1995 until 2007, when I stepped down.

After the success of the Mel Tormé sale, Bruce Marchant, a school friend of mine who I had sold a few posters to, suggested we should open a shop specializing in original vintage film posters. All other poster outlets I had ever been to were usually musty dark shops with piles of folded posters covering every available surface. We wanted to approach the business differently and present the posters in the setting they deserved – in a white gallery space with a few select posters framed on the walls, chosen purely on the aesthetic quality of their design. Inspired by Rebello and Allen's definitive book, we called our new business The Reel Poster Gallery. We rented a small space on the first floor of Great Marlborough Street in Soho on a two and a half years' lease. We had no money, no clients and were unsure if we even had a market. Fortunately, the general public were as excited and intrigued by the new market in movie posters as we were, and our business did extremely well. At the end of our lease, we were able to move to bigger, ground-floor premises in West London's Westbourne Grove, where we stayed for the next 13 years.

In addition to presenting the posters as art, I also believed in the importance of research and archiving. The gallery began printing catalogues, with each poster researched as thoroughly as possible; not always easy in a field where in-house studio artists did not sign their work and where there were many different poster styles or releases made for the same film. My years at The Reel Poster Gallery were an exciting time for me, discovering, documenting and preserving movie posters and helping to form and curate high-end collections for individuals and institutions. One of the highlights was curating *Cinema Posters of the Twentieth Century* in 2001, the first international exhibition solely dedicated to film posters. This exhibition ran for three months at the Suntory Museum in Osaka, Japan, and toured to the newly opened Toppan Printing Museum in Tokyo and the Obihiro Museum in Hokkaido. We also had an opportunity in 2004 to collaborate with the Design Museum in London on their renowned exhibition of work by the late designer Saul Bass, which was an interesting and rewarding time. I am not a wealthy man and part of the pleasure in dealing in movie posters was being able to advise on, handle and display some of the most stunning and valuable posters in the world. I might not have been able to afford a French *Casablanca* or an American *Frankenstein* poster but I could live with it for a few weeks, research it and then find it a suitable new home.

In the mid-1990s, I was a frequent visitor to Ray's Jazz Shop in Shaftesbury Avenue with my friend, Farhad, a jazz enthusiast. A guy called Glyn Callingham was one of the managers at Ray's. He had produced a popular book on jazz album covers with a designer called Graham Marsh a few years previously, *The Cover Art of Blue Note Records* (Collins & Brown, 1991), and he suggested I do a book on movie posters. Glyn and Graham were releasing a follow-up, *The Cover Art of Blue Note Records: Volume 2*, and I was invited to the book launch. I got chatting to Graham and he asked if I would ever consider doing a series of books on movie posters. I said I had absolutely no knowledge of how to put a book together and he told me not to worry because he did. A conversation came back to me from the press calls I had taken during the 1995 Christie's sale. I had been speaking to the author and journalist Gabriele Pantucci and after discussing the auction, we had got chatting about Italian film and food. I told him I had sold a poster for *Rome, Open City* and he told me his father was one of the financiers on the film. Gabriele was also a publisher and at the end of our conversation he told me that if I ever wanted to do a book on film posters, I was to give him a call. After meeting Graham, I went home and dug out Gabriele's contact details. Within six weeks, he had found two publishers interested in doing books with Graham

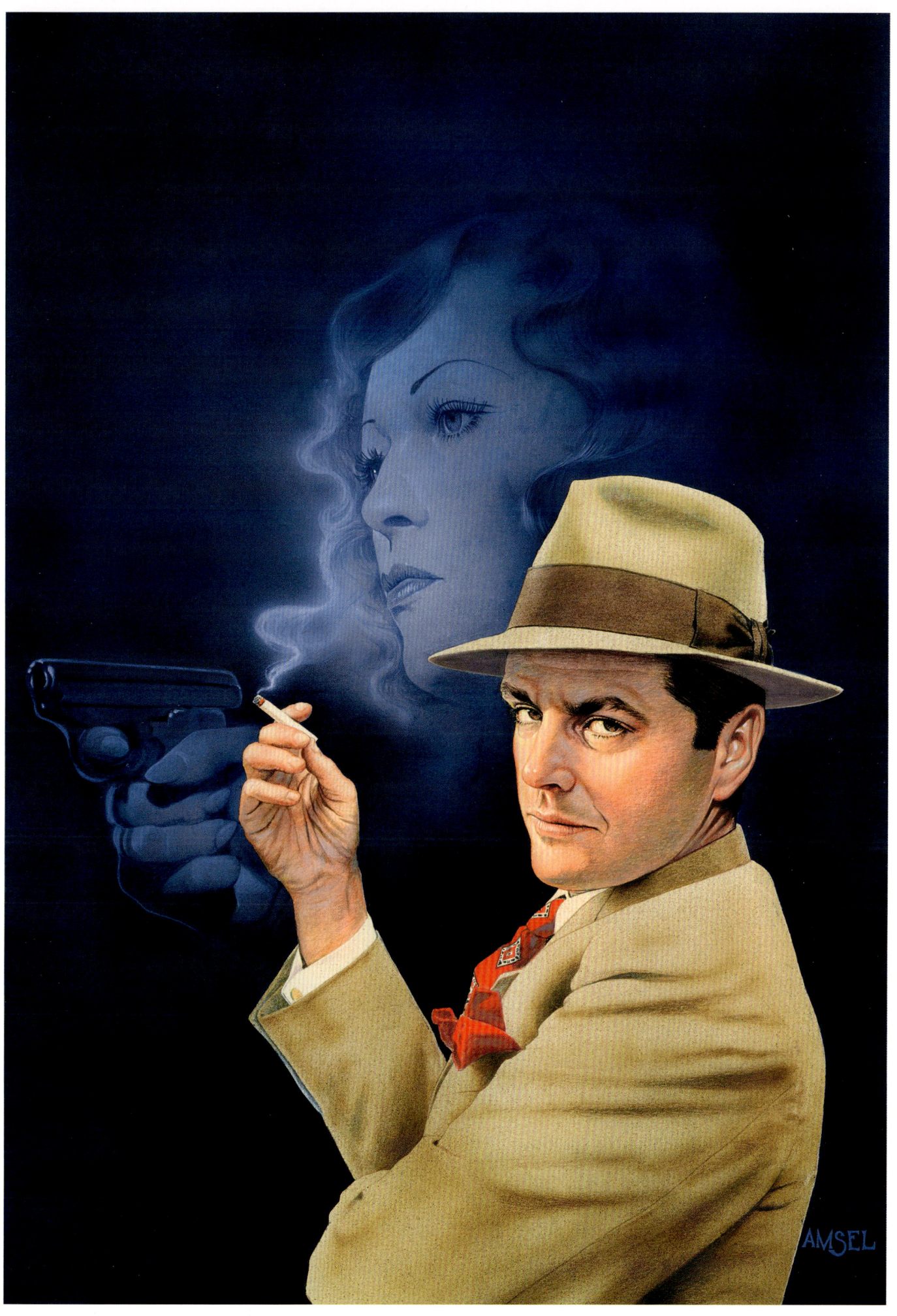

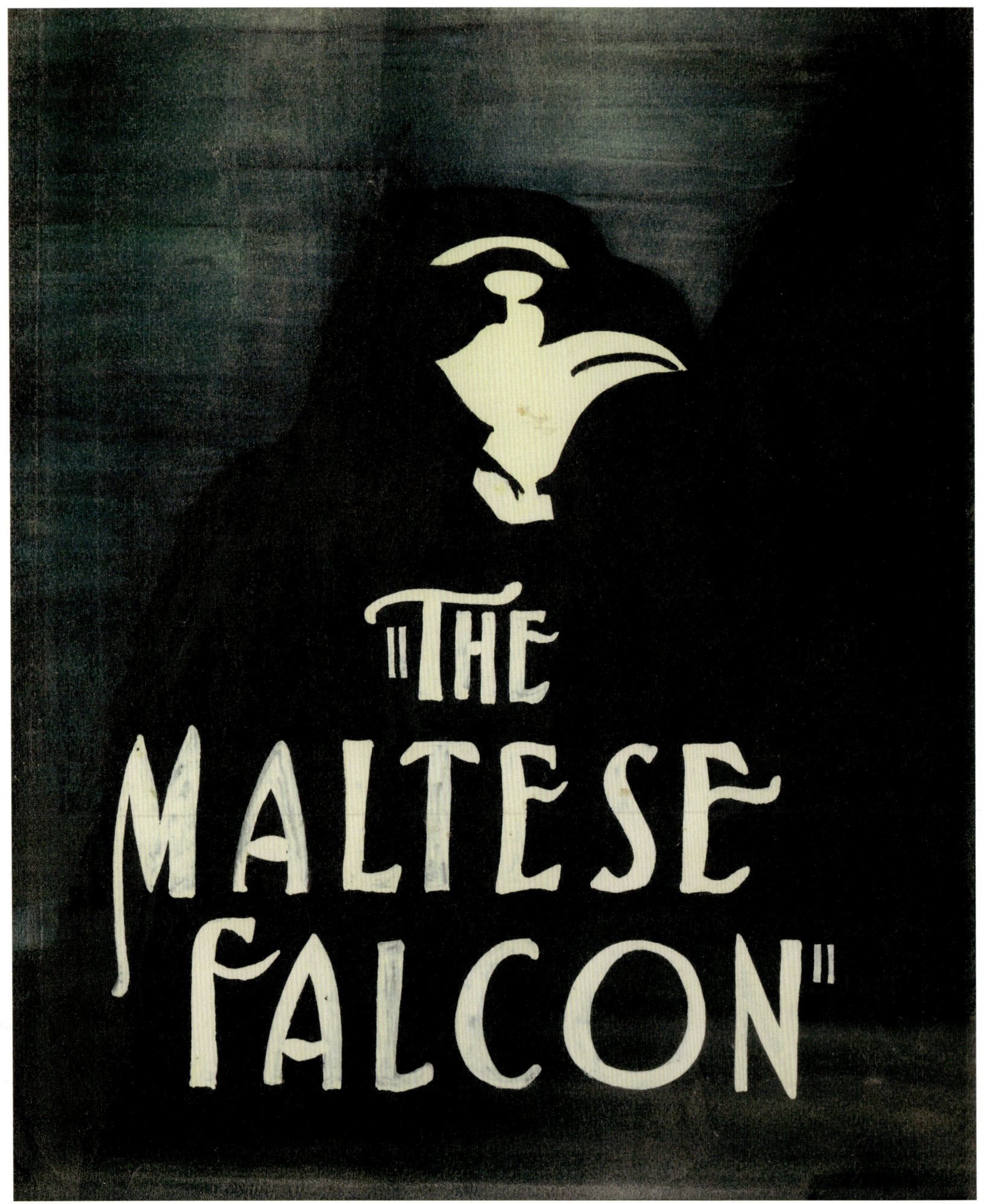

and I – one of which was Aurum Press. After meeting with Aurum, we agreed to do our first book, *Film Posters of the 60s*. At this point, Gabriele asked if he could pass us on to his wife, Leslie Gardner, who was a book agent. Since that first contract with Aurum, Leslie has been involved in every single book I have ever produced and I could not have asked for a better agent. She is dedicated, fierce, ruthlessly intelligent and always on my side. After *Film Posters of the 60s* turned into a bestseller, Aurum gave Graham and I carte-blanche to produce at least one book a year of our choice for the next several years. We eventually produced 11 books with Aurum and several with other publishers, including the worldwide bestsellers *James Bond Movie Posters* and *Audrey Hepburn: The Paramount Years*.

A few years ago I embarked on a book project that was to change my life. In 2009, I was introduced to a designer called Bill Gold. Bill is the most important and prolific movie poster designer of the twentieth century, responsible for over 2000 film campaigns from *Casablanca* to *Mystic River*. His archive included thousands of iconic movie posters, unseen designs, alternative versions, sketches, drafts, notes, photographs and diaries. All of this incredible history had never been accessible to the public. I realized that only a significant book publication could begin to do Bill's work justice, so I set up a new publishing company, Reel Art Press, in order to produce the book to the quality and level I wanted. The resulting limited edition opus, *Bill Gold: PosterWorks*, featured 450 pages of glorious illustrations with a foreword by Clint Eastwood and accompanying text by Christopher Frayling. It was a magnificent publication and opened the doors to working on other book projects, including the limited edition *The Rat Pack*, featuring over 85 per cent unseen photography. Reel Art Press now produces around seven books a year, each with an emphasis on high production values and stunning, mostly unseen, photography.

Establishing Reel Art Press meant leaving The Reel Poster Gallery completely in 2010. Leaving has also allowed me the time to focus on what I love best – creating beautiful publications, forming collections, curating and consulting privately. Despite leaving my gallery years behind me, I have not lost any of my enthusiasm for movie posters, which has ultimately led to the publication of this book. During my years as a full-time dealer, people would always ask me, 'What is your favourite poster?' This was a very difficult question for me to answer and would depend on my mood or what I was most excited about that week, month or year. I would sometimes skirt the question entirely by discussing my favourite original artwork instead – the painting for *Chinatown* by Richard Amsel that I had first fallen in love with all those years ago. Celebrated American designer Merv Bloch hired Amsel to do the artwork for the main campaign, but it was never used – only badly reproduced on the German and Australian posters, which fail to do the piece justice, and with a font that was never quite right. In 1991, the original painting by Amsel turned up at an auction in New York. I bid and bought it despite having no money. Over the next six months, I slowly sold all of my collection in order to buy it. It remains my favourite artwork for my favourite film.

This book, then, is an attempt to finally give a more direct and thorough answer to that question, 'What is my favourite poster?' It has been a much harder task than I had anticipated. Even as we go to press, I cannot say with 100 per cent certainty that this is my definitive list and there are inevitably several posters that I am sad to have not been able to include. This selection is *not* based on The 100 Best, The 100 Rarest or The 100 Most Expensive. It is not based on posters for the 100 Best Films Ever Made. There are many important films missing from this list, including *Citizen Kane, Gone With the Wind* and *The Wizard of Oz*. There are whole genres missing, such as musicals and war films. There are also no posters for films from some of my favourite directors, like Martin Scorsese, Terrence Malick, Francis Ford Coppola and Nicholas Ray. That is not what this book is about.

The Essential Collection is very much my own idiosyncratic selection. It is based on personal taste and what I would like to have hanging on my wall; on what I believe are the most effective posters in terms of design and impact. The vast majority are original release posters, but there are a couple of re-releases thrown in. Occasionally, the original just doesn't get it quite right. A good example is the original American release poster for *The Maltese Falcon*, which is a mess. It uses an old photo of Bogie as 'Mad Dog' Earle in *High Sierra* and a tagline – *A story as explosive as his blazing automatics!* – that has absolutely nothing to do with the movie. Original release posters for *The Maltese Falcon* from other countries also fail to do the film justice. The only design that has ever been a worthy representation of the film is a poster designed in-house for Warner Bros executives on the fiftieth anniversary of the film's release. I have included the artwork opposite to illustrate what the original should and could have been had more foresight gone into the design.

As I look through these pages, I realize that there is a preponderance of guns, drugs, gorillas and dames and I don't know, and would hate to think, what a psychiatrist would make of this selection. What I do know is that for months, perhaps years, after this book is published, I will wake up in the middle of the night thinking, 'Why didn't I include *that* poster or *this* poster?' Because it never ends and the list is never complete. At the very least, this book is an attempt to begin to answer the question. So, after several years of prevaricating, here, finally, are 100 of my favourite posters. My 100 essentials.

Tony Nourmand
March 2013

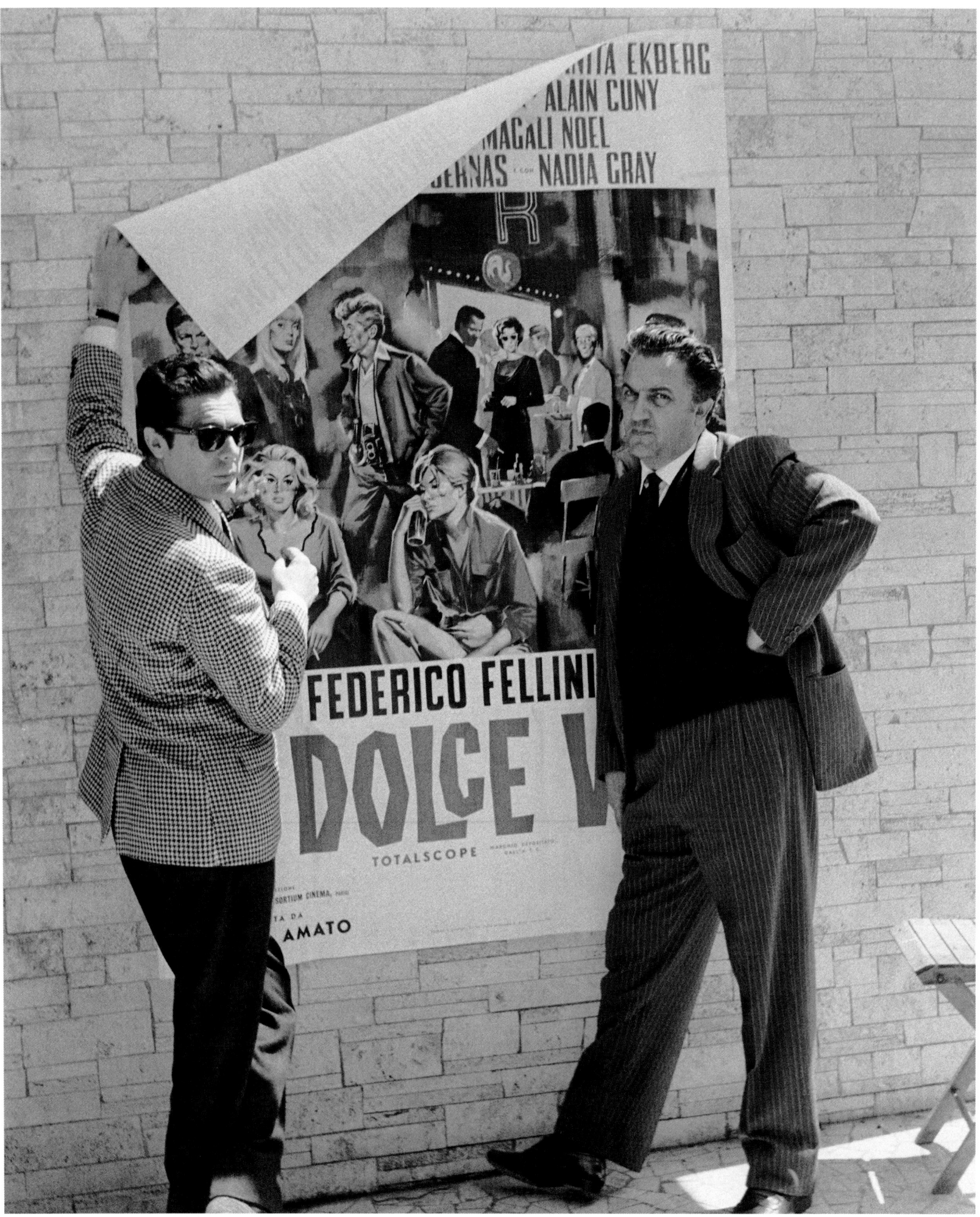

100 Movie Posters

LE AVVENTURE STRAORDINARISSIME DI SATURNINO FARANDOLA 1913
ITALIAN POSTER, ART BY ALBERT ROBIDA

Frenchman Albert Robida (1848-1926) was an illustrator, caricaturist and novelist. A contemporary of Jules Verne, Robida had an extraordinary ability to convey – both in illustration and prose – extravagant, and often prophetic, visions of the future.

Between the 1870s and the 1890s, Robida wrote a series of popular futuristic novels and also illustrated for the popular French weekly serial, *La Guerre Infernale*. He predicted many twentieth century advances with an uncanny accuracy. One of his works from 1883 imagines a television reporter in 1963 covering a guerrilla war in North Africa, which is simultaneously watched by a family thousands of miles away on a full-colour, wall-mounted display in their living room. Many of his visions involved the future of warfare and conflict and as *Life* magazine commented in 1942, 'Robida foretold ... what the flowering of the machine age would mean to the arts of war.'

Based on one of Robida's own fictional novels from 1879, *Le avventure straordinarissime di Saturnino Farandola* was an Italian silent film directed by Marcel Fabre. It is one of the earliest cinematic examples of 'science fiction' and is a tale of adventure in the known and unknown worlds on land, sea and under the sea. Robida's remarkable poster artwork for the Italian release of the film imagines chemical and underwater warfare and is characteristic of Robida's ability to combine insight with a fantastical wicked wit. Only one copy of this poster is known to exist.

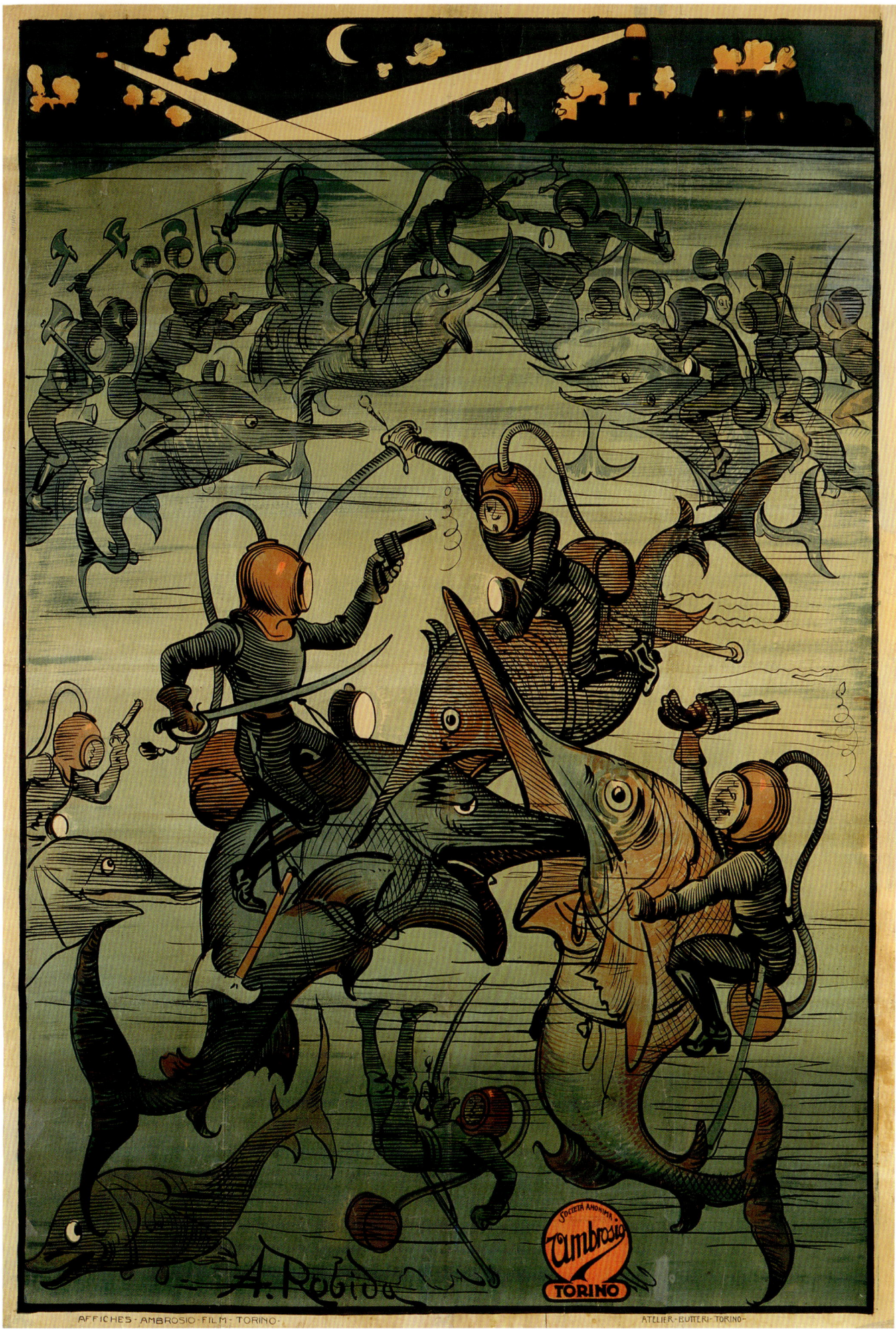

LES VAMPIRES 1916
FRENCH POSTER, ART BY ACHILLE LUCIEN MAUZAN

Louis Feuillade is considered the father of movie serials. His critically acclaimed work in the genre is often seen as a forerunner of the experimental films of Luis Buñuel and Alain Resnais and of the crime thrillers of Fritz Lang and Alfred Hitchcock. Feuillade was director of Gaumont Studios between 1907 and 1925, directing over 800 films and establishing Gaumont as one of the biggest studios in France. He remains most famous for his trilogy of silent crime serials, *Fantômas* (1913), *Les Vampires* (1915) and *Judex* (1916).

Les Vampires was formed of ten episodes of differing lengths, which were shown in France between November 1915 and June 1916. If seen in its entirety, it is one of the longest films ever made at six and a half hours. It starred the beautiful acrobat Musidora in her iconic black bodysuit as 'Irma Vep' – an original 'vamp' character and leader of a criminal gang of the same name as the serial's title, 'The Vampires'. The serial was criticised for its glorification of violence and was nearly banned by the police until a personal public appeal by Musidora.

Musidora was also the focus of artist Achille Lucien Mauzan's poster for the serial. Achille Lucien Mauzan (1883-1952) was a serious painter, sculptor and poster artist. Born in France, he studied art in Lyon before moving to Italy in his early twenties. He became a successful poster designer, particularly in the field of advertising. In 1924, he set up his own publishing house in Milan, Mauzan-Morzenti, and in 1926 he set up a second publishing house in Argentina, Affiches Mauzan. He produced over 2000 posters, which were noted for their humour and bright colours.

BLIND HUSBANDS 1919

AMERICAN POSTER, ARTIST UNKNOWN

Erich von Stroheim was one of the greatest directors of the silent era, frequently cited as one of cinema's earliest 'auteurs'. *Blind Husbands* was his accomplished directorial debut and it bears the hallmarks of the epic realism and grand cynicism that would characterise his later work. It received rave reviews on its release, with *The New York Times* commenting that, 'If the promise that is borne of his first performance as a director is fulfilled, the screen will be greatly enriched.' *Variety* was more emphatic, exclaiming, 'This picture is exceptional. It marks an epoch.'

This 'window card' poster for the film is one of the most art deco and unusual American posters of the period. At the time, it was cheaper to print in just two or three colours, however, on this occasion, such budget constraints only add to the impact of the design. The curve and multiplicity of the disembodied heads are also suggestive of the Dolomites mountain range – a key location in the film's climax between the central characters. The film had actually originally been titled *The Pinnacle* and, according to *The New York Times*, Stroheim strongly objected to the 'cheapening title' of *Blind Husbands*.

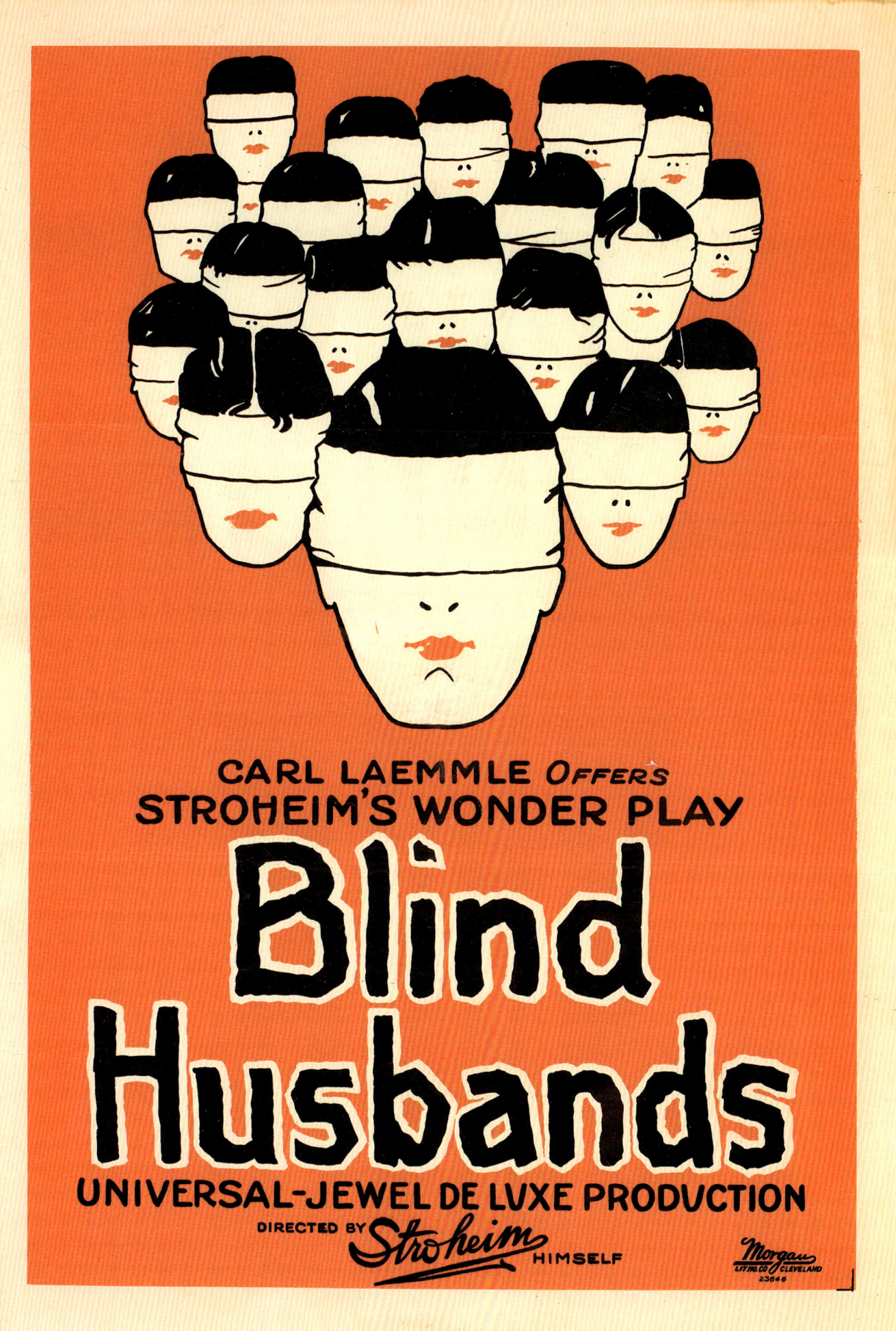

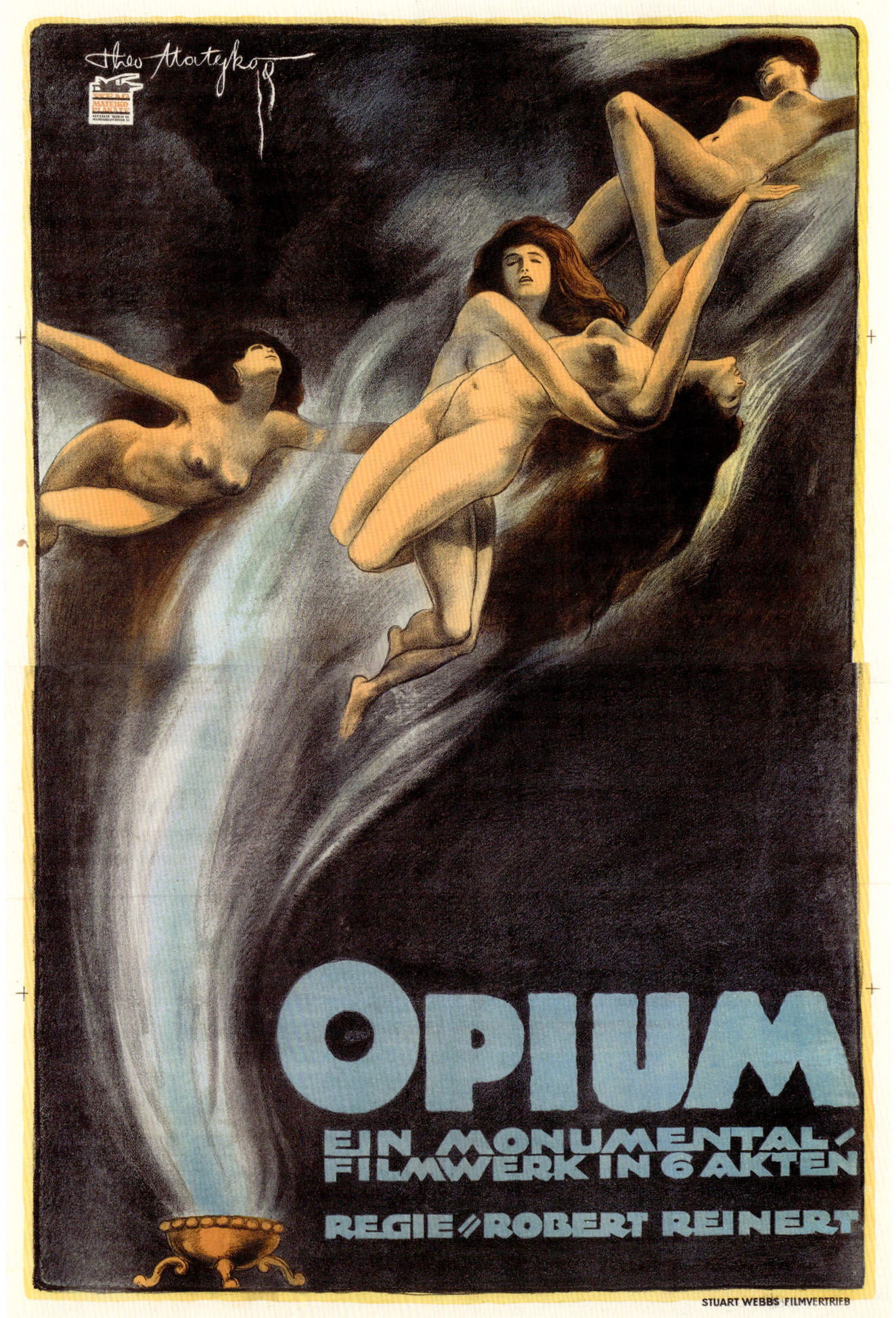

OPIUM 1919
AUSTRIAN POSTER, ART BY THEO MATEJKO

Theo Matejko's poster for *Opium* is a beautiful and striking design. It is also a historically interesting piece as an unusual example of uncensored paper and an early example of 'exploitation' poster art; the film may have been a dud, but the alluring poster artwork seduced a prospective audience with the promise of drugs and naked flesh. This risqué masterpiece was pasted across Vienna's billboards during a brief 18-month period when censorship was relaxed following the end of the First World War.

Theo Matejko (1893-1946) was born in Vienna and began his career as an interior designer and cabinet-maker, before moving into the realm of commercial art, designing movie and advertising posters. He was a war correspondent throughout the First World War and then, in 1920, he moved to Berlin where he worked as a poster designer for UFA, the leading German film studio (where his second wife was also an actress). Notable posters from this later UFA period include *Dr Mabuse* (1922) and *The Ten Commandments* (1923).

HOLLYWOOD 1923
AMERICAN POSTER, ART DIRECTION ATTRIBUTED TO VINCENT TROTTA

Hollywood was released in 1923, the same year that the 'Hollywoodland' sign was erected in the Hollywood Hills and the industry arrived as the go-to destination for every starlet with a dream. A silent comedy, *Hollywood* was released as competition to rival studio Goldwyn's *Souls for Sale*, which also focussed on the industry and its stars. *Hollywood* allegedly featured over 30 cameos of actors playing themselves, including 'Fatty' Arbuckle. Now a lost film, it is unlikely that the full list of those involved will ever be uncovered. In contrast, this rare American poster is one of the most enduring representations of Hollywood in the Roaring Twenties. Although uncredited, the poster was likely designed by Vincent Trotta, who was Paramount's art director at the time (see p.59). It remains a fitting depiction of Tinseltown today – a dark smiling gullet swallowing a never-ending stampede of hopefuls.

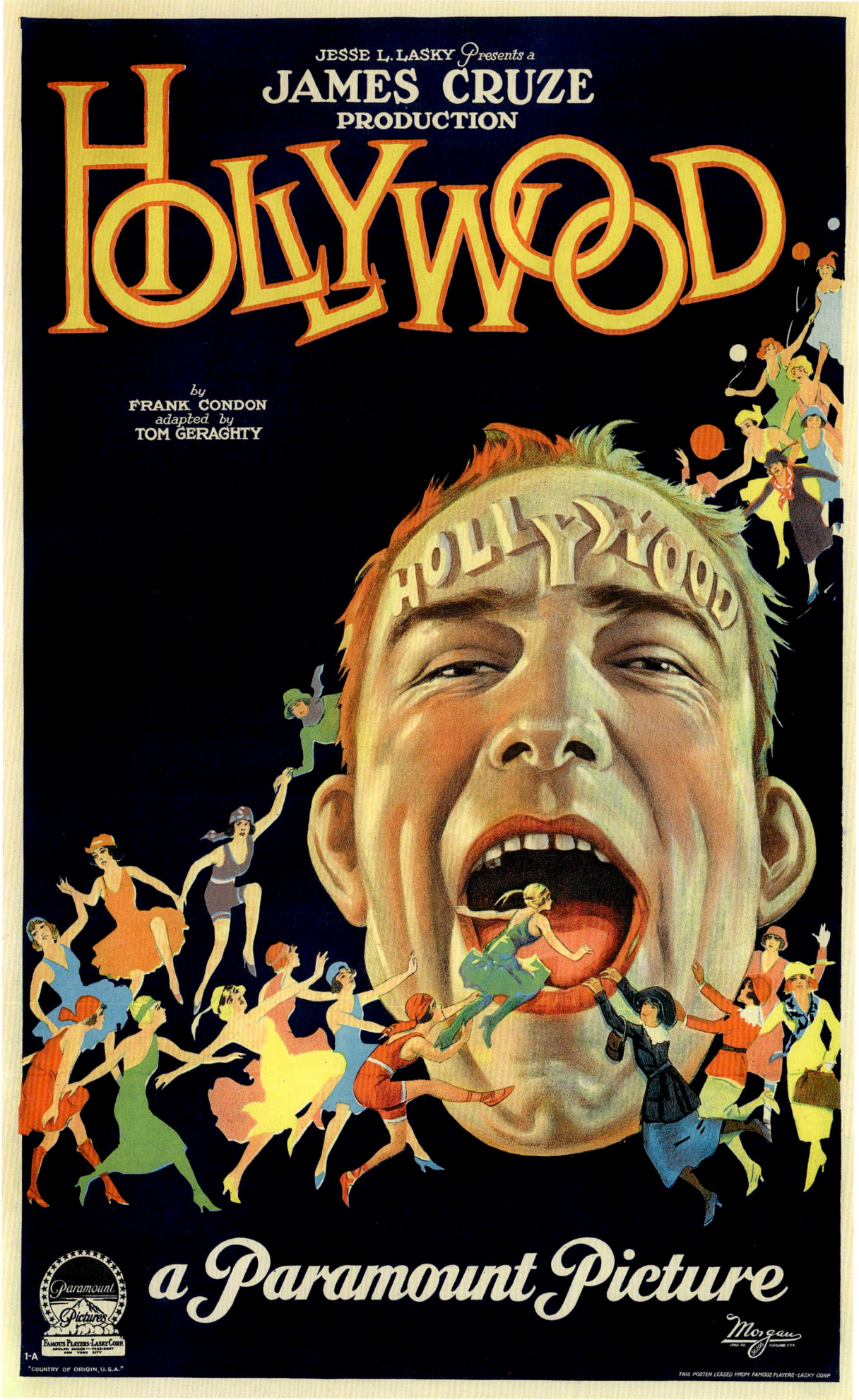

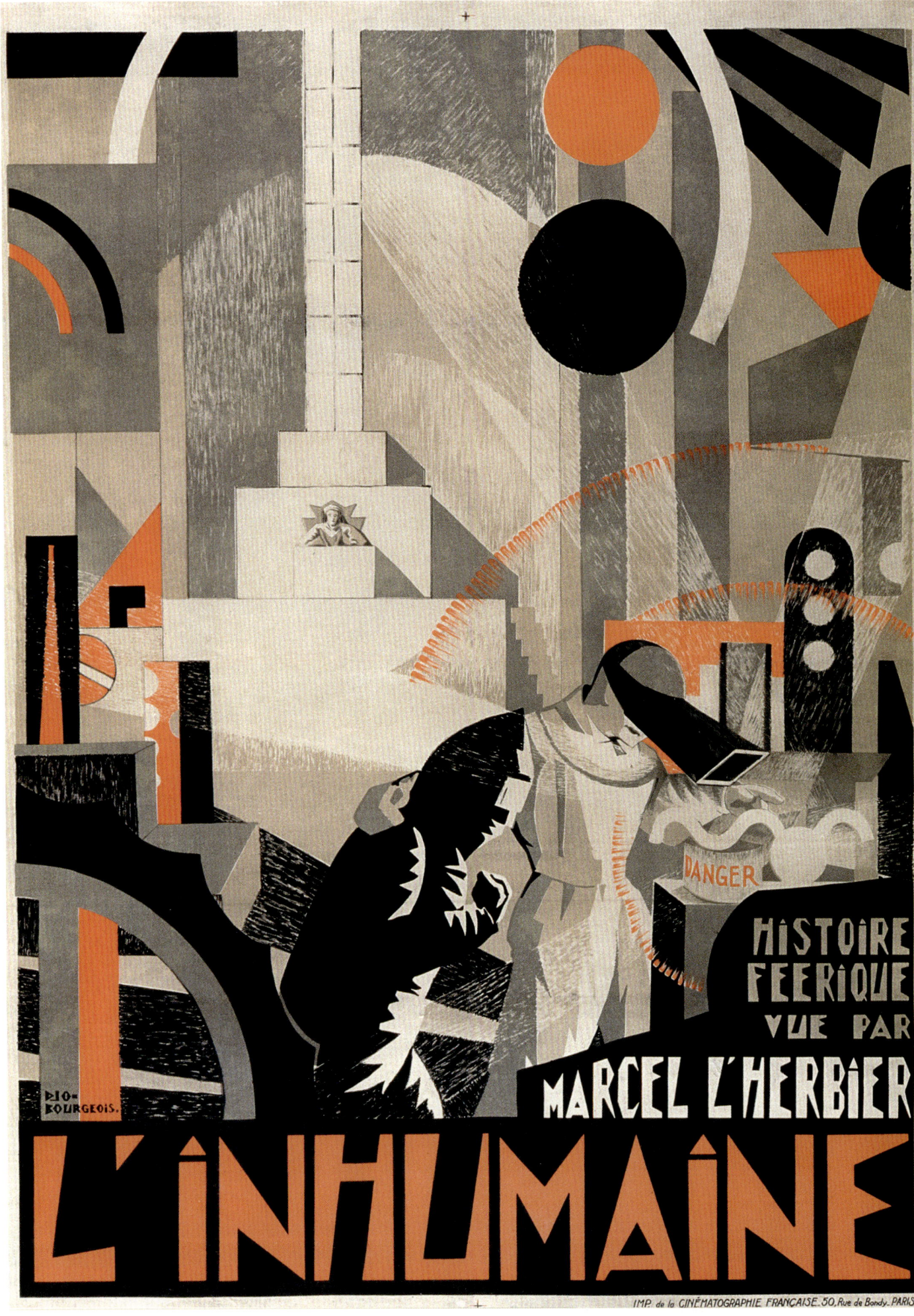

L'INHUMAINE 1924
FRENCH POSTER, ART BY GEORGES 'DJO' BOURGEOIS

Marcel L'Herbier's *L'inhumaine* was a hymn to the avant-garde. An ultramodern science fiction melodrama, it was a comment on art and technology. Writing at the time, the renowned architect Adolf Loos commented that, 'The final images of *L'inhumaine* surpass the imagination. As you emerge from seeing it, you have the impression of having lived through the moment of birth of a new art.'

L'Herbier involved all of his avant-garde friends in the production – costume design was by Paul Poiret, dance sequences choreographed by Rolf de Maré and allegedly everyone from Picasso to Man Ray and James Joyce were extras. The extraordinary Cubist sets were designed by painter Fernand Léger and architect Robert Mallet-Stevens. The magnificent French poster was designed by Georges 'Djo' Bourgeois and it depicts Léger's and Mallet-Stevens's glorious sets in the background.

Georges 'Djo' Bourgeois (1898-1937) was an architect and designer. He set up his own workshop in 1924, becoming one of the most respected and original furniture designers of the period. He was dedicated to a simple, modern aesthetic influenced by the functional lines of Bauhaus. He exhibited at the esteemed Salon d'Automne and Salon des Artistes Decorators and made furniture for a number of prestigious clients. He designed a number of posters, the most notable of which is *L'inhumaine*.

BERLIN: DIE SINFONIE DER GROSSTADT 1927
FRENCH POSTER, ART BY VENABERT

Walter Ruttmann's *Berlin: Symphony of a Great City* is an important work of silent-era experimental film. A documentary style montage in the manner of Eisenstein or Vertov, Ruttmann's poetic masterpiece was a tribute to the vibrancy and life of a cosmopolitan city in the Roaring Twenties. This rhythmic collage of candid and staged scenes, originally accompanied by a rousing score by Edmund Meisel, follows one typical day in the life of Berlin's inhabitants. As well as its artistic importance, the film is also poignant as a piece of historical footage, shot just a few years before the rise of National Socialism and the destruction of the city.

The artist Venabert managed to mirror the exact mood of Ruttmann's work in his stunning poster design. Unfortunately, little information is known about this extraordinary artist.

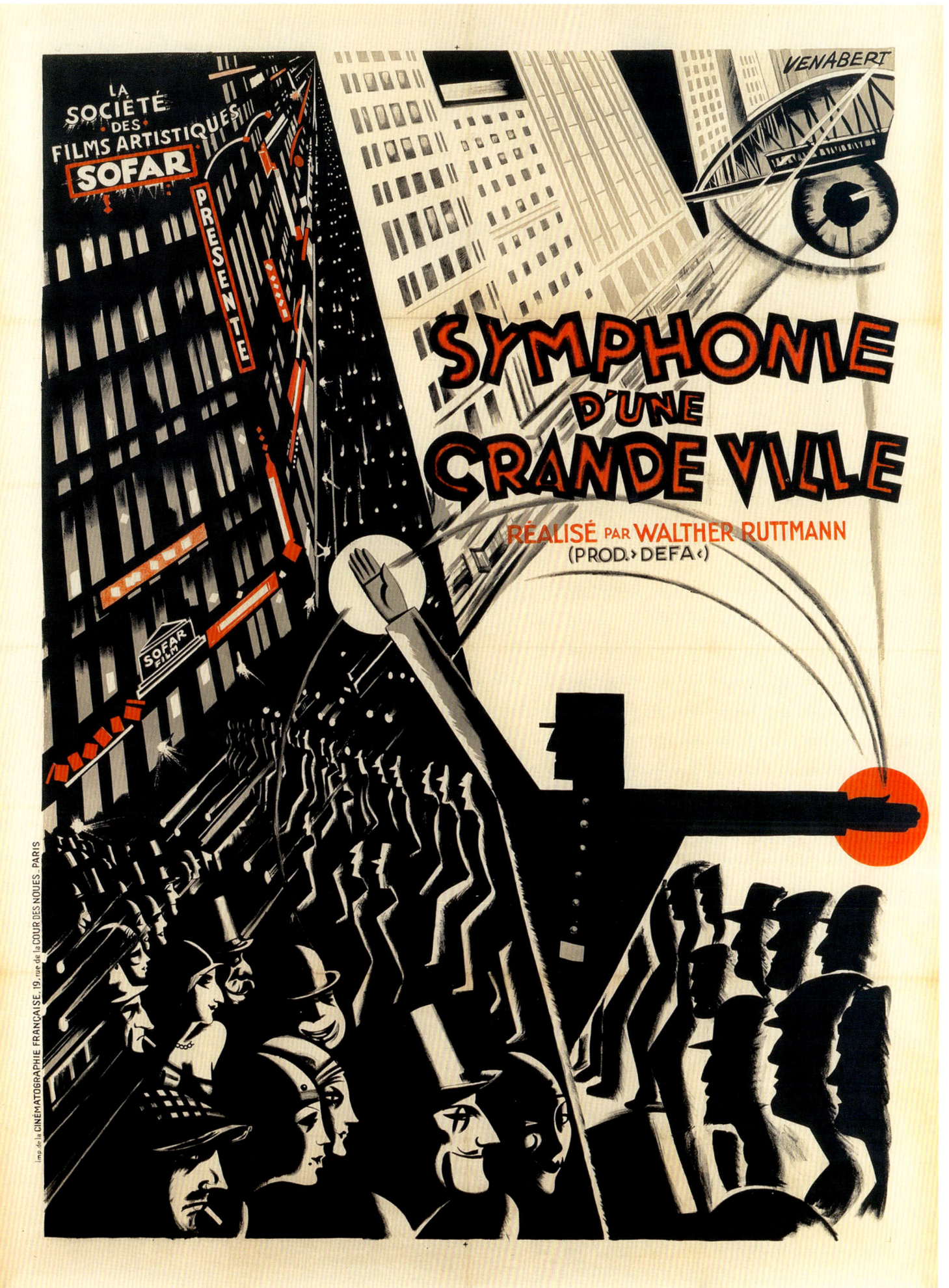

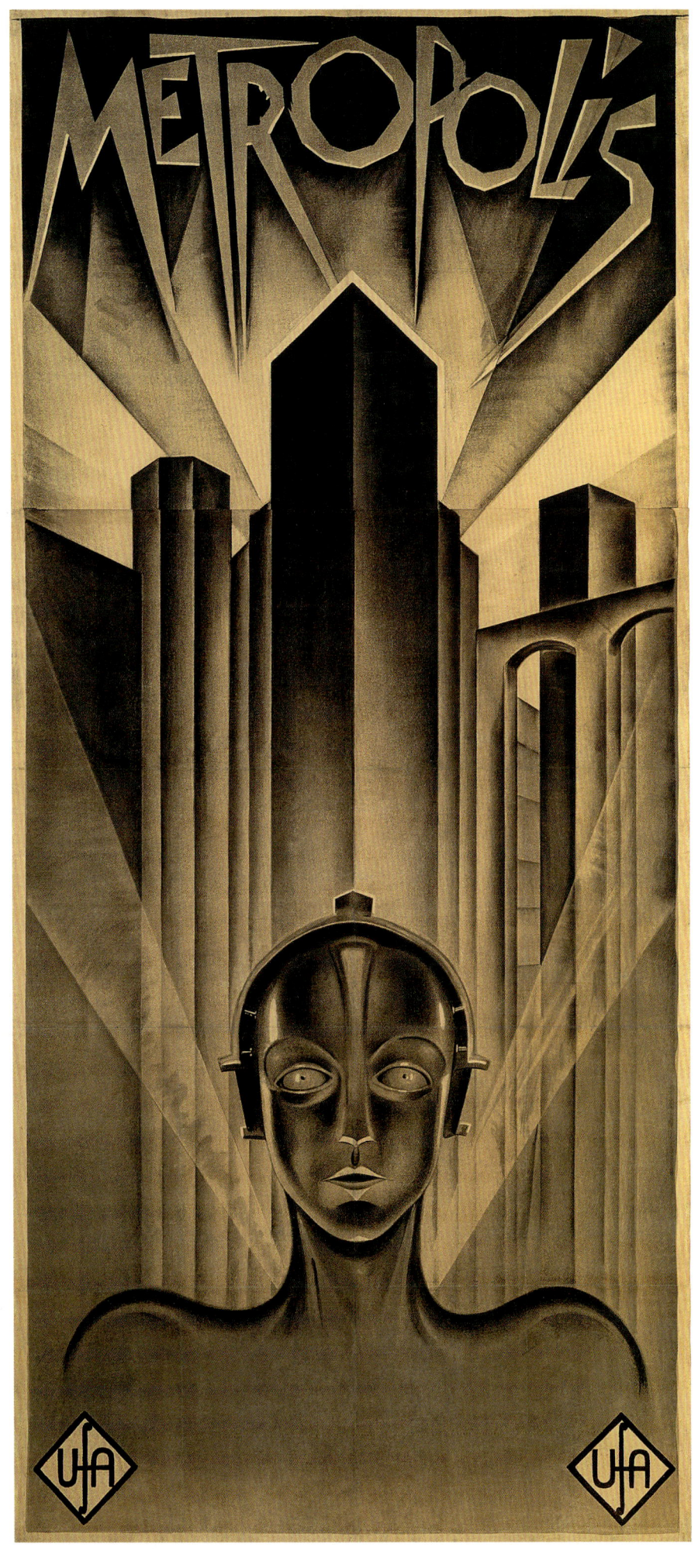

METROPOLIS 1927
GERMAN POSTER, ART BY HEINZ SCHULZ-NEUDAMM

Metropolis is a masterpiece of German Expressionist Cinema. Director Fritz Lang's staggering futuristic gothic opera examined powerful themes of class struggle and growing industrialisation during a period of economic and political discontent in Europe. This seminal work was also the first full-length science fiction film. With its colossal sets, cast and production costs, the film very nearly bankrupted UFA studio and received mixed reviews on its original release. Writing for *The New York Times*, H.G. Wells called it, 'The silliest film. I do not believe it would be possible to make one sillier.' Today, it is recognized as one of the most innovative and important works in cinema history.

The Modernist themes in *Metropolis* were reflected in the poster artwork used for the film's promotion around the world. The two most stunning and awe-inspiring posters are the German three-sheet and the French billboard poster.

The German three-sheet poster for *Metropolis* was designed by graphic artist Heinz Schulz-Neudamm (1899-1969). Two versions of Schulz-Neudamm's artwork were printed: one with title and screen credits at the bottom, which was used in German theatres; and a second, completely free of text, which was exported for screenings around the world. Without text, the poster is Modernist design in its purest form. It is something of a 'holy grail' amongst poster collectors and one of the most sought after vintage posters of all time. In 2005, I brokered the sale of one of only two known copies of this text-free version of the poster. Although no-one realised we were doing it at the time, the sale broke the world record for a vintage poster in *any* genre, including previous records set by advertising posters by Toulouse-Lautrec. *Metropolis* sold for $690,000.

Lang's dystopic future was dominated by monumental skyscrapers and gigantic steel structures. His inspiration came from the construction of Manhattan that was taking shape in the 1920s. In an interview with Peter Bogdanovich in 1965, Lang commented, 'I first came to America briefly in 1924 and it made a great impression on me ... I looked into the streets – the glaring lights and the tall buildings – and there I conceived *Metropolis*.'

This vision of the urban-industrialisation of the future is captured to greatest effect on artist Boris Bilinsky's dramatic artwork for the French billboard poster. Boris Bilinsky (1900-1948) was one of the most interesting designers in Europe at this time, flourishing in a period where poster artists were afforded a huge amount of artistic freedom of expression (he was also a film-set architect and costume designer). Bilinsky's Modernist approach also took influences from Russian Constructivism and Dadaism. Only one copy of Bilinksy's billboard poster for *Metropolis* is known to have survived and it belongs to the Film Museum in Berlin.

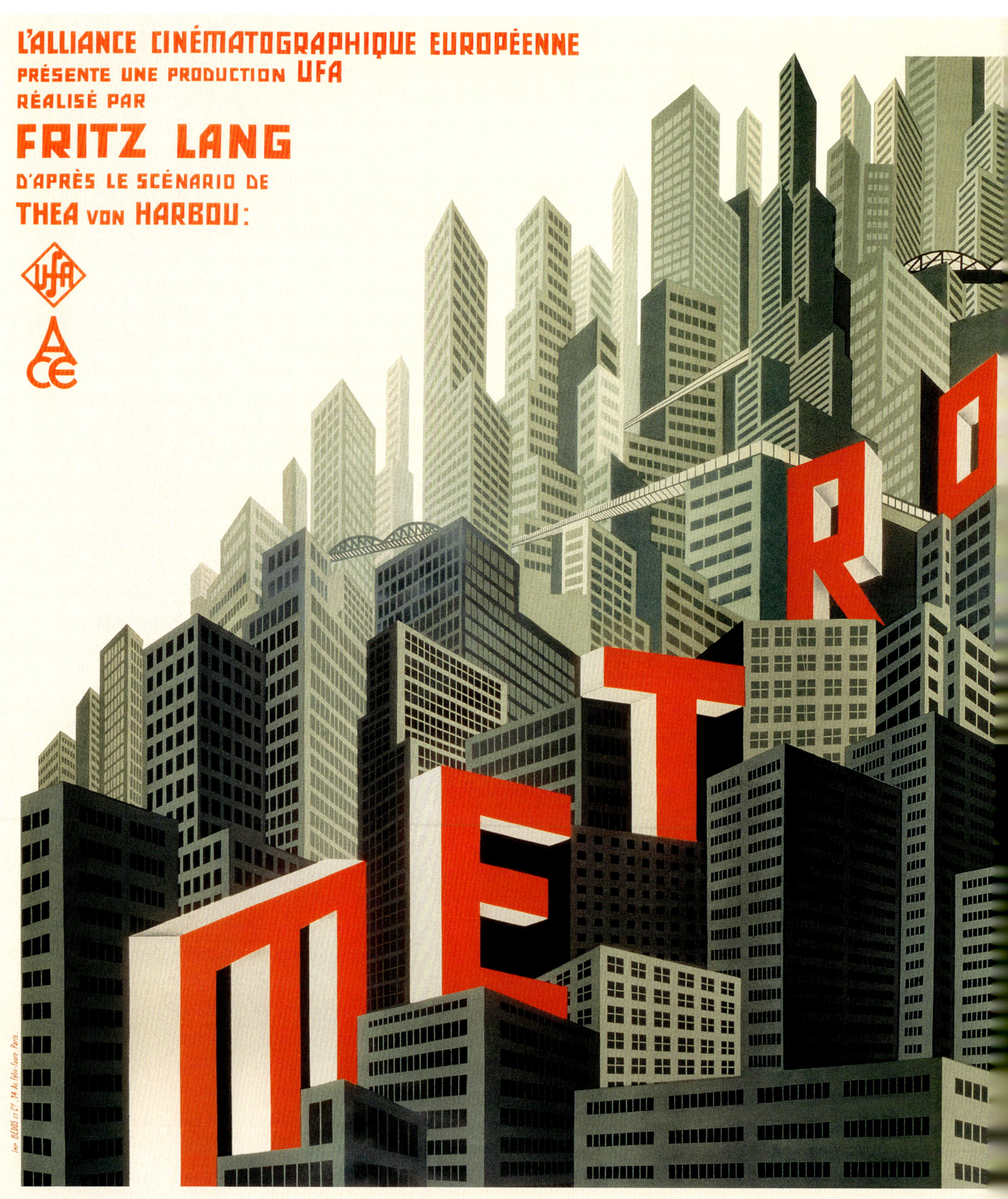

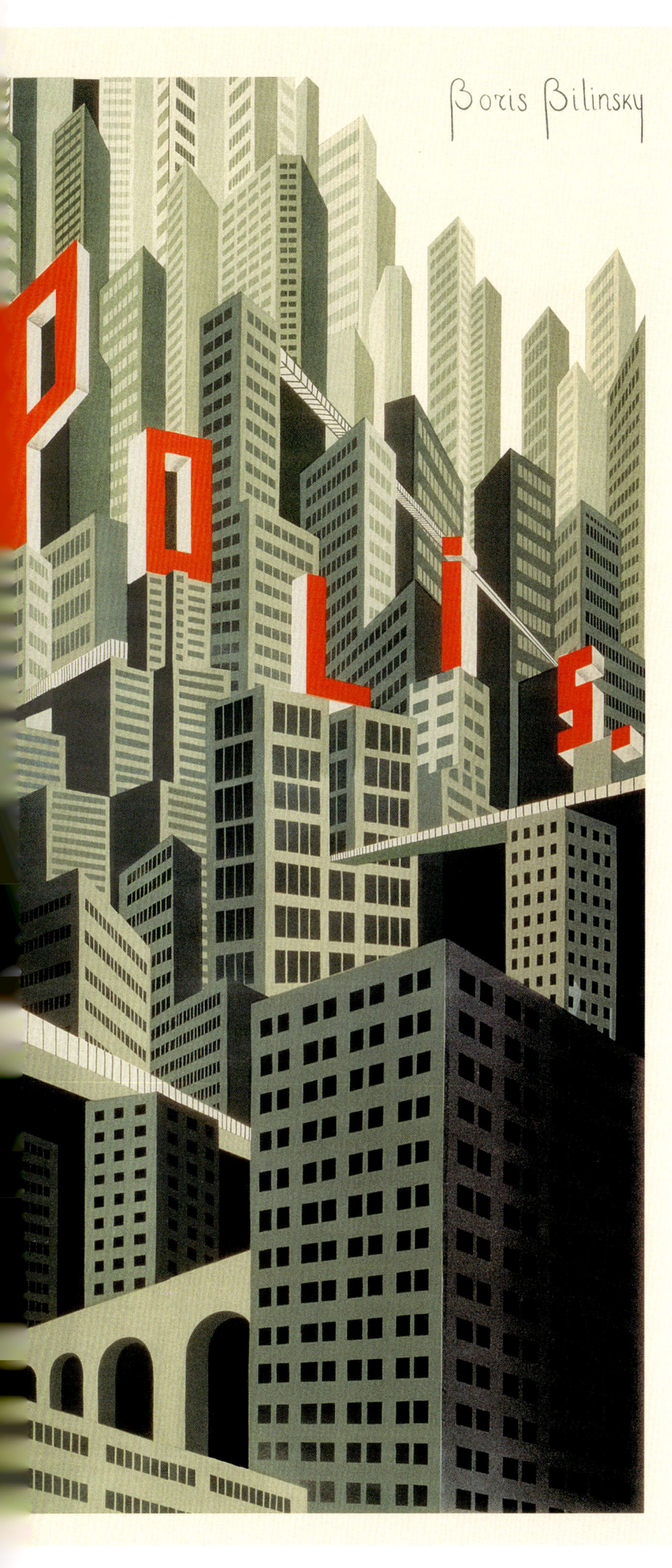

METROPOLIS 1927
FRENCH POSTER, ART BY BORIS BILINKSY

Grass: A Nation's Battle for Life 1925
American poster, Artist unknown

Grass: A Nation's Battle for Life was one of the first silent films I ever watched. As an Iranian, I had heard about the film and was interested to see its depiction of 'the old country'. Sitting down to watch this epic early documentary, it completely mesmerised me. Years later, when I found a poster for the original release – the only one to ever surface – I fell in love with its clean design and the simple 'Grass' title.

The filmmaker of *Grass* was Merian C. Cooper and his life reads like a gripping adventure novel. After being thrown out of the US Naval Academy (allegedly for daring to suggest that planes would replace ships in warfare), he went on to become a bomber pilot during the First World War. At one point during the conflict, his family received a telegram informing them Cooper had been killed in action. The truth was in reality much more dramatic. During a particularly gruelling dogfight, Cooper's plane caught fire and his co-pilot was shot through the neck. Determined to save him, he threw the plane into freefall and managed to extinguish the flames, although not before badly burning his hands. Unable to hold the controls, he managed to land the craft safely using only his elbows and knees.

After the Armistice, Cooper travelled to Poland and helped to establish a volunteer squadron of US pilots to fight the Bolsheviks. One of his fellow airmen was Ernest B. Schoedsack, who became his lifelong friend and business partner. Cooper flew in over 70 missions before being shot down and captured by the Red Cavalry. He was held for nine months before escaping back to the States. Cooper and Schoedsack became interested in documentary filmmaking and embarked on a series of intrepid expeditions to some of the most inaccessible corners of the globe.

For their first collaboration, the friends decided to make a film about nomadic tribes. With little experience, however, they had trouble tracking down an appropriate story, before eventually coming into contact with the Bakhtiari tribe – a nomadic people who were embarking on their epic and harrowing annual trek over the mountains from summer pastures in Angora (modern-day Ankara, Turkey) to winter pastures in the Bakhtiari country of south west Iran.

Cooper and Schoedsack followed the Bakhtiari tribe on their annual pilgrimage and the resulting piece of film, *Grass: A Nation's Battle for Life* is a stunning achievement. A moving documentary, it follows the 50,000-strong tribe as they move families and animals over the high peaks of the snow-covered Zagros mountains to safety. The footage includes breathtaking shots of families struggling barefoot through deep snowfields and swimming through fast-flowing rivers. It remains an amazing document of a culture and time.

Grass was originally intended for the lecture circuit but after Jesse Lasky, the head of Paramount Pictures, saw it, he was so impressed that it was given a theatrical release in New York, receiving enthusiastic reviews.

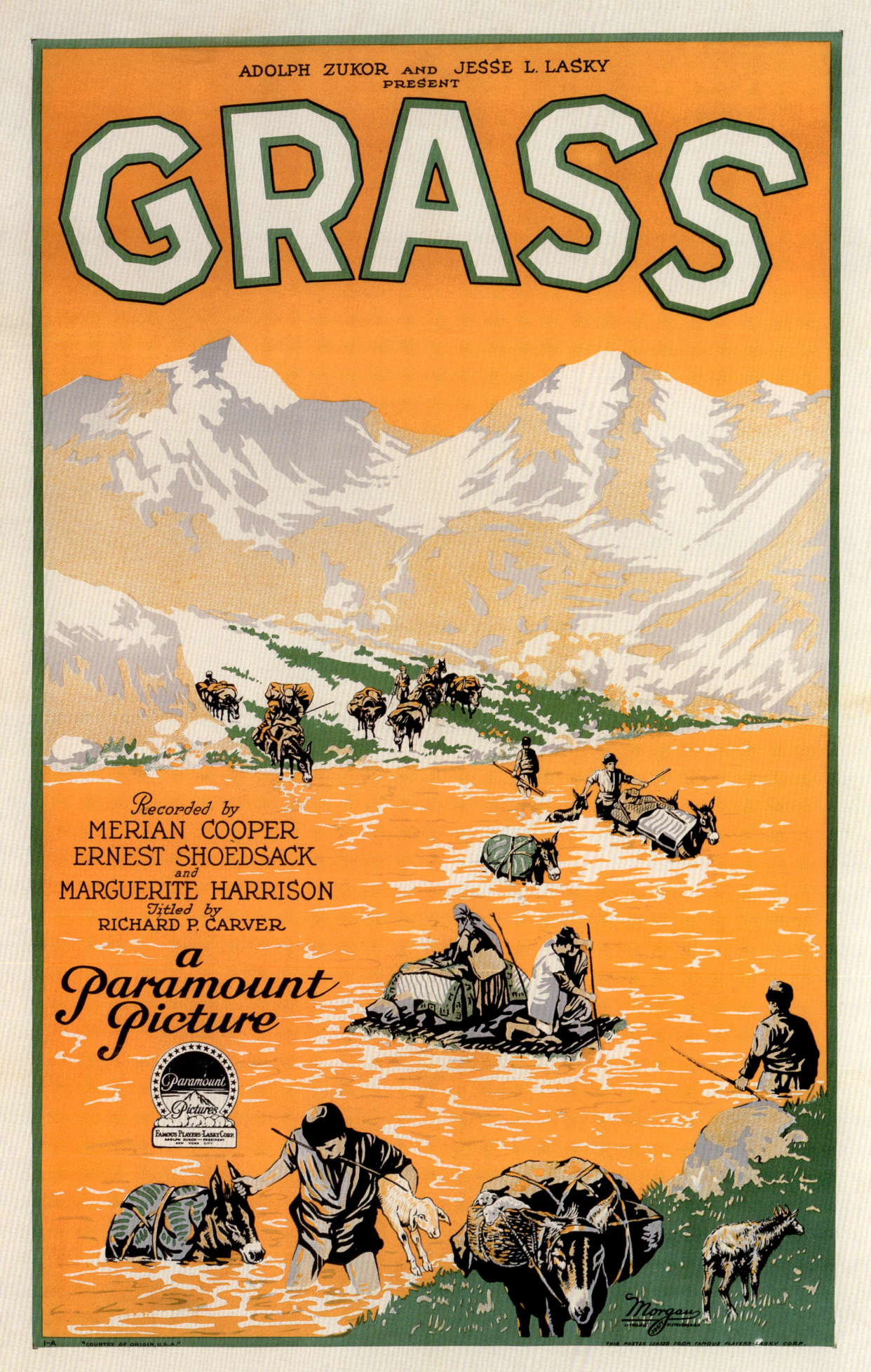

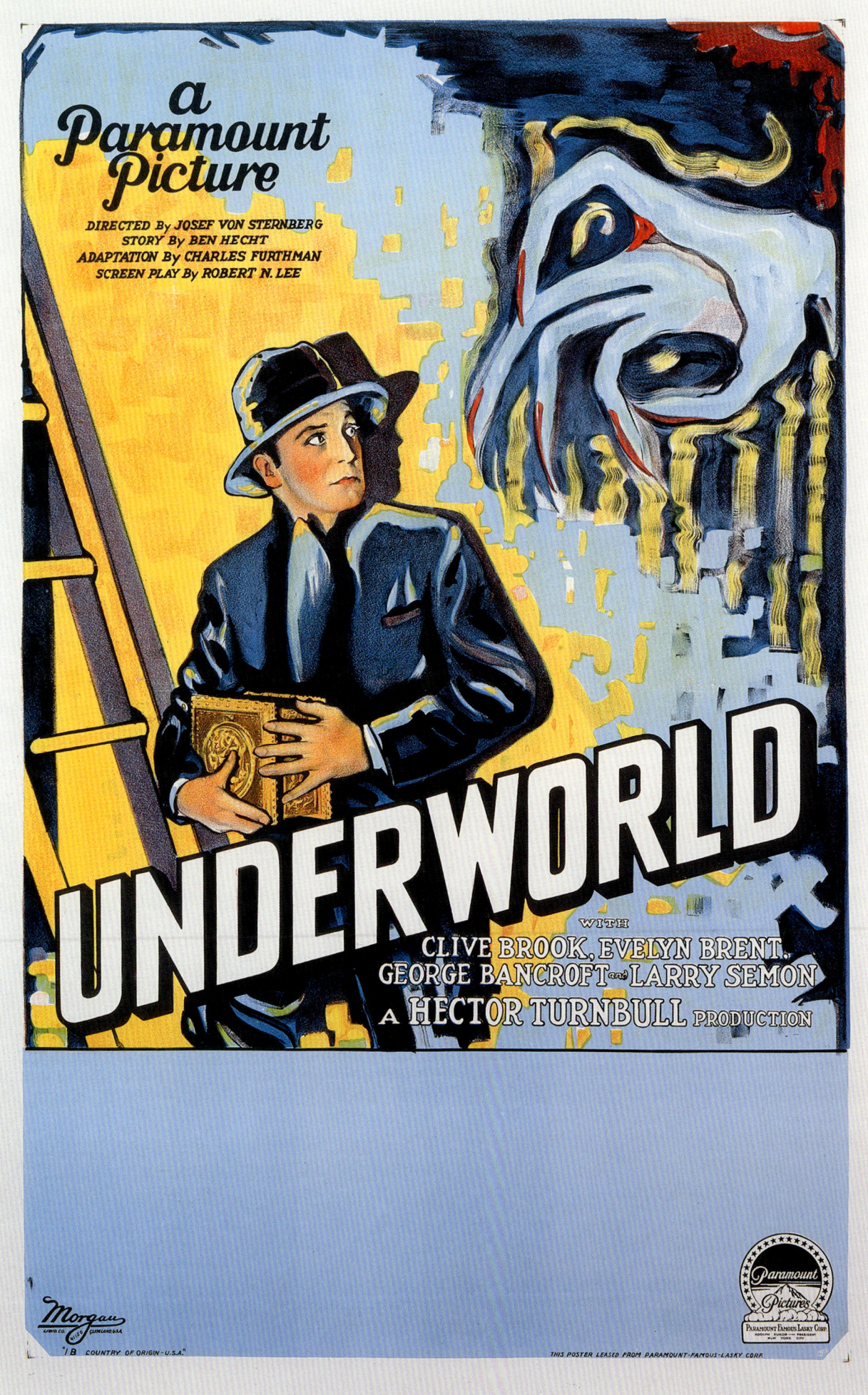

UNDERWORLD 1927

AMERICAN POSTER, ARTIST UNKNOWN

Underworld is widely regarded as one of the earliest gangster films and the movie that launched the genre in Hollywood. One of the first films to deal with organised crime, it starred George Bancroft as a criminal kingpin. It was written by Ben Hecht and apparently based on his own experiences as a crime reporter in Chicago (he would also use his experiences in his script for *Scarface* a few years later – see p.51). The movie was directed by Josef von Sternberg, at the time a relatively unknown name, and this was only his second feature. When filming was finished, Hecht was so unhappy with what von Sternberg had produced that he tried to have his name taken off the picture before its release. Paramount also thought it would be a flop and the film was very nearly shelved. It was only released at a single cinema, New York's Paramount Theater. Against expectations, however, von Sternberg's approach proved successful and *Underworld* became a massive hit. An eager, queuing public had the theatre rushing to arrange all-night screenings and the film was finally given a nationwide release a few months later. Paramount rewarded von Sternberg with a bonus of $10,000 and presented him with a gold medal. Hecht also won the Academy Award for screenwriting at the first Oscars in 1929.

Underworld is an extraordinary piece of cinema. Underpinned by Hecht's crime writing, the mood is von Sternberg at his best – expressionist, atmospheric and almost noir in feel. This rare, alternative style American poster is the most evocative poster on the film, capturing von Sternberg's expressionist mood. It is also the only known copy. The space at the bottom of the poster was for a cinema to add their own screening information before hanging it outside the theatre.

THE CANARY MURDER CASE 1929
AMERICAN POSTER, BASED ON PHOTO BY EUGENE ROBERT RICHEE

The poster for *The Canary Murder Case* was painted by an unknown Paramount artist meticulously copying a still by the famous photographer Eugene Robert Richee (with the dramatic addition of a monstrous killer arm).

Eugene Robert Richee (1896-1972) was head of Paramount's portrait studio from its inception in 1921 until the early 1940s. His muse was Louise Brooks and he shot several beautiful portraits of the star throughout her reign as Hollywood's original flapper girl. Richee's most famous portrait of the star features Brooks shot in profile against a black background with her classic sharp black bob and black dress blending into the background. Only the whites of her face, hands and a long string of pearls remain visible.

Known for her fiercely independent spirit, *The Canary Murder Case* effectively ended Brooks' Hollywood career when she incited the studio's anger by resolutely refusing to return from Germany to record sound retakes.

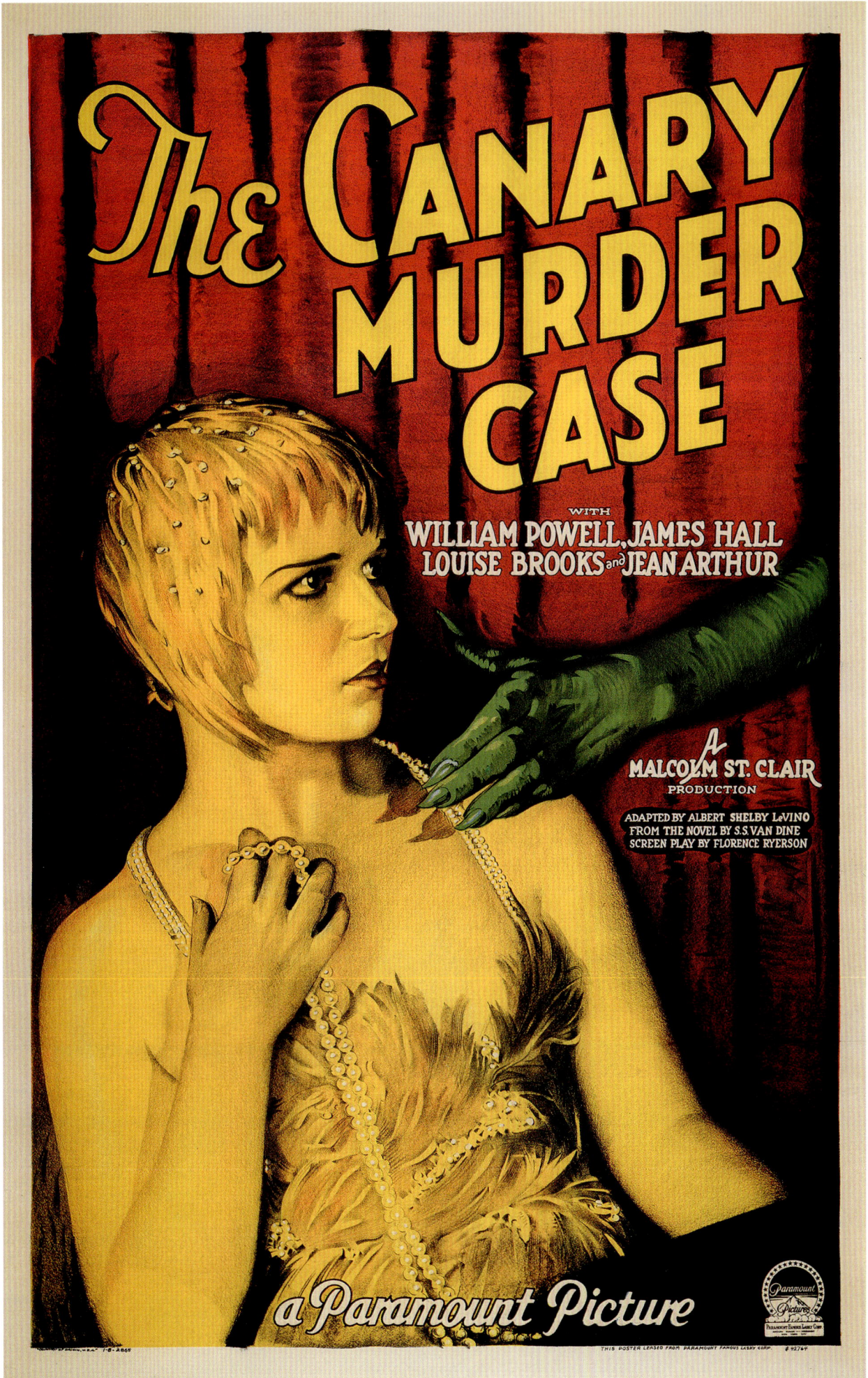

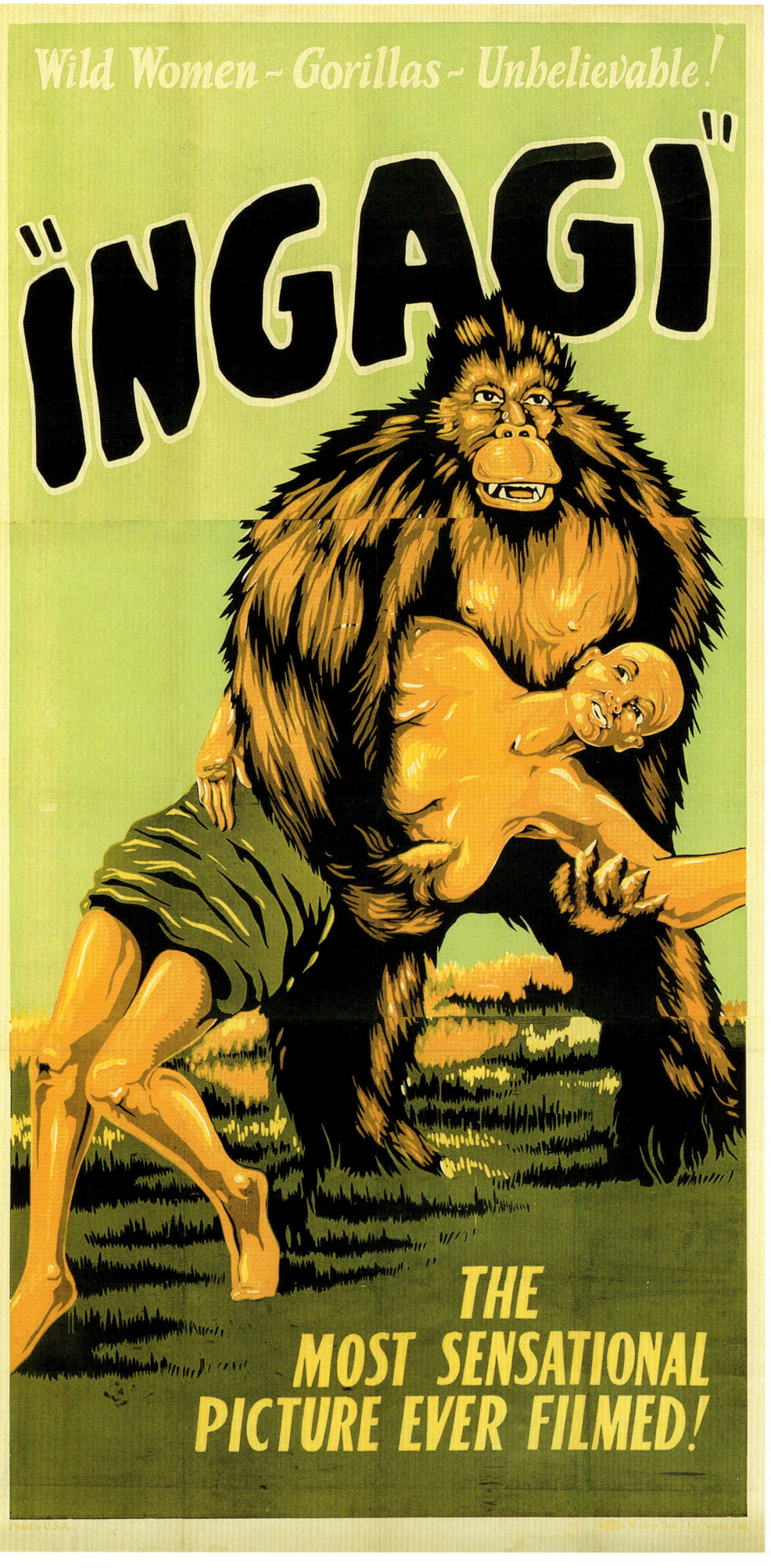

INGAGI 1930
AMERICAN POSTER, ARTIST UNKNOWN

Wild Women – Gorillas – Unbelievable! How can you go wrong…? Printed cheaply in three-tone colour, this poster for *Ingagi* is B-movie exploitation cinema at its best and is one of my favourite posters from the genre – replete in all its disturbing immorality.

Released in 1930, *Ingagi* was presented to the public as a simple ethnographic documentary, before running into controversy after accusations that scenes had been faked. Many people believed that this tale of a British expedition stumbling upon a tribe where innocent woman were offered to gorillas for sex – and which featured hitherto unknown jungle creatures – was based on fact. The Hays Office launched an urgent investigation. It was rather quickly revealed that the creatures were, in fact, turtles with stuck-on wings and tails, 'pygmies' were Californian children from the local neighbourhood and, most painfully, large chunks of the film were in fact 15-year-old expedition footage from an old silent-era documentary. Unsurprisingly, the film's producers were sued, which ensured the notorious *Ingagi* played on the exploitation circuit for several years.

M 1931
FRENCH POSTER, ART BY CECCHETTO

Fritz Lang's *M* is a masterpiece of Expressionist Cinema and is credited as the director's finest work. It is the tale of a German city terrorised by a child murderer, played with disturbing sympathy by Peter Lorre. The film was Lang's first 'talkie' and sound is used to powerful effect: ticking clocks, long silences and the fateful whistling of the murderer create an atmosphere of ominous dread.

M was a sophisticated and chilling allegory for the tide of fear that swept Germany before the Nazis' rise to power, and was made just two years before the director was forced to flee his homeland for America. Stylistically and thematically ahead of its time, *M* was a key influence on the development of film noir. Serial killer thrillers from the 1930s to present day also bear the hallmarks of Lang's genre-defining work.

It is rare that a film's key moment appears in the advertising campaign. The French poster for *M*, by artist Cecchetto, is the only original release poster from around the world to feature the pivotal scene where Lorre's murderer realises his crimes have been discovered. It has become one of the most iconic images of twentieth century cinema.

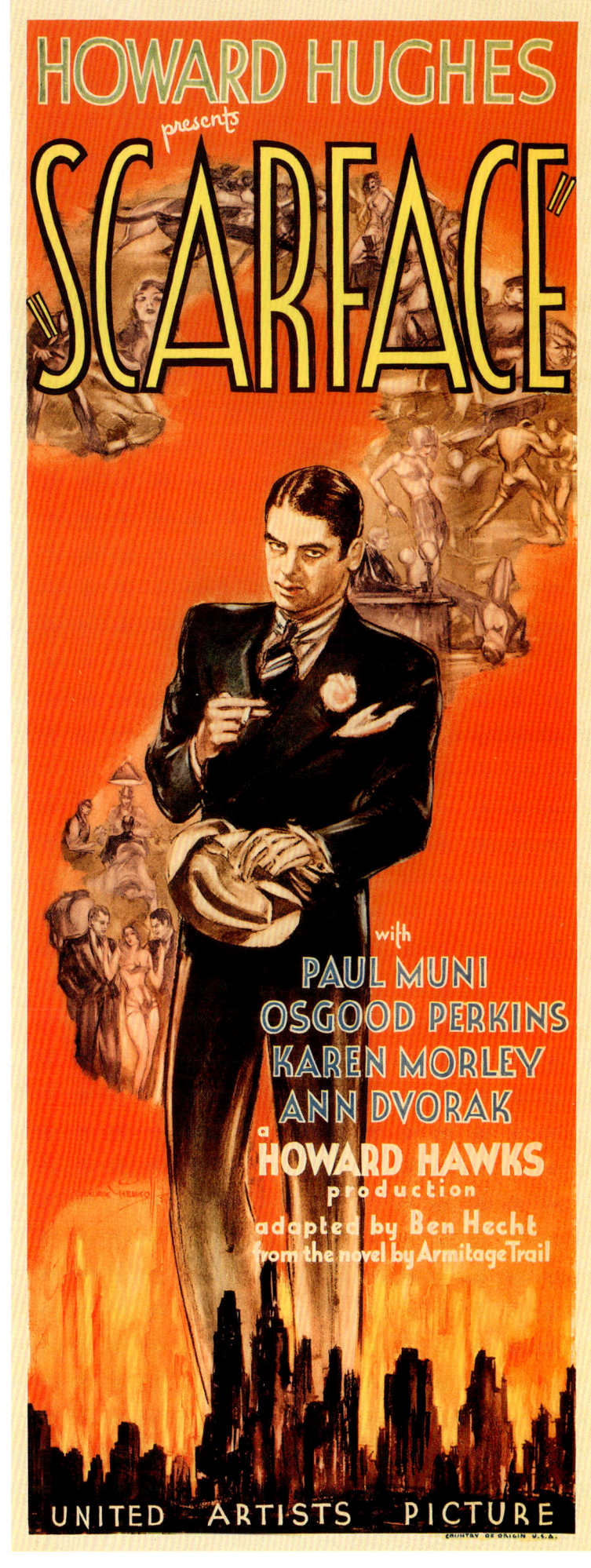

FRANKENSTEIN 1931
AMERICAN POSTER, ART BY KAROLY GROSZ

During the 1930s, Universal Studio was responsible for the most influential horror cycle in the history of cinema, bringing vicarious frights to the masses for the first time and ushering in a bloody new era for the genre.

Born in Hungary, Karoly Grosz was the art director for Universal Studios in their glorious horror heyday and he was responsible for the majority of their posters from this period, including *Dracula* (1931), *Frankenstein* (1931), *The Old Dark House* (1932), *The Mummy* (1932), *Murders in the Rue Morgue* (1932) and *The Bride of Frankenstein* (1935). Grosz usually worked in oil and watercolour and his posters were explosions of colour that depicted a number of key elements: the monster, a damsel in distress, eye-catching title font and studio credits.

In sharp contrast, Grosz's artwork for the teaser poster for *Frankenstein* took a deliberate and markedly different approach. The poster is a strikingly modern design: the face of the staring monster, looming in red from the blackest of depths, is spine-tingling, an effect enhanced by the blood-soaked typography and lack of credits. Today we are numb to the constant blare of shock advertising, yet Grosz's *Frankenstein* still has the power to arrest. Standing in front of a copy of this poster in person is chilling. It is the best of all Universal's horror posters and features the best tagline: *Warning! The monster is loose!* ... And it was.

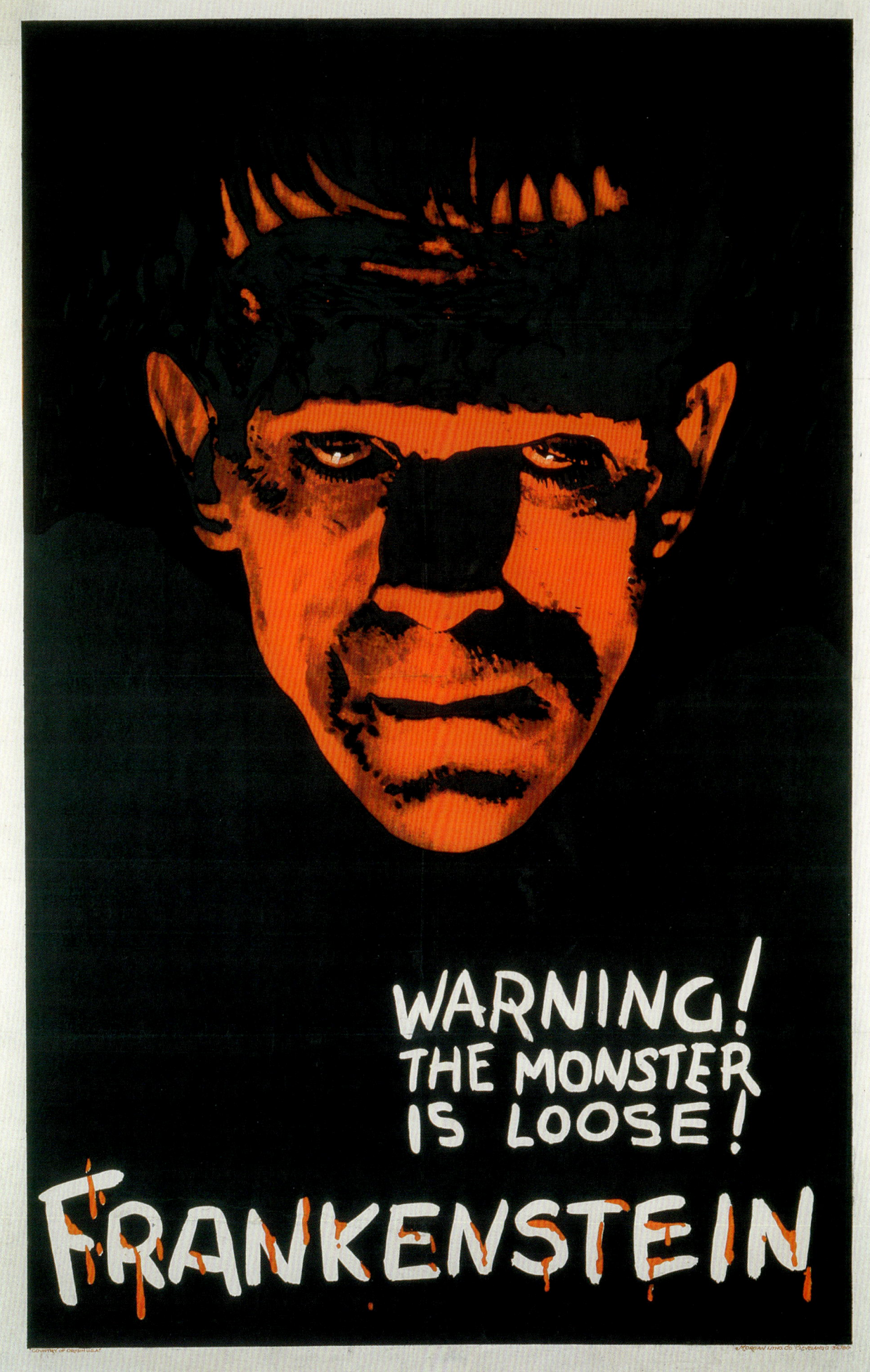

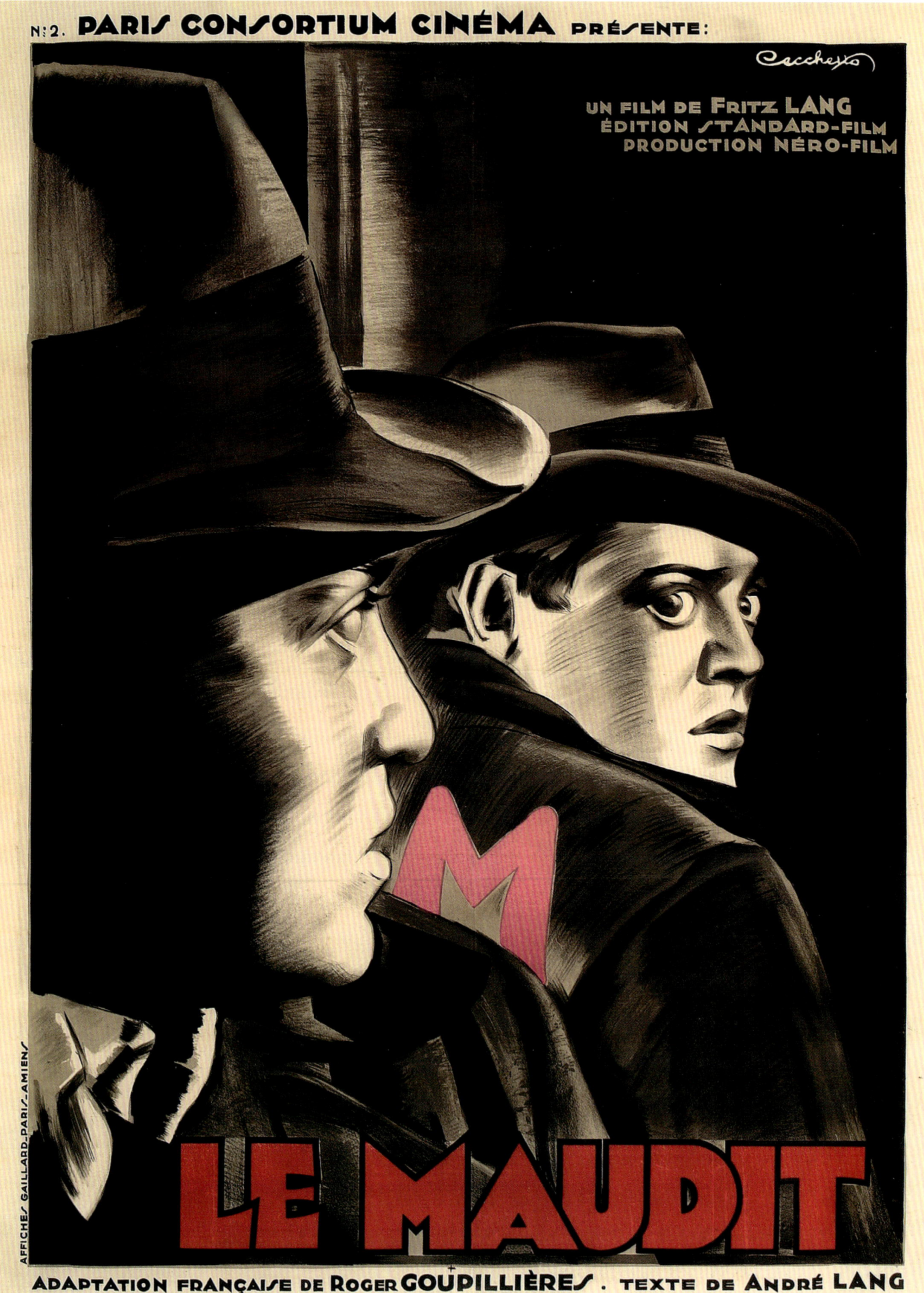

SCARFACE 1932

AMERICAN POSTER, ARTIST UNKNOWN

Released in 1932, *Scarface* is a seminal work and possibly the most influential gangster film ever released (and famously remade by Brian De Palma in 1983). Produced by Howard Hughes and directed by Howard Hawks, the film was written by Ben Hecht, who based his script on the novel of the same name by author Armitage Trail and on his own experiences as a crime reporter in Chicago. It starred Paul Muni as Tony Camonte, a fictional character loosely based on Al 'Scarface' Capone. Apocryphal tales abound of Capone's henchmen turning up to threaten Hecht, only to end up as script advisors on the film, taking a final print back to a delighted Capone to hold his own private screenings.

Scarface was a brutal and savage portrayal of violent mob warfare. *The New York Times* wrote in its original review that, 'The slaughter ... is like that of a Shakespearean tragedy, for after the smoke of machine guns and pineapple bombs has blown away and the leading killer has gone to his death on the gallows, the only one of a group of principal characters left is a blonde with carefully plucked eyebrows.' Its boundary-pushing savagery and too-close-for-comfort parallels to Capone led to controversy with the censors. They forced a rewrite of the ending and insisted that the tagline *Shame of a Nation* be added after the title in advertisements for the film. Ever the renegade, however, Hughes insisted on releasing his original version in states with minimal censorship control. He also attempted to sue the Hays Office for their interference.

Original posters for the film hardly ever surface and of the few examples that have appeared, this is one of the best. Muni's *Scarface* looms over the city in an overriding stance that was fittingly reflected in *The New York Times* comment that, 'The picture is dominated by Mr. Muni's virile and vehement acting.' Girls and fisticuffs swirl in the smoke behind him, which is curled into a question mark asking, perhaps, where such a ruthless pursuit of power will end.

WHAT PRICE HOLLYWOOD? 1932
AMERICAN POSTER, ARTIST UNKNOWN

What Price Hollywood? was director George Cukor's first big hit and starred Constance Bennett in one of her finest performances. Often referred to as the earliest version of the *A Star is Born* tale – a young ingénue's rocketing fame paralleled by her lover's downfall – on its release, it was also one of the most realistic portrayals of Hollywood that had been seen on screen. The screenplay was by Adela Rogers St. Johns who based her script on the real-life experience of actress Colleen Moore and her alcoholic husband. The true story of director Tom Forman, who committed suicide after a breakdown, was also threaded into the plot.

The film was produced by David O. Selznick. Four years after its successful release, he approached Cukor to direct his new film, *A Star is Born* (1937). Cukor declined as it was too similar to *What Price Hollywood?* However, several years later, Cukor decided to return to the subject, directing the successful musical remake of *A Star is Born* with Judy Garland in 1954. (The film was again remade in 1976 as a rock version starring Barbara Streisand.)

The American poster for *What Price Hollywood?* was a great graphic representation of the film's realistic edge. Indeed, the film's original title had been *The Truth About Hollywood*. In the book, *Memo from David O. Selznick*, Selznick commented, 'I believed that ... the trouble with most films about Hollywood was that they gave a false picture ... that they were not true reflections of what happened in Hollywood.' In contrast, in *What Price Hollywood?*, 'Ninety-five percent of the dialog ... was actually straight out of life and was straight "reportage" so to speak.' This reportage element is emphasised in the tabloid headlines screaming across Constance Bennett's face.

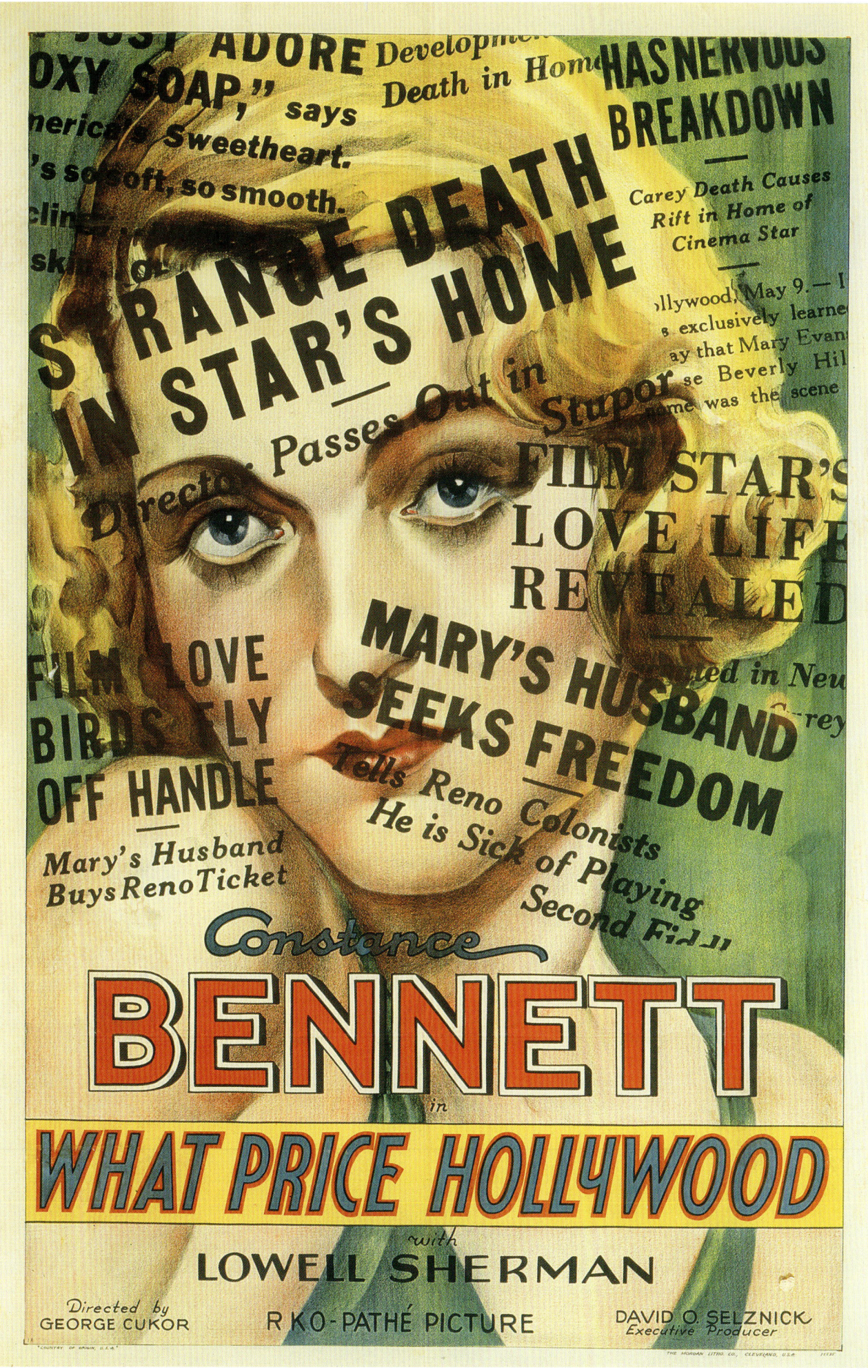

EXTASE 1933
FRENCH POSTER, ART BY CARLO MARIANI

Gustav Machaty's *Extase* is an important work of early European Cinema and was revolutionary in its enlightened portrayal of female sexuality. It was something of a cause célèbre on its release in 1932 and was banned in America. The furore arose from Hedy Lamarr (then still Hedy Kiesler) appearing naked on screen for a full ten minutes. The fact that the camera also lingered on a close-up of her face while she was sexually aroused only added to the frenzied uproar. Artist Carlo Mariani captured this scene in his sensual and masterful artwork for the French poster that manages to convey an erotic glamour.

    The film made a star of Hedy. At the time, she was married to Fritz Mandl, a rich German and a Nazi sympathiser. Unable to handle his wife's notoriety, Mandl tried, in vain, to buy all copies of the film after its release. He also became increasingly possessive, never letting Hedy out of his sight. Isolated and unhappy, the actress allegedly finally made her escape by drugging a maid and escaping from their hotel room in disguise. She made her way to America where she became one of Hollywood's most alluring stars. (As a rather irrelevant aside, Hedy was also a gifted electrical engineer and was honoured by the Electronic Frontier Foundation in 1997 for her co-invention of 'spread-spectrum broadcast communications technologies'.)

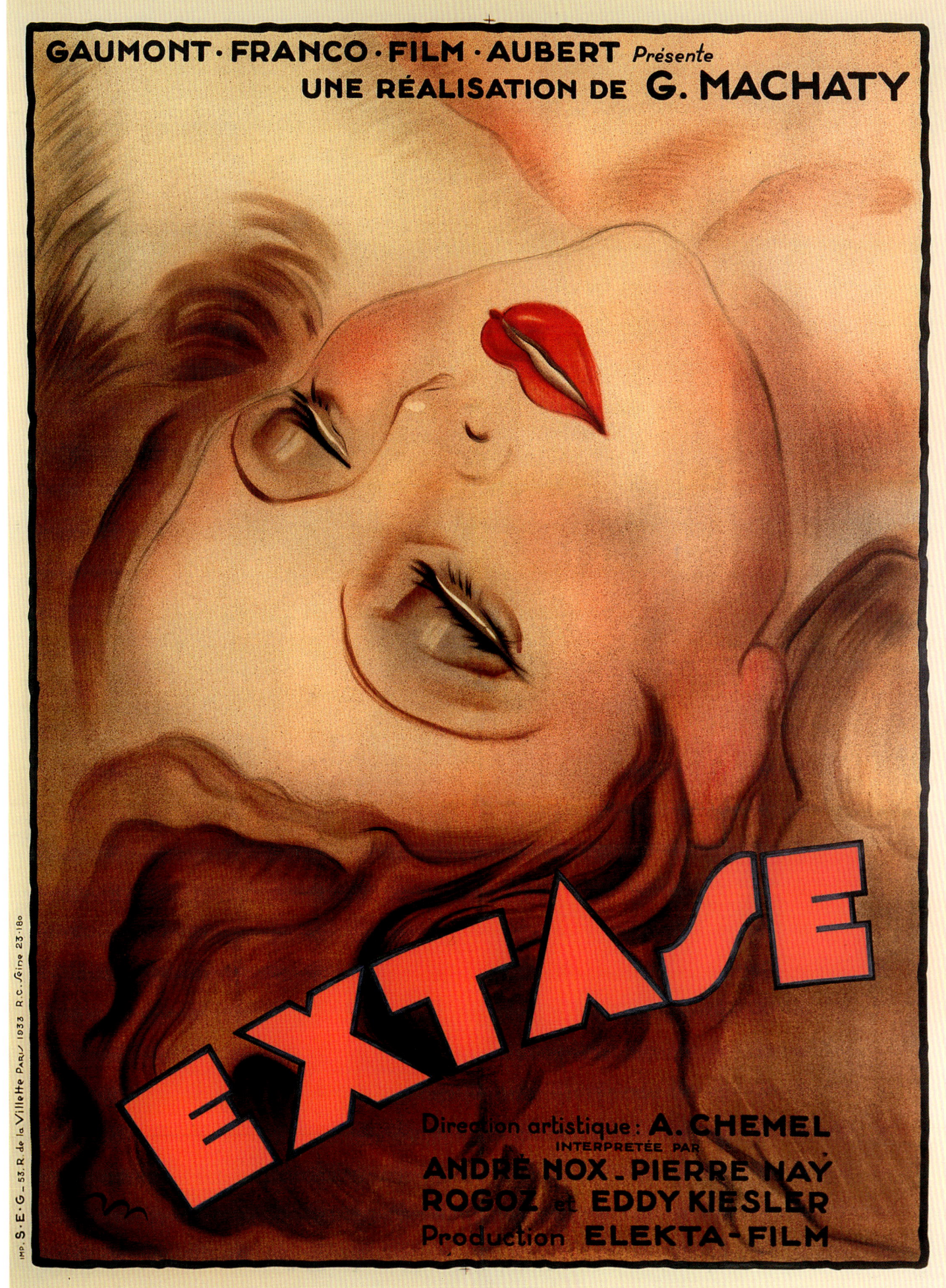

KING KONG 1933

AMERICAN POSTER, ART DIRECTION BY DAVID L. STRUMF, ART BY S. BARRETT MCCORMICK AND BOB SISK

A perfect blend of adventure, science fiction and horror, *King Kong* is the ultimate monster movie and the definition of a blockbuster. It has fuelled numerous sequels, spin-offs and two notable remakes in 1976 and 2005.

Kong was the brainchild of Merian C. Cooper, whose lightbulb moment supposedly came after he dreamt that a giant gorilla was terrorising New York. Cooper was something of a real-life Indiana Jones and based the character of Carl Denham on his own madcap adventures in far-flung lands (see p.38).

In a shrewd marketing ploy, a novelisation of *King Kong* was published in advance of the film's release. Based on an early screen draft, the book actually contained scenes that never made it into the final script (such as the renowned spider-pit scene that Peter Jackson would re-incorporate into his 2005 remake). The film was eagerly anticipated worldwide with colourful poster campaigns that focussed on the monster in various awe-inspiring poses. The image of Kong on top of the Empire State Building on this American poster is iconic and one of cinema's most celebrated images. With art direction by David L. Strumf and art by S. Barrett McCormick and Bob Sisk, it is by far the best poster on the film and its impact is all the more dramatic because of the larger poster size.

I remember reading an article in the 1980s that discussed the most instantly recognisable images in Western culture. At the top of the list were the Coca-Cola logo, Mickey Mouse, the Swastika and King Kong on top of the Empire State building – quite an achievement for an entirely fictional creation.

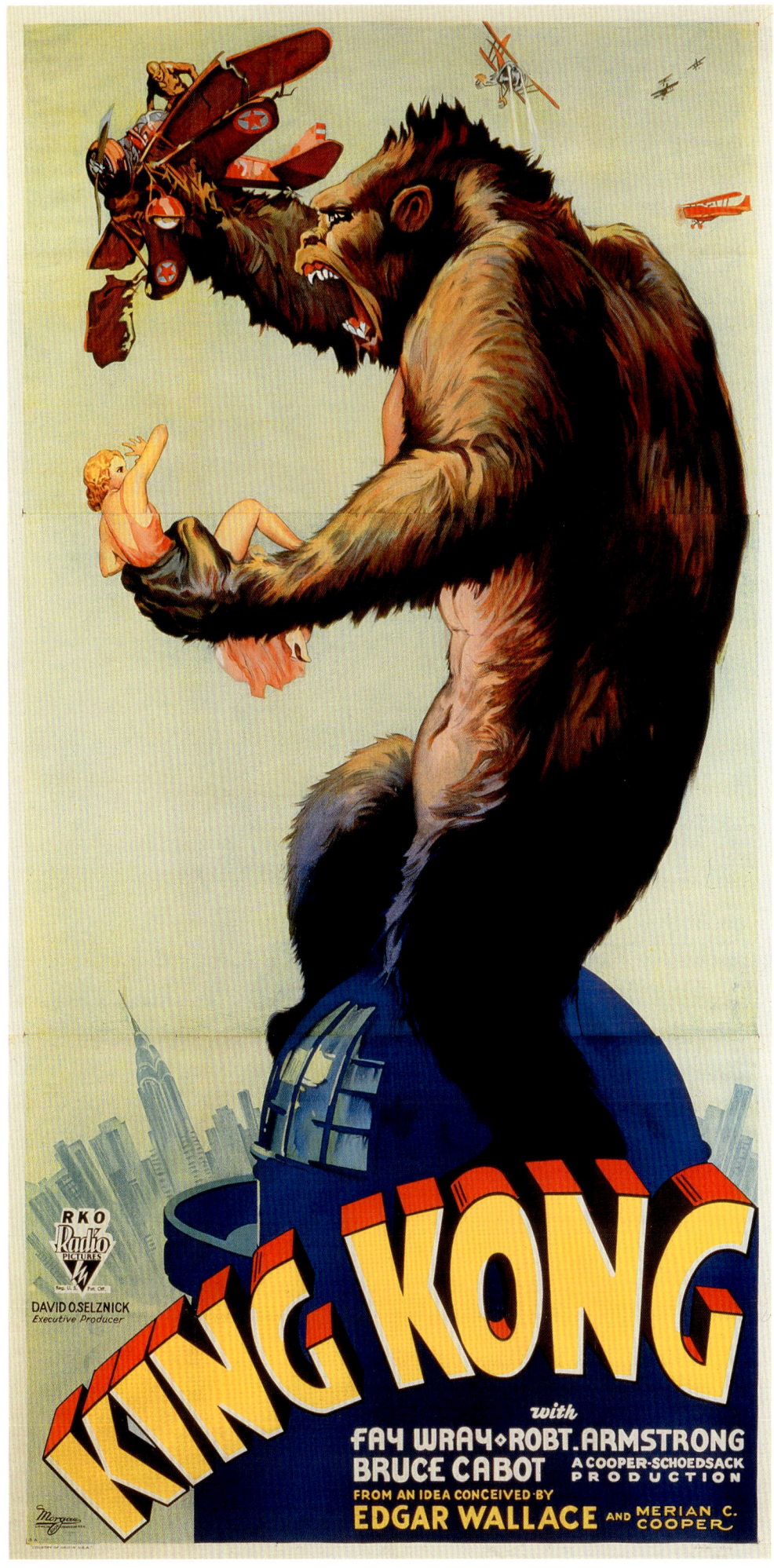

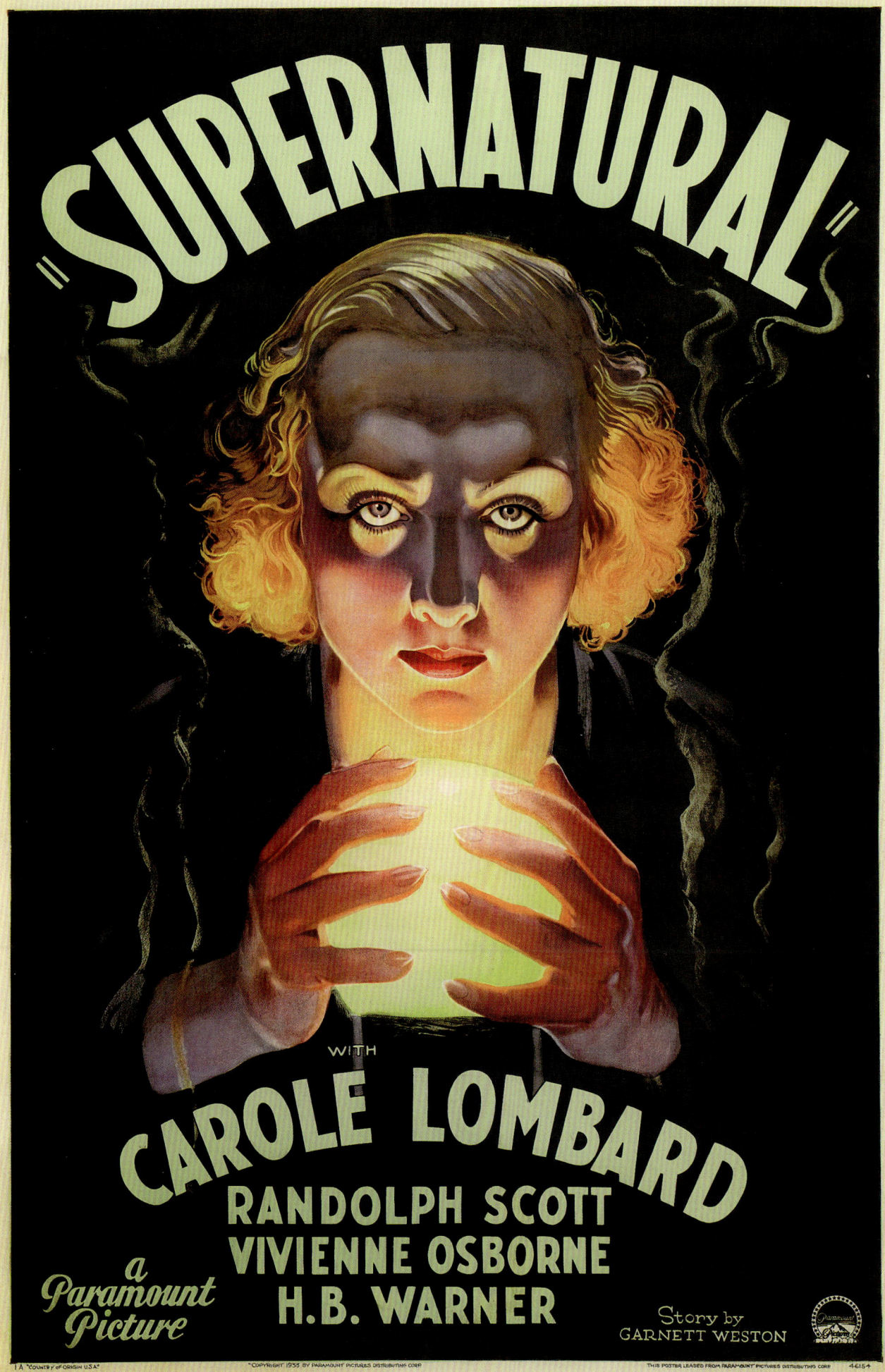

SUPERNATURAL 1933
AMERICAN POSTER, ART DIRECTION BY VINCENT TROTTA AND MAURICE KALLIS

The American poster for *Supernatural* is chilling and one of the best horror posters of the twentieth century. The artwork was designed by Vincent Trotta (1886-1970), chief art director at Paramount during the 1920s and 1930s (and later renowned as chief judge of the Miss America pageant), and his assistant, Maurice Kallis (1903-1988). The poster's vibrant colours and haunting shadows are all the more surprising for depicting Carole Lombard, usually synonymous with light screwball comedies and a gentle smile.

Lombard was the highest paid actress in the business when she was approached by the Halperin Brothers – fresh from their success with Lugosi-led horror *White Zombie* – to star in *Supernatural*. Supposedly tension grew on set as Lombard felt she was more suited to comedic roles and not the possessed, revenge-seeking murderess she was expected to play here. The resulting film, however, is one of her finest performances. This unsettling tale is also notable for being one of the earliest Hollywood films to deal with the theme of spirit possession.

LADIES THEY TALK ABOUT 1933
AMERICAN POSTER, ART BY ALBERTO VARGAS

Barbara Stanwyck has always been one of my favourite actresses. She was also one of the most notorious of the pre-Code dames. 'Ladies they talk about' just about summed it up and her husky, brazen sexuality was exactly the type of femininity the Hays office desperately tried to stamp out after 1934. The American poster by Alberto Vargas is one of the most beautiful depictions of the actress – with Stanwyck's posture and slipping silk gown a perfect reflection of her unabashed appeal.

Legendary for his pin-up paintings of the female form, Alberto Vargas (1896-1982) was one of America's most famous commercial illustrators and his 'Varga Girls' are icons of Americana. Born in Peru, Vargas was educated in Europe, before moving to New York in 1917. In 1919 he was hired as the official painter of the renowned Ziegfeld Follies. For the next 12 years, Vargas painted several portraits of Ziegfeld's beautiful starlets (one of whom, Anna Mae Clift, later became his wife). In the early 1930s, Vargas moved west to Hollywood where he established himself as a painter of the stars and also worked on set design. He worked for all the major studios and painted portraits of the leading ladies of the day, including Garbo, Dietrich and, of course, Stanwyck in *Ladies They Talk About*.

In 1940, Vargas began working for *Esquire* magazine, taking the place of *Esquire*'s renowned in-house artist, George Petty. At *Esquire*, Vargas developed his iconic 'Varga Girl', dropping the 's' from his name at the suggestion of the magazine's publisher, David Smart. Vargas's aim was to create, 'A Varga Girl so beautiful, so perfect, so typical of the American girl, that I can put that picture in any part of the world, without any signature ... and they will say, that is the Varga Girl.' For the next six years, from 1940 to 1946, his Varga Girls appeared across the pages of *Esquire*, on their calendars and special editions. His pin-up illustrations became a breast-pocket favourite of American soldiers serving overseas. Such was the morale-raising role of Vargas's scantily-clad girls that the US Government awarded him an official decoration for his work.

In the 1950s, Vargas completed a legendary series of 12 'Legacy Nudes' that he had been working on for several years. They confirmed his status as one of America's foremost artists and opened the door to working for *Playboy* in the 1960s and 1970s. Over 30 years after his death, Vargas's name continues to rank amongst an elite group of artists that have been able to capture the beauty and sexuality of the female form for the American masses.

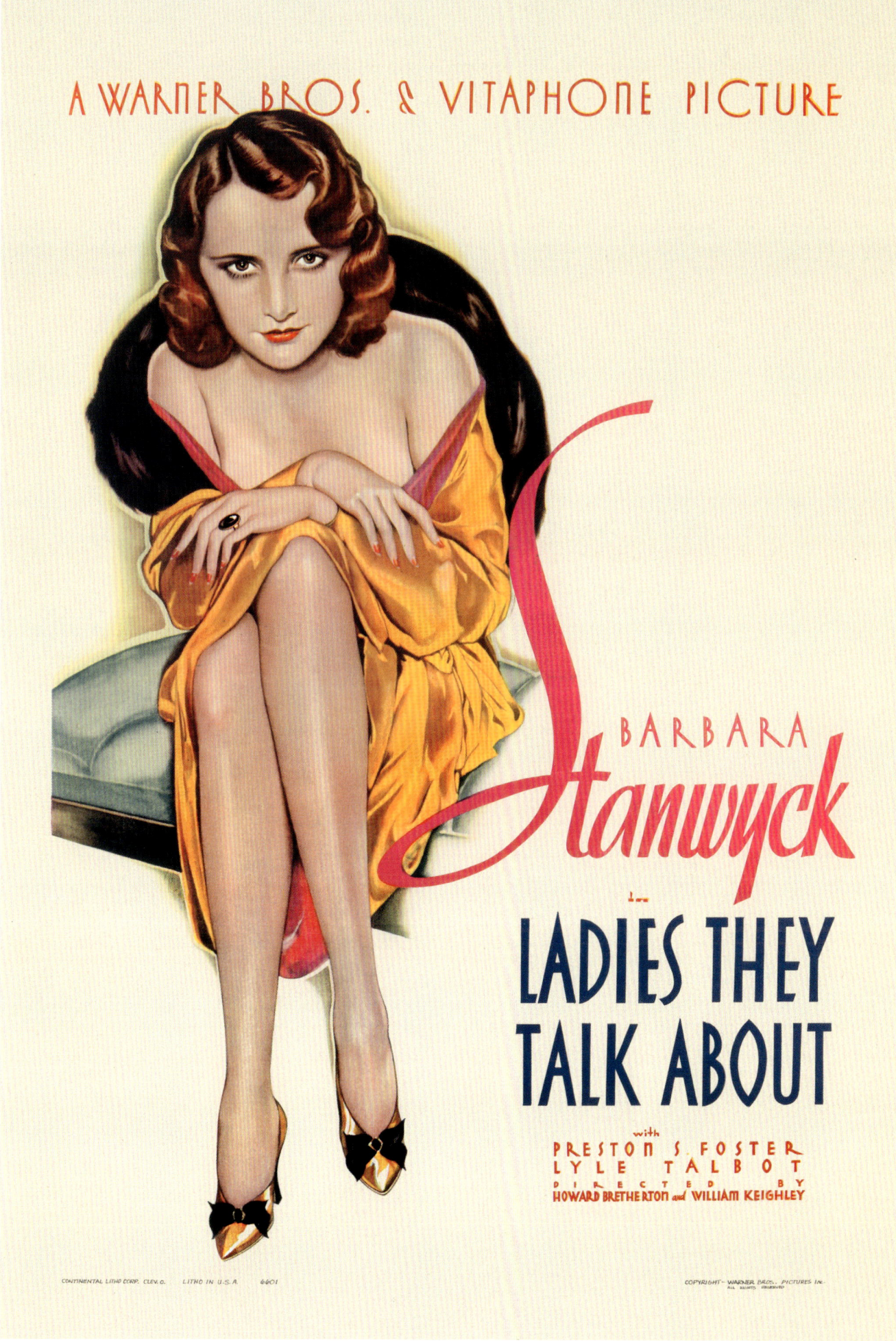

LE SEXE FAIBLE 1933
FRENCH POSTER, ART BY PAUL COLIN

In 1993, I attended one of my first ever movie poster auctions in France. This poster for *The Weaker Sex* – the first film Robert Siodmak made in France after fleeing Germany – was not in the main auction but was instead being shown to someone else in the room by an old-time French collector. It was one of many moments in my life when I have slightly lost my mind over a poster, and I simply had to have it. I did not realize at the time that it was the only known copy of the poster in existence. A couple of years later, the same copy turned up again at Christie's, London, in the first dedicated film poster sale by a major auction house in Europe.

This evocative and bold poster was typical of artist Paul Colin's style. Paul Colin (1892-1985) was renowned as one of the most important French graphic designers of the twentieth century and was a true master of his art.

Colin's career break came in the mid-1920s, when a friend commissioned him to create a poster for *La Revue Nègre* in Paris, starring jazz-age siren Josephine Baker. His design proved such a success that he was invited to join the artistic staff at the theatre as a poster and set designer. Meanwhile, Josephine Baker became his one time-lover, lifelong friend and muse.

In 1929, Colin produced an Art Deco portfolio of over 40 colourful pochoir lithographs depicting the jazz-age exuberance of Paris, entitled *Le Tumulte Noir* (*The Black Craze*). This stunning achievement secured Colin's reputation as one of the country's leading graphic design talents. A year later, he opened the first poster design school in Paris, which proved a training ground for a number of respected future graphic designers, including the celebrated FHK Henrion. Colin's complete body of work includes nearly 2000 posters, many of which have been exhibited worldwide.

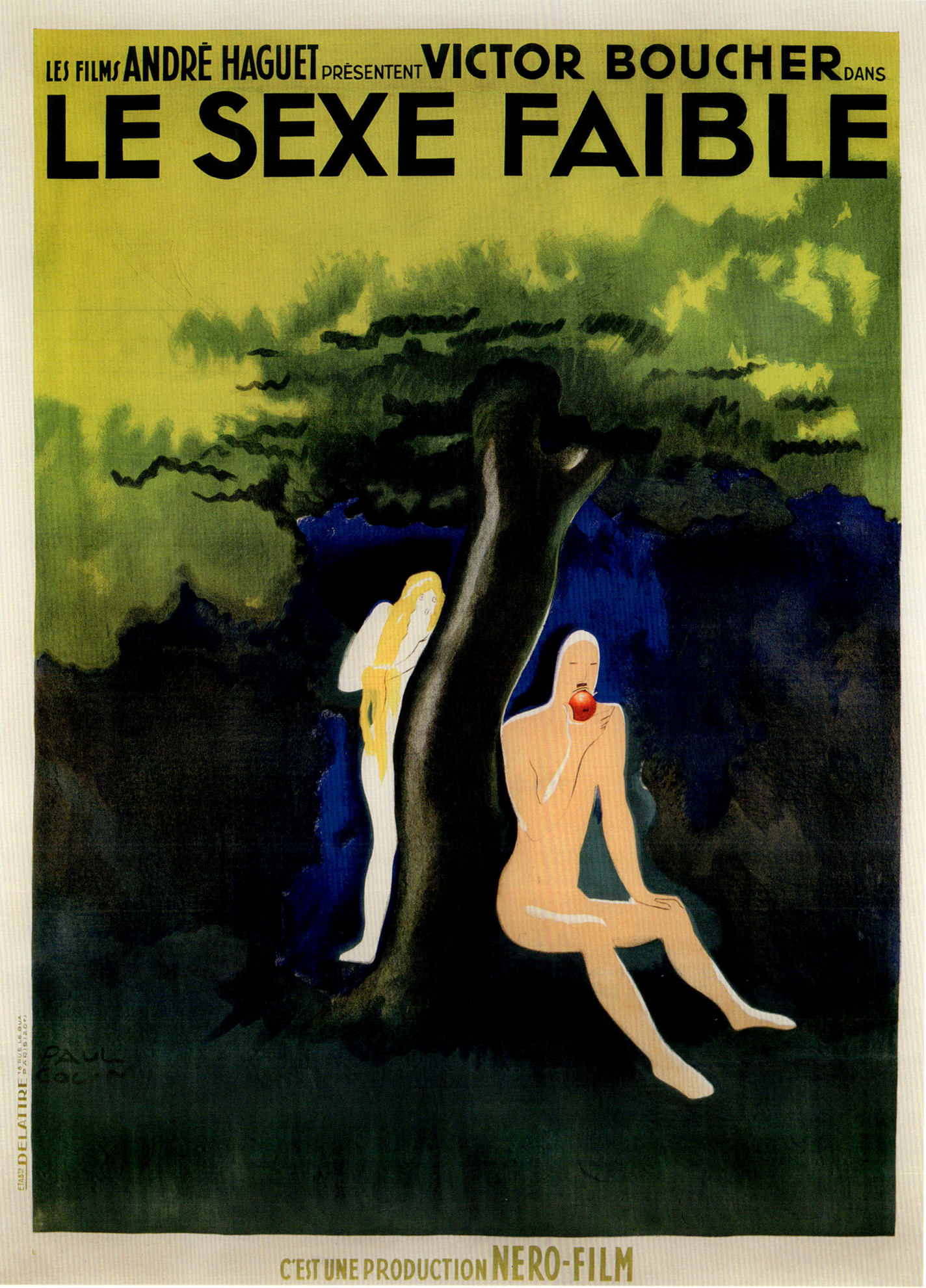

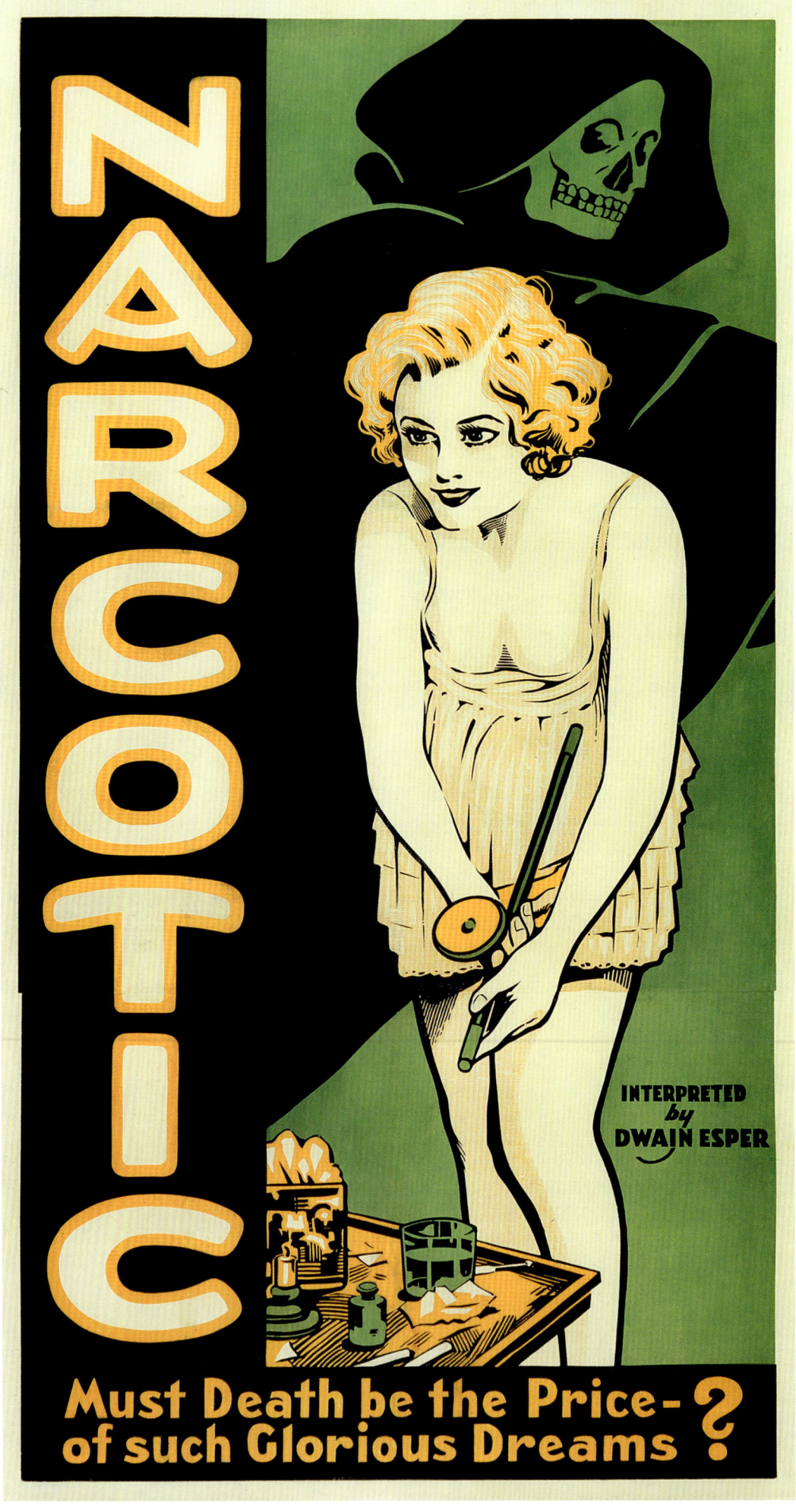

Narcotic 1933
American poster, Artist unknown

Known as 'King of the Celluloid Gypsies', Dwain Esper was one of the renowned 'Forty Thieves' – a small group of independent filmmakers that travelled the country pedalling their films and who had more in common with the carnival and circus tradition than with the mainline movie business. The roadshow men did everything themselves, from writing and directing their films to distributing and promoting them. They would sometimes try to get approval from the Breen Office by screening a heavily censored print of their product, but more often than not they would take the uncensored version on the road, travelling from state to state. They would then either come to an arrangement by which the local theatre owner agreed to screen the film or, if this didn't work, they would set up a tent on the edge of town, with a sheet for a screen and wooden benches for seats. The films were cheaply made, badly acted and of a generally terrible standard, yet they offered audiences something Hollywood could not: brash titillation. Their poster art was likewise not distinguished for its subtlety. Provocative titles promised 'Startling Revelations!' and 'Shocking Truths!' against a backdrop of female flesh.

Esper was the most renowned and the shrewdest of the early exploitation producers. He marketed his films as 'educational', allowing his audience the comfort of convincing themselves that rather than enjoying his steamy movies they were, in actual fact, widening their knowledge of important social issues. 'Informative' pamphlets and books were sold to audiences watching films on venereal disease, while vice films featured a voice-over proclaiming the moral necessity of teaching the young the facts of life. The opening credits of *Narcotic* claimed it an essential piece of film that was, 'Presented in the hope that the public may become aware of the terrific struggle to rid the world of drug addiction.'

Esper was also braver than many of his contemporaries and showed nudity and explicit drug taking when no one else would. Joseph Breen, industry enforcer of the Hays Code, condemned one of Esper's earliest films as the most disgusting film he had ever seen. Not only did he refuse it an official seal, but tried to have Esper imprisoned for making it.

The Golden Age of Esper was the 1930s and some of his better-known titles from this time include *Human Wreckage*, *Sex Madness* and *Marihuana: Weed With Roots In Hell*. His *Narcotic* showed an endless spectrum of drugs and injecting methods and was shocking, even for the exploitation industry, in its detailed depictions. For good measure, it also featured lots of sex and prostitution. While on the road with *Narcotic*, Esper boosted ticket sales by displaying the corpse of 'Elmer The Dope Fiend' by the entrance to the theatre or tent where the screening was taking place. The preserved cadaver was actually that of a former highwayman that Esper had acquired from a circus on the cheap.

HORSE FEATHERS 1932
AMERICAN RE-RELEASE POSTER, ART BY CONSTANTIN ALAJÁLOV

This poster for the 1937 re-release of the Marx Brothers' *Horse Feathers* is a great example of the mischievous wit and tremendous skill of caricature artist Constantin Alajálov (1900-1987). Born and raised in Russia, the Red Revolution interrupted Alajálov's studies at 16. He painted Soviet murals and posters to survive, before travelling to Persia – where he was a court painter for a khan – and then to Turkey, where he earned enough money for the $100 boat fair to America, arriving in New York in 1923. By 1926, Alajálov had his first cover published with *The New Yorker* and over the next 40 years, he designed numerous covers for *The New Yorker*, *Vanity Fair*, *Vogue* and *The Saturday Evening Post*. At this time, *The New Yorker* and *The Saturday Evening Post* had exclusivity contracts and Alajálov remains one of only a handful of artists that worked for both publications simultaneously. He was also a serious painter and art teacher for many years and his work is in the permanent collections of the Museum of Modern Art in New York and the Brooklyn Museum, amongst others.

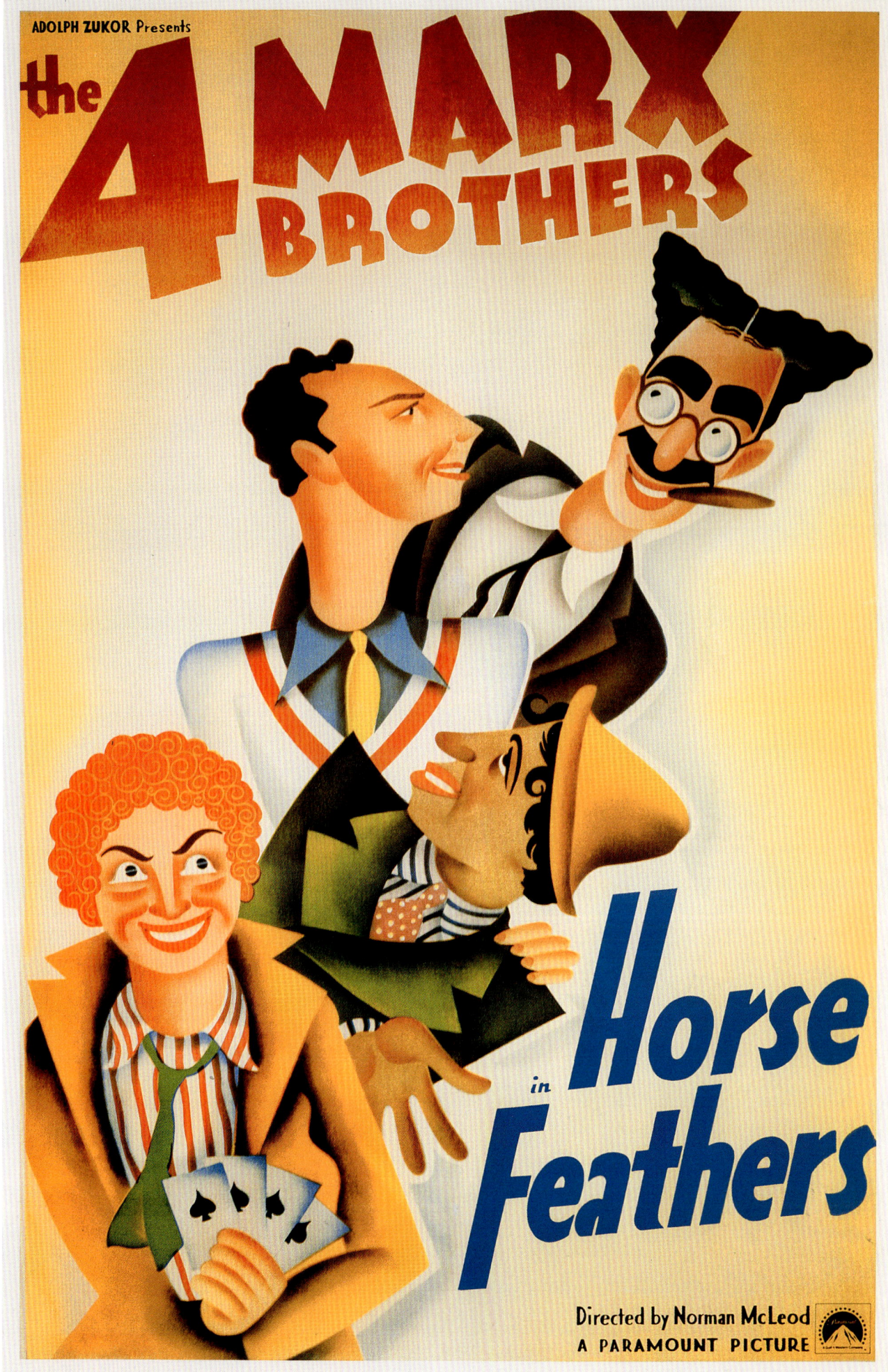

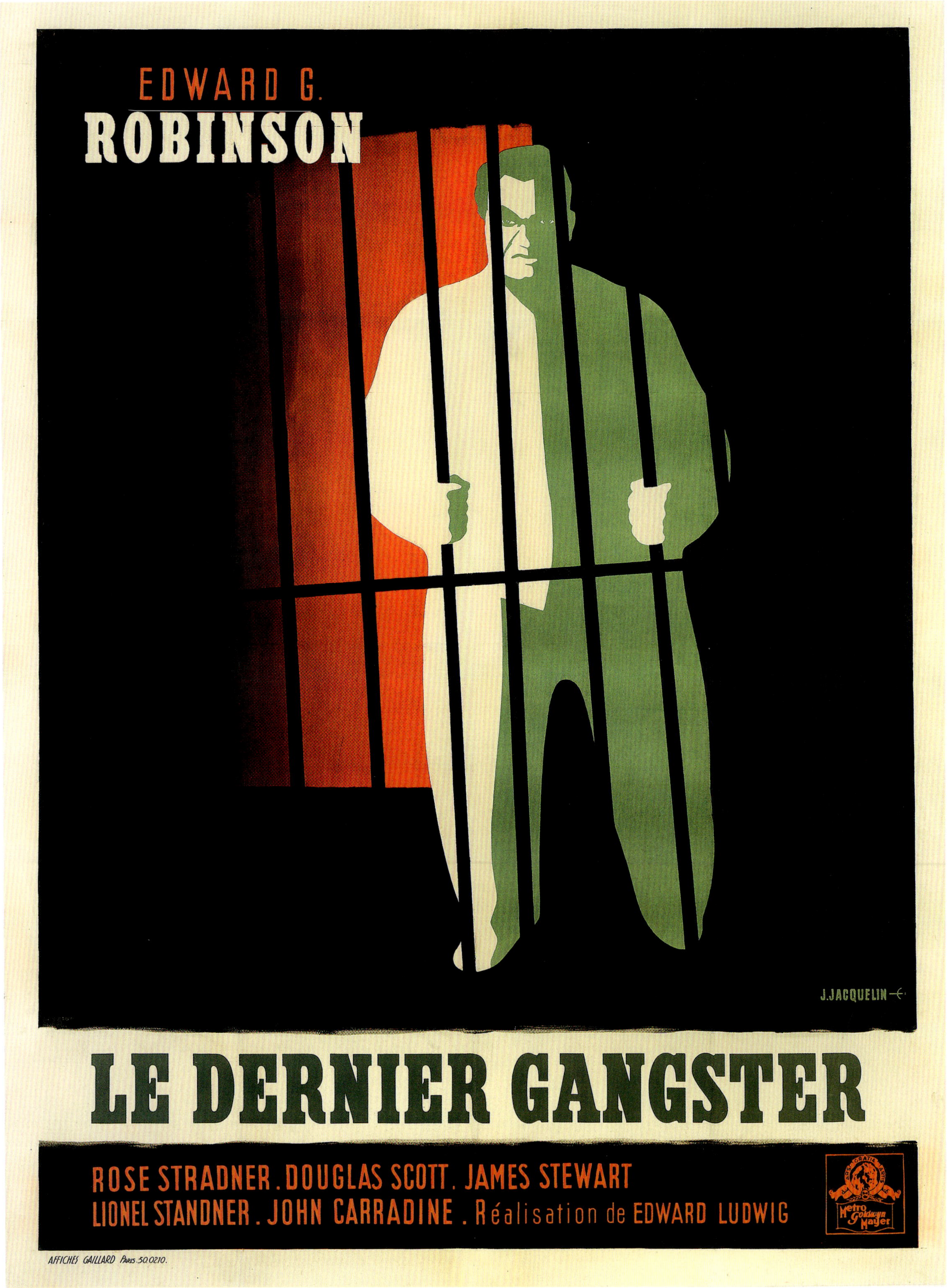

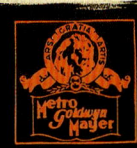

THE LAST GANGSTER 1937

FRENCH POSTER, ART BY JEAN JACQUELIN

I have never seen *The Last Gangster* and I am not in any rush to. However, Edward G. Robinson is one of my favourite actors of all time and his depiction on Jean Jacquelin's French poster for this film is superb. Jean Jacquelin (1905-1989) designed very few film posters and those that he is responsible for show unusual and abstract designs. Because of this, they were often chosen for the alternative style poster, rather than the main campaign. Other examples of Jacquelin's work can be found on the French posters for *Gaslight* (1944), *Dédée d'Anvers* (1947) and *Casque d'Or* (1952).

BRINGING UP BABY 1938

FRENCH POSTER, ART BY BERNARD LANCY

Screwball Comedy – that most American of genres – is ironically captured to greatest effect on this French poster for *Bringing Up Baby*. Bernard Lancy's artwork encapsulates the essence of screwball and all of its chaotic comedic tropes. In marked contrast are the much plainer American posters for the film, which are a crude marriage of slapped together photography and caricature.

Bernard Lancy (1892-1964) was recognised as a master in the field of French poster art. In 1945, he was named Honorary President of the Union of Cinema Poster Artists, a fitting position for a man responsible for posters such as *Bringing Up Baby*, *La Grand Illusion* (1938), *Notorious* (1946) and *The Third Man* (1949).

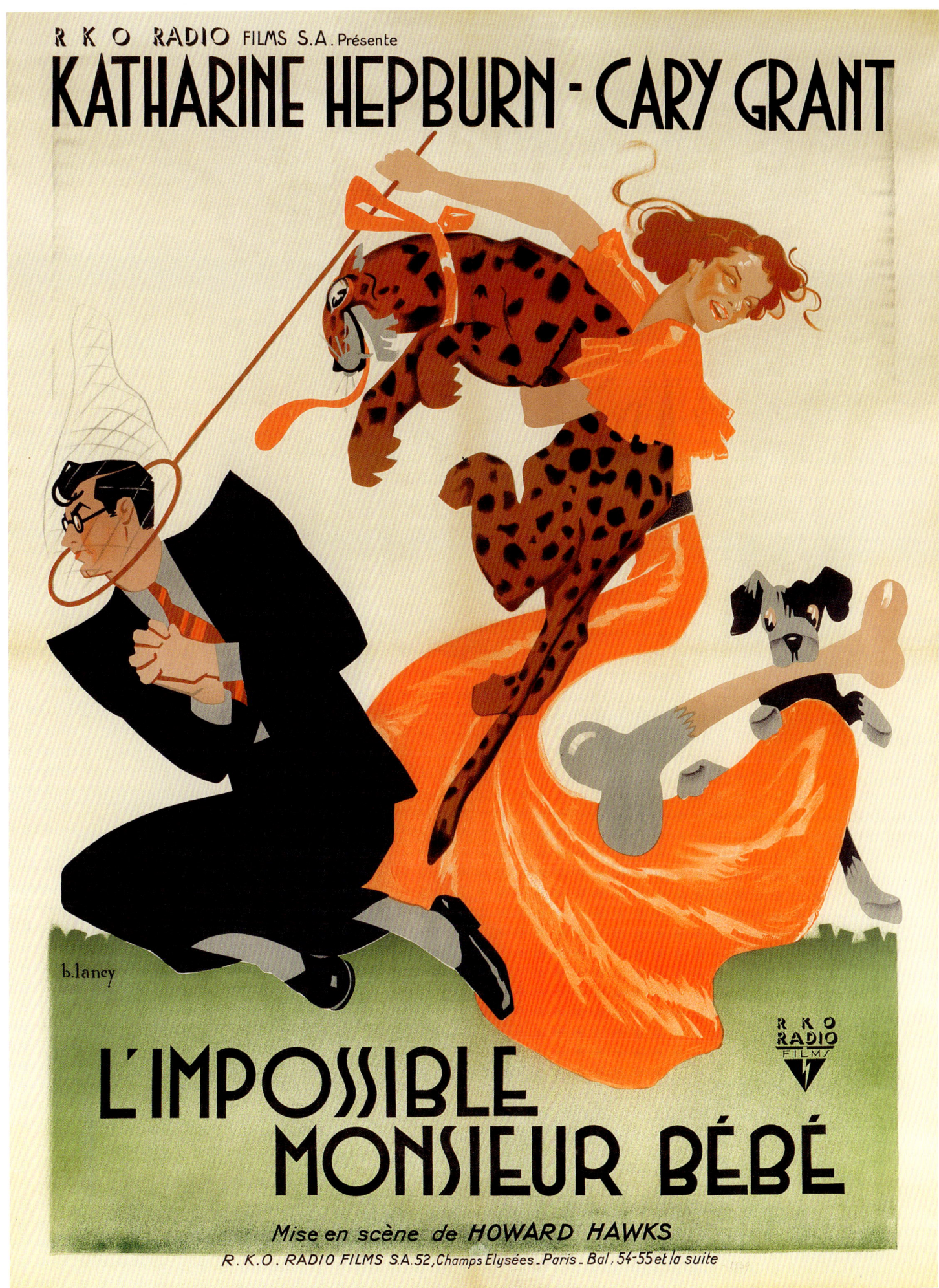

STAGECOACH 1939

AMERICAN POSTER, ART DIRECTION BY HERBERT JAEDICKER

John Ford and John Wayne made over 20 westerns together that defined the genre. They are one of the great director-actor partnerships of twentieth century cinema and *Stagecoach* was their first collaboration. It was also Ford's first 'talkie' western and he insisted on using Wayne, despite studio opposition at an unknown name. Wayne had starred in around 40 westerns at this point – from extra to bigger parts – but this was his breakthrough role. Over the next five decades, Ford and Wayne would go on to make such classics as *She Wore a Yellow Ribbon* (1949), *The Quiet Man* (1952) and *The Searchers* (1956).

Stagecoach centred on nine strangers sharing a stagecoach on a gripping journey across dangerous Apache land. In an unusual decision, Ford gave fairly equal weight to each character and it is an impressive ensemble piece. This is reflected in the stunning American poster that chose not to depict any of the actors and to simply emphasise the story not the stars. The thrill of the action is, instead, captured by the horses' faces and the sharp angle of the title font. The film was shot on location in Monument Valley and the poster also manages to capture something of the beauty of the landscape, with the orange of the setting sun contrasting against the dark blue twilight of the foreground.

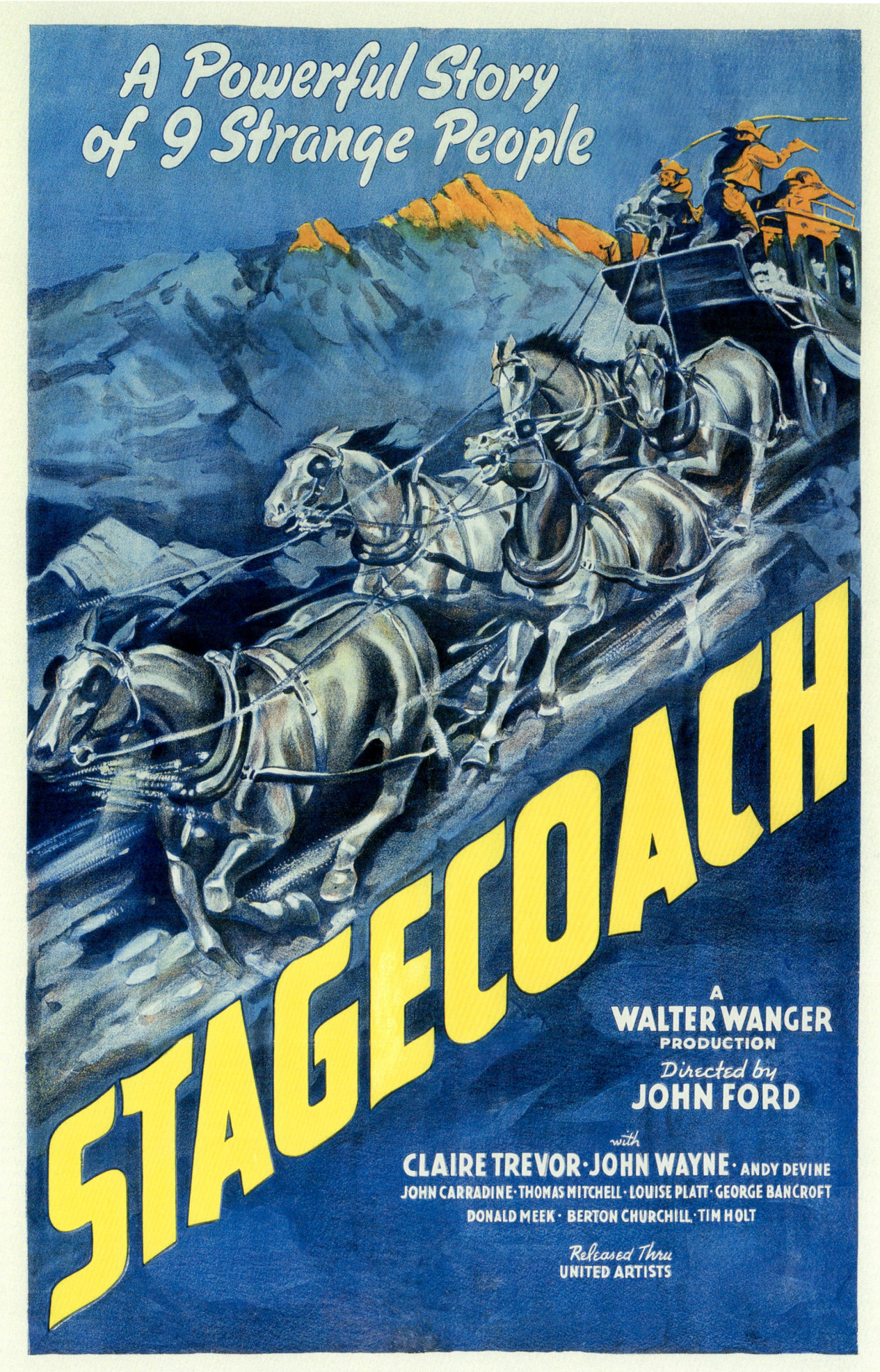

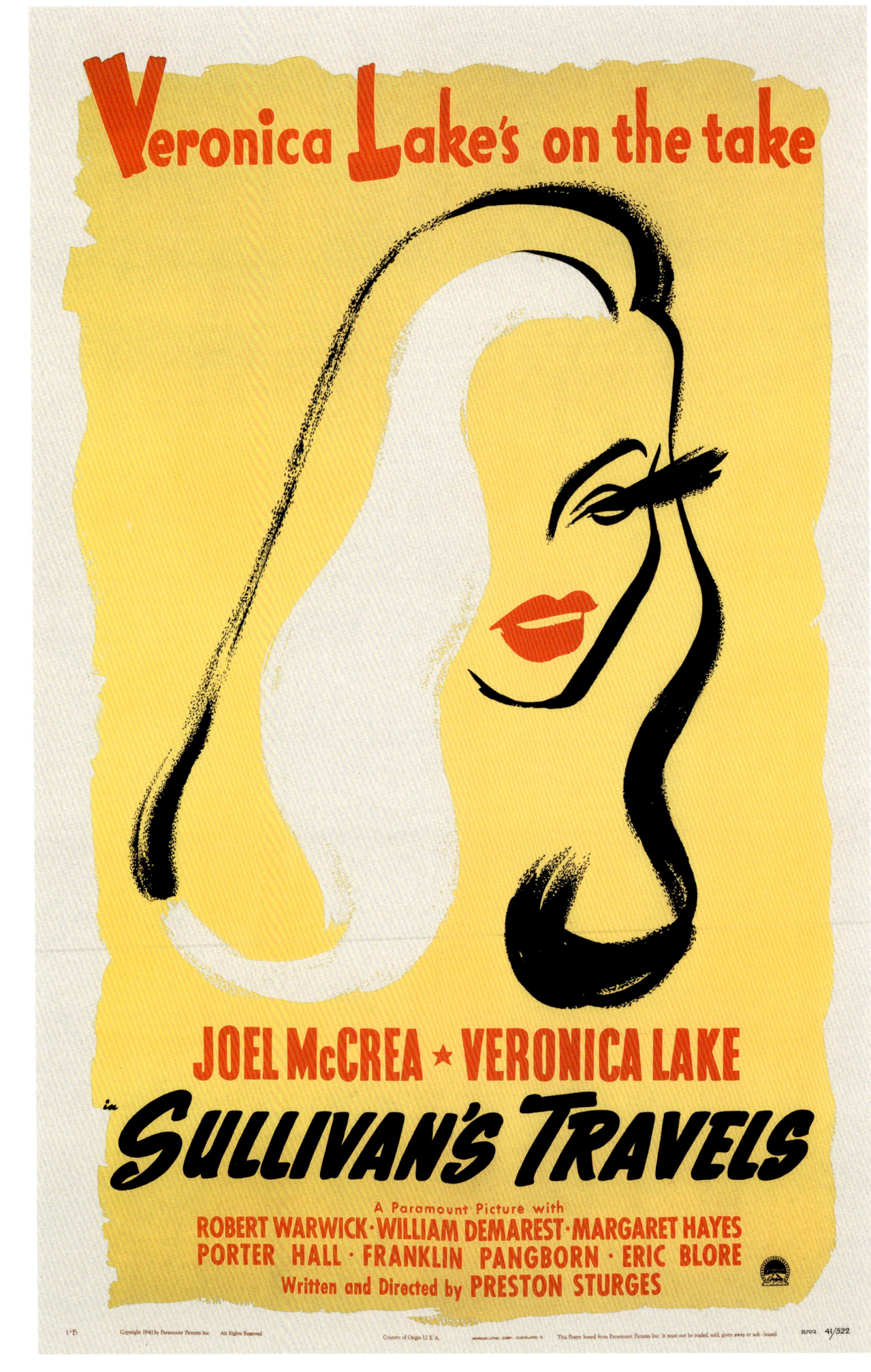

SULLIVAN'S TRAVELS 1941
AMERICAN POSTER, ART DIRECTION BY MAURICE KALLIS

The father of screwball comedy, Preston Sturges' genius was borne of an ability to combine clever, witty dialogue with poignant comments on American society. *Sullivan's Travels* is celebrated as one of his greatest works, with the film highlighting the irreconcilable opportunities gap between rich and poor in America, while also being a fast-paced comedy and a subtle satire of Hollywood.

Lake was being billed as Paramount's bright new star and was a fresh favourite with the public. This American poster, designed by Maurice Kallis, emphasised the peek-a-boo pin-up's greatest assets and summed up her box-office appeal. The simplicity of the poster's paired-down graphics was an unusually modern approach for a Hollywood studio at this time and it was only used as an alternative, 'style B' poster.

THIS GUN FOR HIRE 1942
AMERICAN POSTER, ART DIRECTION BY MAURICE KALLIS

I am not generally a fan of 'Lake and Ladd' film noirs, but I have always had a weakness for this poster – the combination of the archetypal noir title, the remorseless eyes of the hitman, *that* face. It was designed by Maurice Kallis, who had learnt his craft working as an assistant to Paramount's art director, Vincent Trotta, in the 1920s and 1930s (see p.59). In 1942, Veronica Lake was one of the biggest hitters at the box-office and this was the first time she had been paired opposite Alan Ladd. He was only given fourth billing and it is odd that he is even depicted on the poster. *This Gun For Hire* made him a star and Lake and Ladd's winning on-screen chemistry saw them star in a further six films together, including *The Glass Key* (1942) and *The Blue Dahlia* (1946).

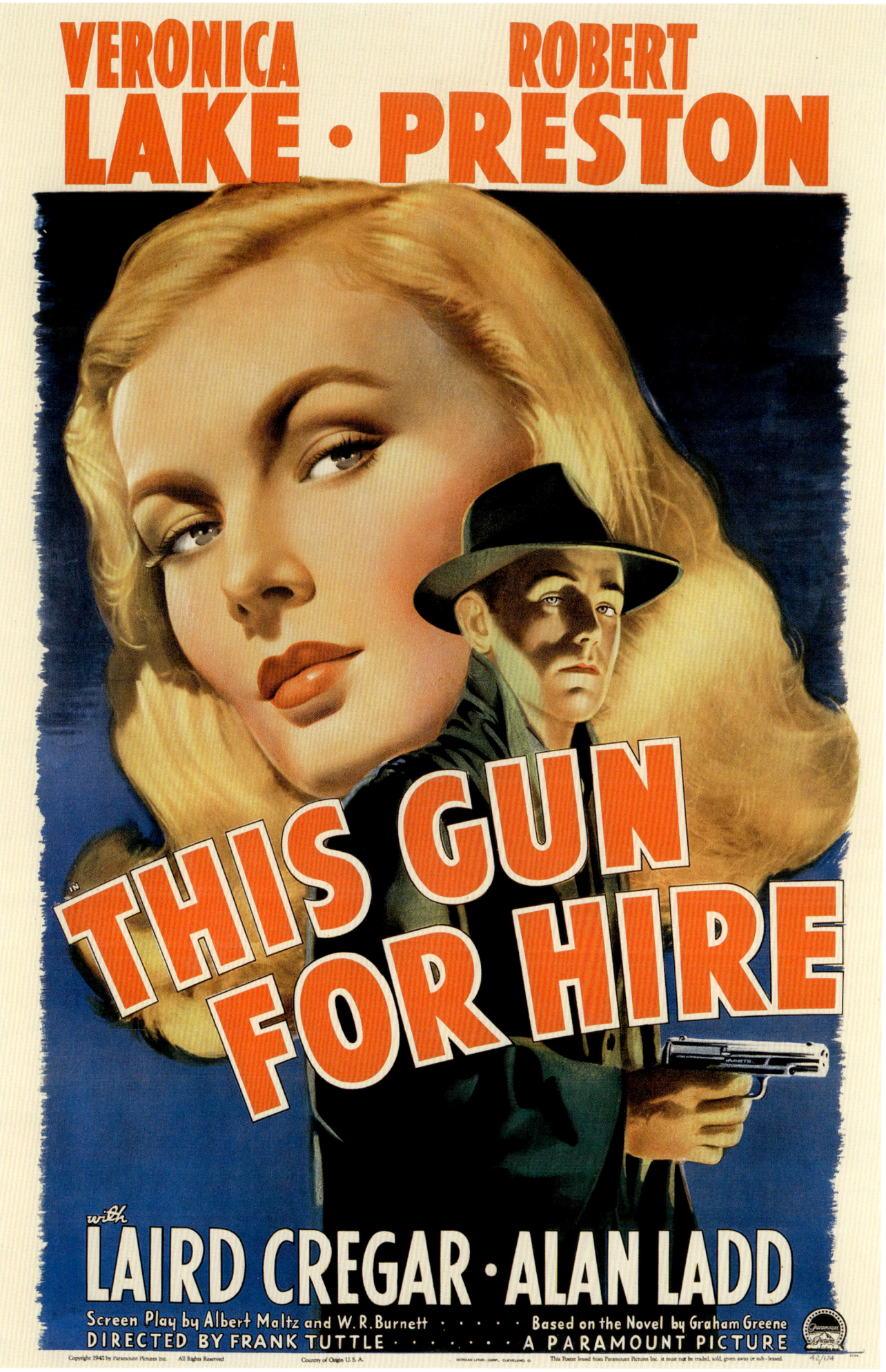

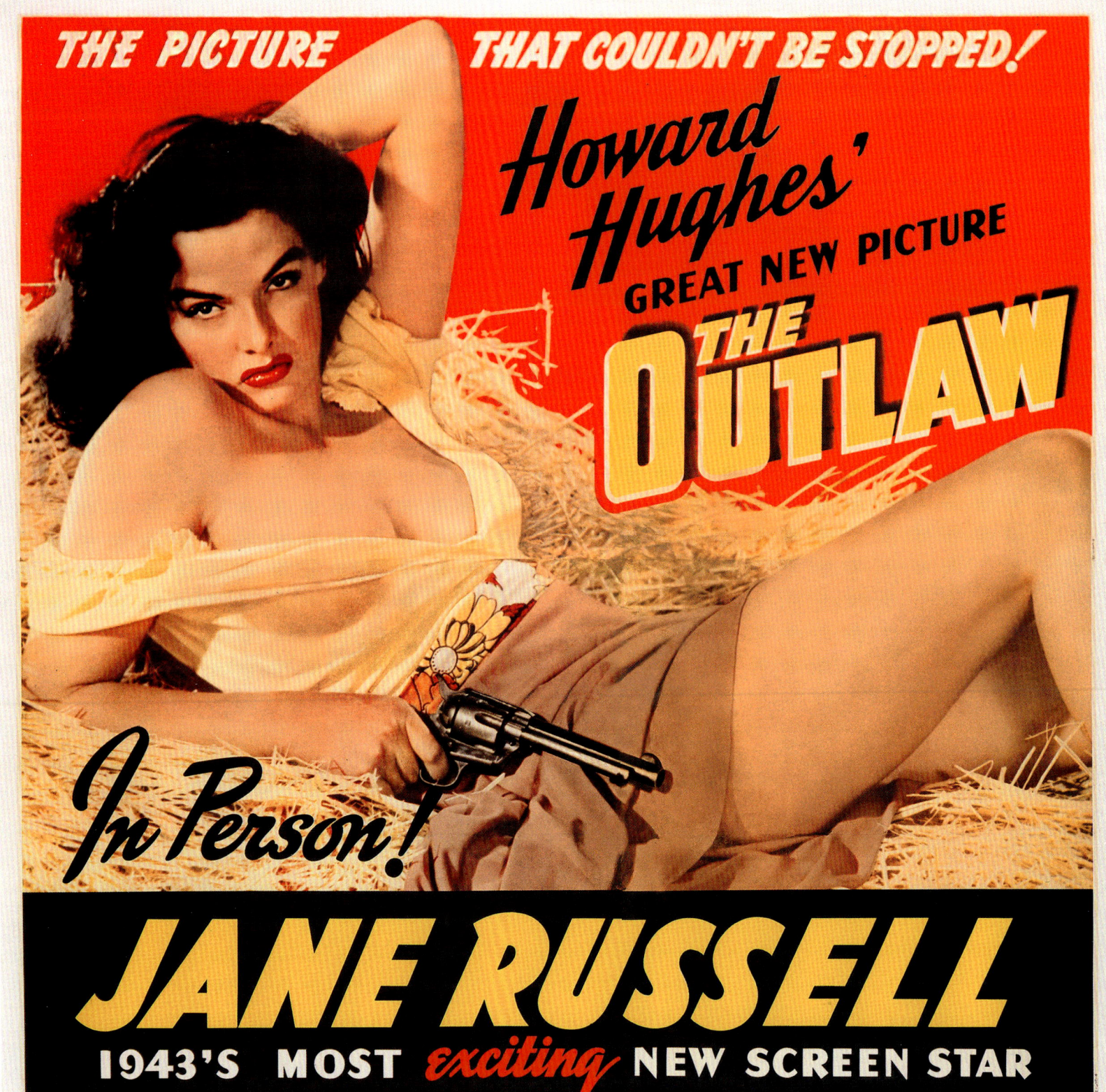

The Outlaw 1942
American poster, Photo by George Hurrell

Howard Hughes was a man of many faces. Shrewd businessman, skilled aviator, notorious womaniser and movie mogul, he was a flamboyant figure in the Hollywood of the 1930s and early-1940s. In 1941, while filming *The Outlaw*, Hughes used his engineering expertise to create a prototype of the push-up bra in a (surely unnecessary) attempt to accentuate Jane Russell's bust – although Russell would later claim that, 'I never wore it … and he never knew. He wasn't going to take my clothes off to check if I had it on. I just told him I did.'

Russell's cleavage, liberally displayed, was a major motif in the film. This was even more so the case in the advertising campaign, which brought Hughes into serious conflict with the censors. He anticipated trouble from the Production Code Administration (PCA) in advance, and thus attempted to release the film under his own steam, premiering it in San Francisco with an accompanying poster declaring, *The picture that couldn't be stopped!* PCA chief Joseph Breen had other ideas, however, and withdrew the picture from circulation. It did not receive an official seal until 1950.

When this 1943 poster from Hughes' original San Francisco premiere surfaced in an auction at Christie's, London, in March 2003, it broke all previous European movie poster auction records, selling for £52,875 ($95,000).

The poster featured a photograph shot by George Hurrell (1904-1992). During the 1930s and 1940s, Hurrell worked with nearly every major studio star in Hollywood. Many would not sit for any other photographer. His groundbreaking techniques, his trademark spotlighting and a rejection of soft focus created a sensuality that came to define Hollywood's Golden Age. *Esquire* magazine wrote in 1936 that, 'A Hurrell portrait is to the ordinary publicity still about what a Rolls-Royce is to a roller-skate.'

Hurrell's incredible black and white publicity stills captured many of Hollywood's most glamorous and famous stars as the movie going public had never seen them before. The reason they all insisted on having Hurrell was simple; he photographed a movie star and created an icon. He photographed all the greats, including Garbo, Bogart, Katharine Hepburn, Harlow, Lombard, Rita Hayworth and Joan Crawford, and he is even credited with creating Veronica Lake's peek-a-boo hairstyle. His portraits of Jane Russell (bra-less) on a haystack for *The Outlaw* were some of the most stunning shots ever taken of the actress and reflected her untamable sexuality.

THE BIG SHOT 1942
FRENCH POSTER, ART BY BORIS GRINSSON

The Big Shot was a pretty average crime caper, however, the French poster for the film is one of the best depictions of Bogie and is also a stunning example of the high standard of French poster design during this period. The artist responsible was Boris Grinsson, who managed to perfectly capture the essence of Bogart's brooding, hardboiled stare. The reclining portrait of Irene Manning in the foreground is beautiful, and I have also always loved the rather abstract figure running away in the distance.

Boris Grinsson (1907-1999) was born in Russia. Fleeing the Bolshevik Revolution, his family settled in Estonia and Grinsson studied art in the Estonian city of Tartu. Moving to Berlin in 1929, he initially harboured acting ambitions, before redirecting his energies into designing film posters for the UFA film studio. In 1933, Grinsson was forced to flee Germany for France after drawing an anti-Nazi election poster that depicted a caricature of Hitler as the Angel of Death.

Settling in France, Grinsson continued to pursue film poster design. Post-war, he became one of the major names working in Paris, alongside contemporaries René Péron and Roger Soubie. At this time, Grinsson would often design the alternative 'style B' poster, while another artist, like Péron or Soubie, would design the main poster for a film's release. In 1947, Grinsson helped to establish a union of film poster designers. The commissions kept coming and he became one of the most sought-after talents in the business. From the 1930s to 1972 (when he retired from the increasingly photographic profession), Grinsson produced some 1800 posters across a variety of genres. His most notable works include *This Gun For Hire* (1942), *Gilda* (1946), *The Lady from Shanghai* (1948) and *From Russia with Love* (1963).

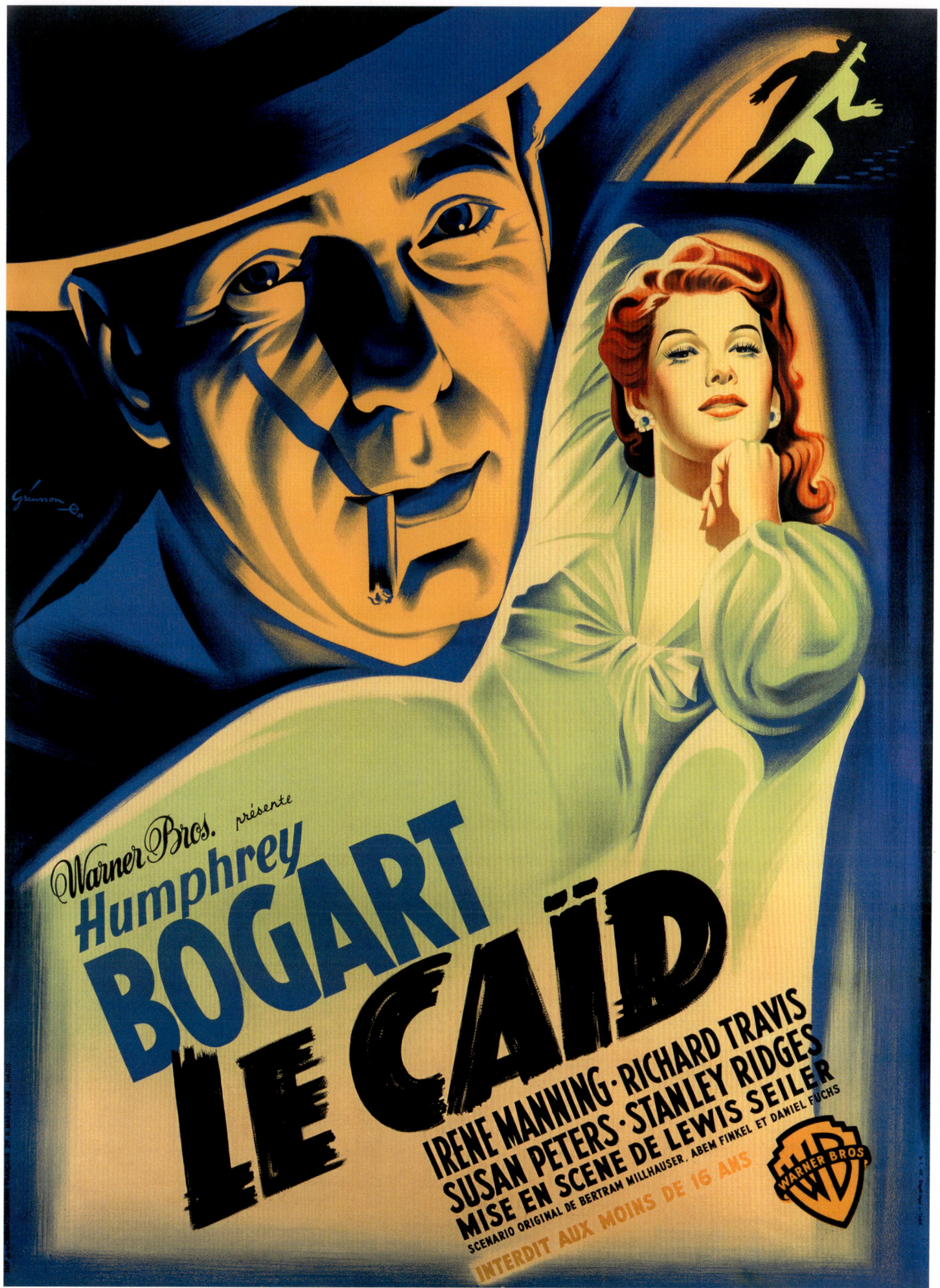

Casablanca 1942

French poster, Art by Pierre Pigeot

Artist Pierre Pigeot's French poster for *Casablanca* is a beautiful piece and by far my favourite poster on the film. Bergman's oversized profile and the lines of smoke streaking across the poster, depicted in warm hues of pink and orange, are an unusual and striking design choice. The ambiguity of the film's outcome is also conveyed in the decision to depict the chess scene.

As a French poster designer, Pierre Pigeot was very active during the 1930s and 1940s and he mainly worked on Warner Bros studio releases. This poster for *Casablanca* is his most famous work. It is a great example of the artistic freedom afforded to European artists during this period.

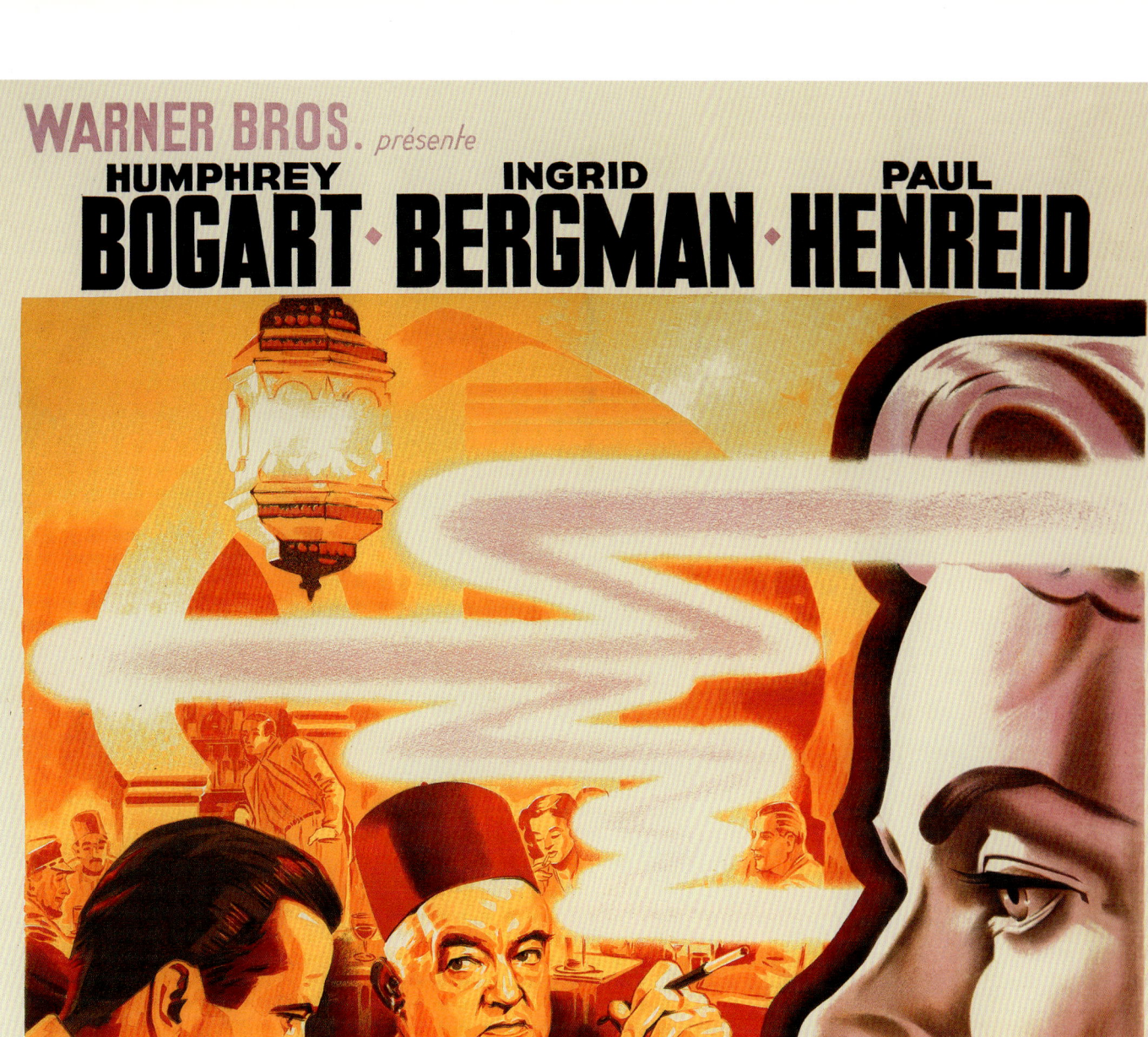

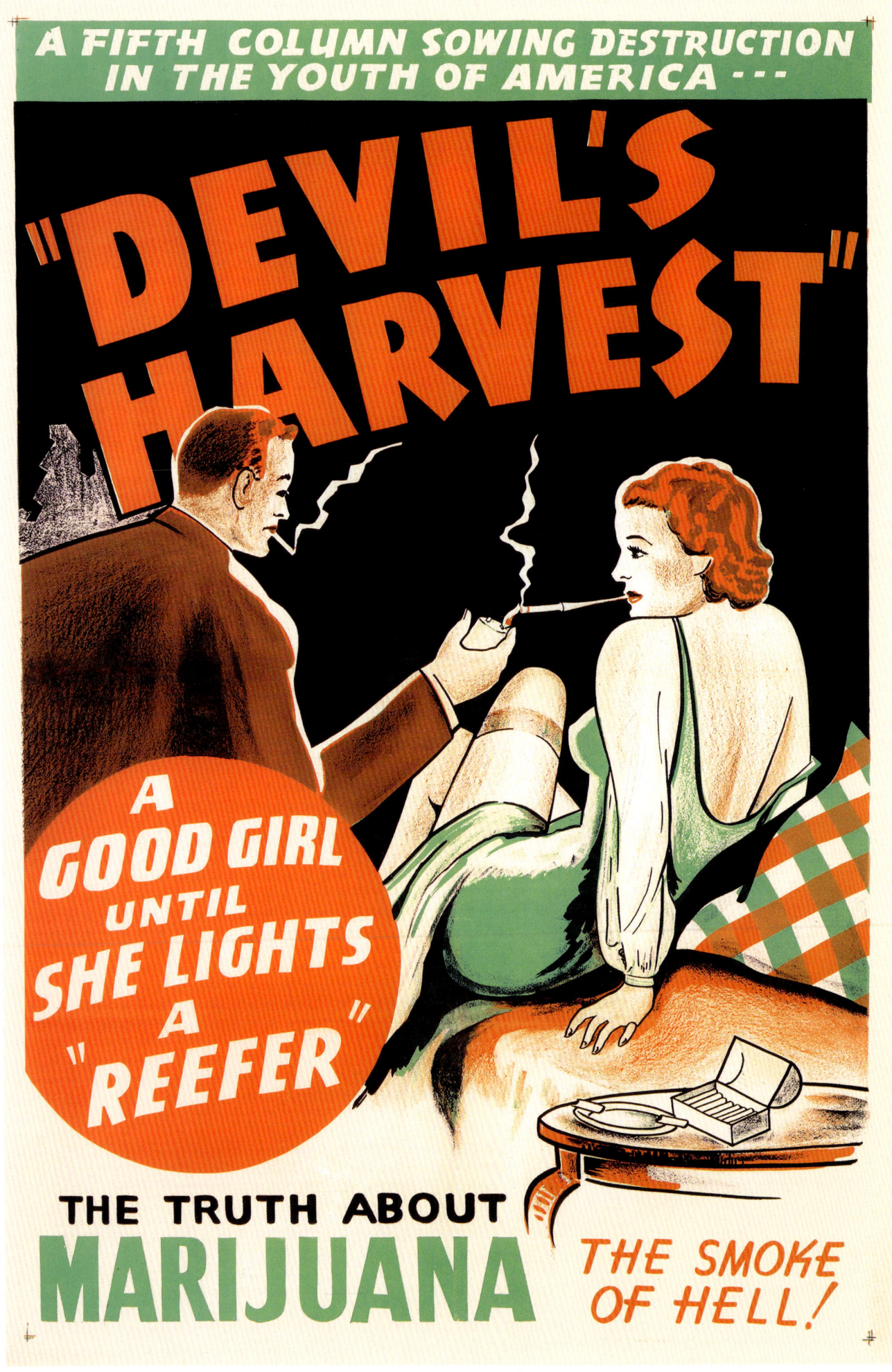

DEVIL'S HARVEST 1942
AMERICAN POSTER, ARTIST UNKNOWN

This poster for *Devil's Harvest* is an excellent example of exploitation-era poster art and a personal favourite. I originally saw it at the first Christie's movie poster auction I attended in New York in 1992. Without thinking, I stuck my hand up but was unsuccessful – perhaps a blessing considering my finances at the time. I had to wait another 15 years before I had another opportunity to acquire the poster and it is now one of the few pieces I have hanging in a prominent position in my home.

In the 1920s and 1930s, marijuana flicks were a hot topic of cinema's bottom feeders, with shrewd producers playing on society's fears of the drug's debauched effects. In the 1940s, however, with America now at war, the silver screen was supposed to portray Americans as happy warriors engaged in a noble mission overseas – no one wanted to dwell on domestic problems such as drug abuse. There was also a practical issue; as Japanese sources of rope began to dwindle, growing American hemp became a patriotic activity. This was especially true after 1942 when the US government introduced its 'Hemp For Victory' campaign, releasing films that showed farmers wading through fields of luscious cannabis plants. Such footage naturally took the edge off the marijuana paranoia. The exploitation industry, however, was reluctant to abandon a theme that had proved profitable for so many years and *The Devil's Harvest* gave the marijuana staple a new and topical twist by attributing America's drug problems to the Nazis and an insidious Fifth Column.

CABIN IN THE SKY 1943
AMERICAN POSTER, ART BY AL HIRSCHFELD

The American poster for *Cabin in the Sky* is one of the most stylish posters from this period and it makes me happy every time I look at it. The artwork is by Al Hirschfeld (1903-2003), one of the most important and influential American caricaturists of the twentieth century. Hirschfeld's skill in creating the most incisive satirical portraits using the simplest of lines was unparalleled and he was a true genius of his art.

Displaying a prodigious talent from childhood, Hirschfeld studied at the Art Students League in New York while still in his early teens and, at 17, he was working as an art director at Selznick Pictures. He also began working as a sketch artist for the *New York Herald Tribune* and *The New York Times*. The popularity of his line drawings soon led to commissions from every leading magazine and publication in the country, including *The New Yorker, Time, Life, TV Guide, Collier's, Look, Rolling Stone* and *Reader's Digest*. He also worked on movie and theatre posters, album covers and as an art consultant. In 1991, he became the first artist in history to have his name on a US postage stamp booklet.

In 1996, an Oscar-winning documentary, *The Line King*, was made about Hirschfeld's life. Four years later, in 2000, the Library of Congress officially declared him a 'Living Legend'. In 2002, he was awarded the National Medal of Arts: presented by the President of the United States, the medal is the very highest honour bestowed upon an artist on behalf of the people.

Hirschfeld's subjects were mostly drawn from Broadway or Hollywood. This, combined with the longevity of his career, has resulted in his work serving as a 'Who's Who' of the leading figures in entertainment in the twentieth century. Permanent collections of his drawings are housed in the Metropolitan Museum of Art, the Museum of Modern Art and in private and public collections around the world.

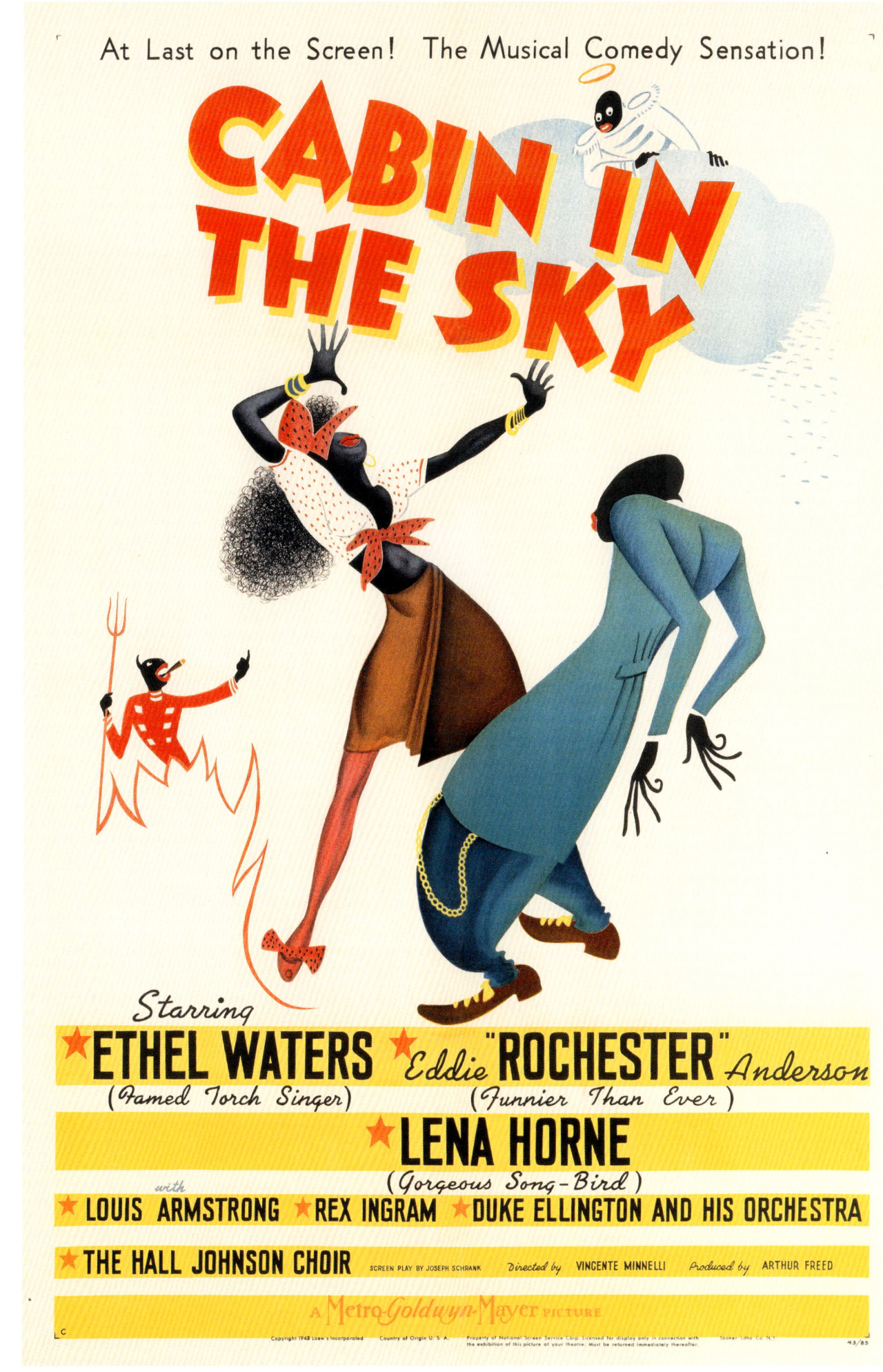

TEEN AGE 1944

AMERICAN POSTER, ARTIST UNKNOWN

This poster for *Teen Age* is one of the most beautiful examples of exploitation poster art that I have encountered. Simple graphics and few colours were a hallmark of the genre, which lends the design a strikingly modern feel. I have only ever seen one copy of this poster.

Made in 1944, *Teen Age* was a zero-budget exploitation flick that recycled footage from *Gambling With Souls* (1936) and *Slaves in Bondage* (1937). It played on society's fears of a rise in wartime juvenile delinquency. The film took its title from the hot new phrase of 1944, 'teen age' – a term that had been coined to label the distinct spending power of the hormone-fuelled group aged between 14 and 18. In the April 1945 issue of *American Speech* it was listed in the 'new words' section, while in 1947 *Encyclopædia Britannica* identified 'teen ager' as a new word that had been coined in 1944.

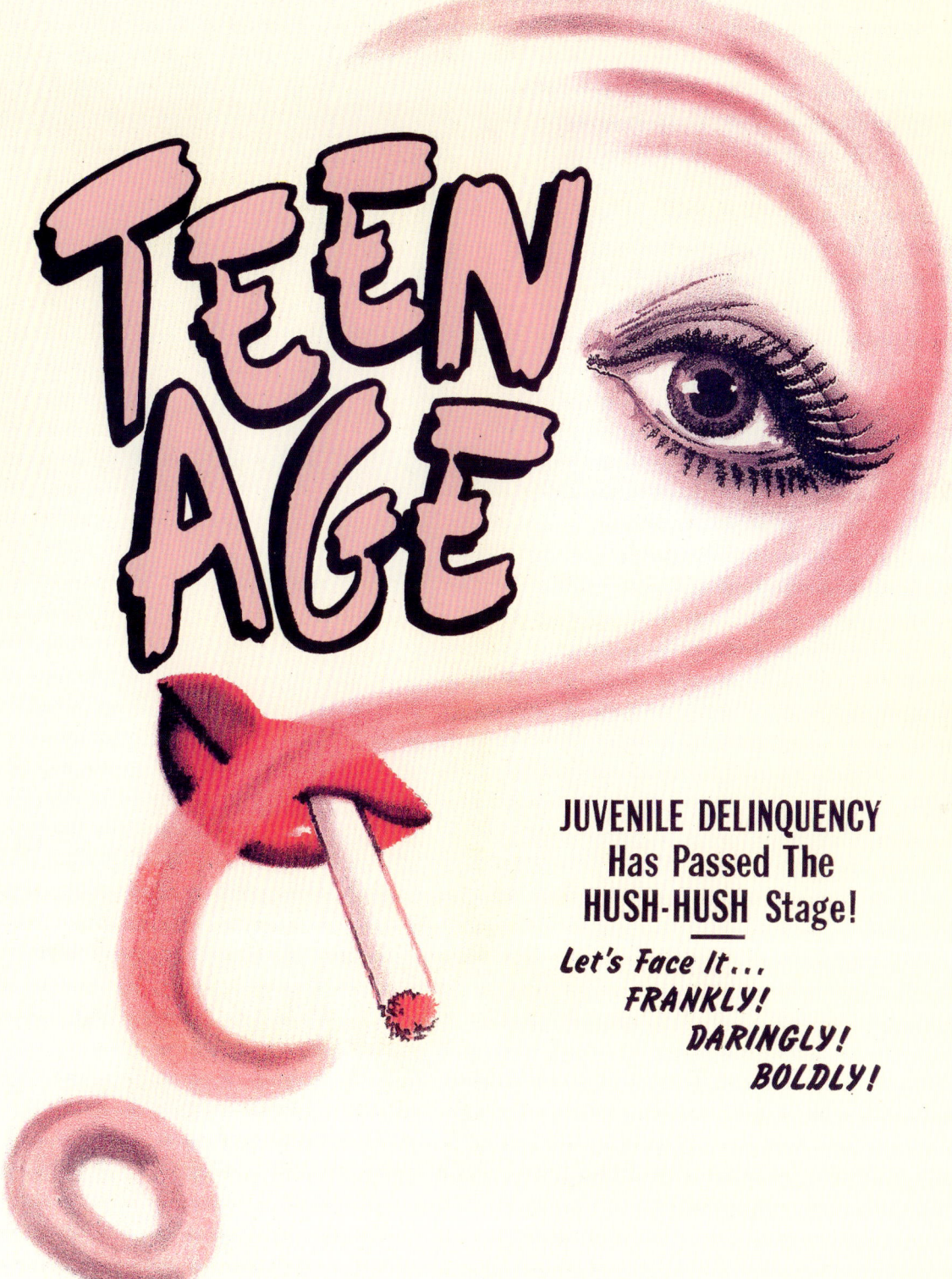

TO HAVE AND HAVE NOT 1944
ITALIAN POSTER, ART BY LUIGI MARTINATI

Luigi Martinati's Italian poster for *To Have and Have Not* is the most beautiful and captivating poster from all of Bogart and Bacall's screen outings together and it is also my favourite work of Martinati's. The film was Lauren Bacall's screen debut. She was only 19 at the time but had an uncommon maturity – in her speech, the way she carried herself and her trademark, knowing look – that Martinati managed to capture to such superb effect on this poster.

From their opening scene together, Bogart and Bacall had a magnetic, powerful chemistry. They were married within a year and were one of the strongest couples in Hollywood until Bogart's death in 1957. At his funeral, Bacall placed a small gold whistle into the urn with Bogart's ashes, inscribed with a line nodding to *To Have and Have Not*, 'If you want anything, just whistle.'

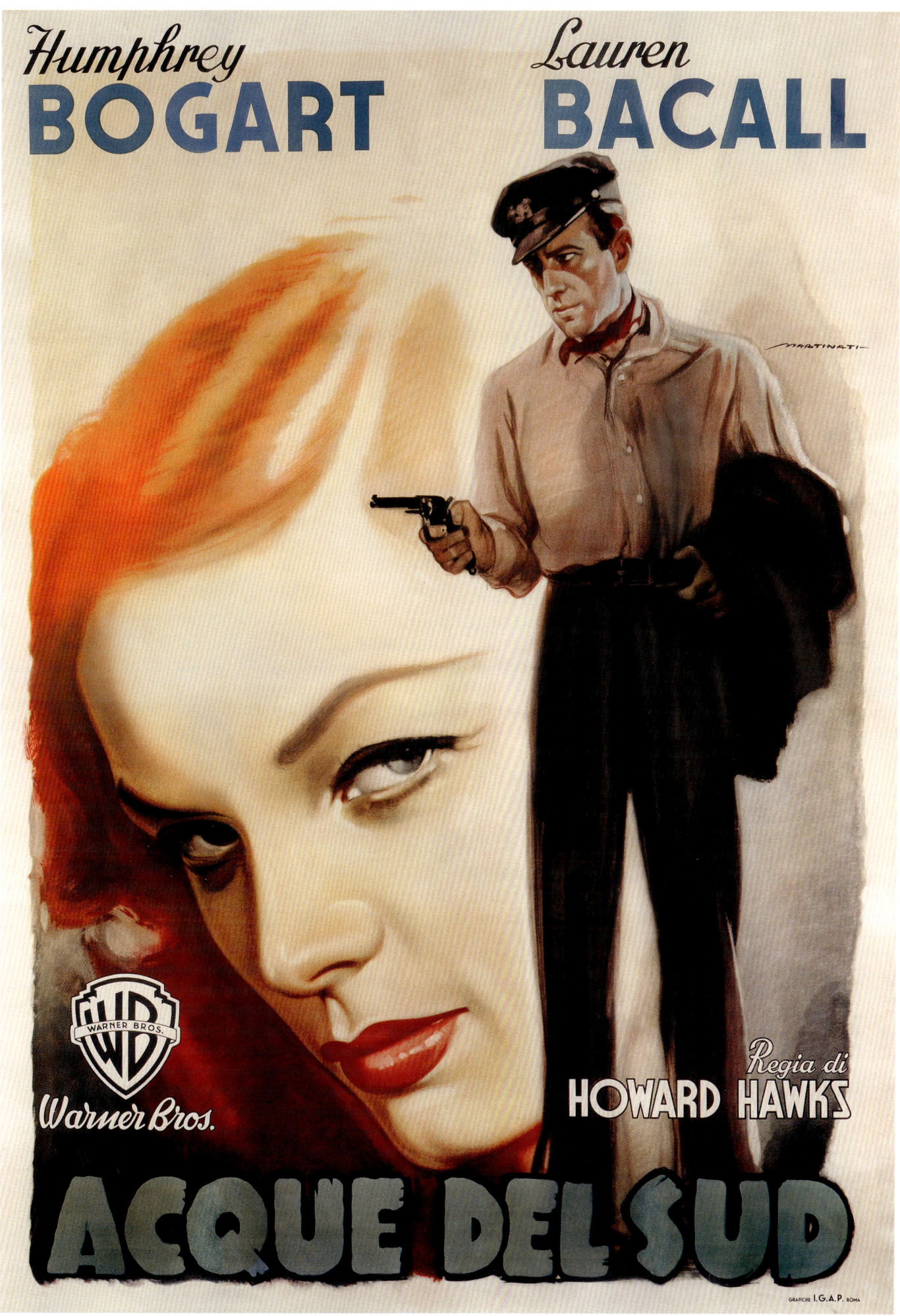

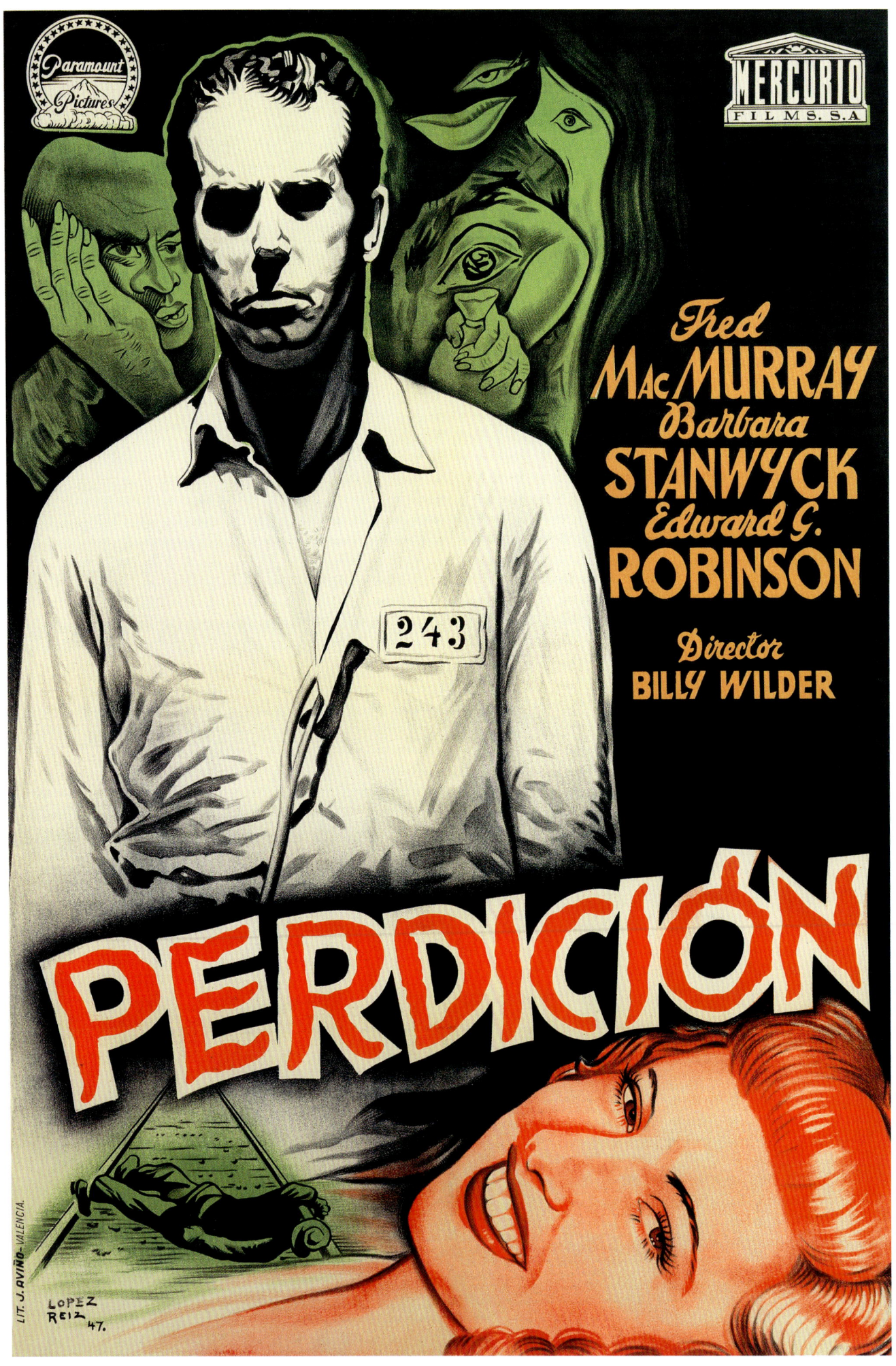

DOUBLE INDEMNITY 1944
SPANISH POSTER, ART BY LOPEZ REIZ

Billy Wilder's genre-defining noir, *Double Indemnity*, is one of his finest works. Based on James M. Cain's hardboiled novel, this bitter tale was translated to the big screen by Wilder and one-time co-writer, Raymond Chandler. Barbara Stanwyck starred as the consummate femme fatale who tempts Fred MacMurray's corruptible salesman into a murderous plot against her husband. Edward G. Robinson completed a trio of powerful performances as the claims investigator trying to get to the bottom of the suspicious case.

The Spanish poster by artist Lopez Reiz is the only poster from around the world that managed to convey the darkness at the centre of the film. Reiz depicted Wilder's original ending, which saw MacMurray executed in the San Francisco gas chamber for his crimes. This scene was ultimately cut because Wilder believed it unnecessary (and with the added advantage of making the film an easier sell to the censors). Although not used, Reiz's use of the scene on his design perfectly captures the essence of the duped fool, haunted by his weak-willed inner demons – depicted by Reiz in a surreal style reminiscent of Picasso's *Guernica*. Even the Spanish title, 'Perdición', translates as 'un-doing' or 'ruin'. The image of the condemned prisoner would have been powerful for a Spanish audience living under Franco's oppressive dictatorship.

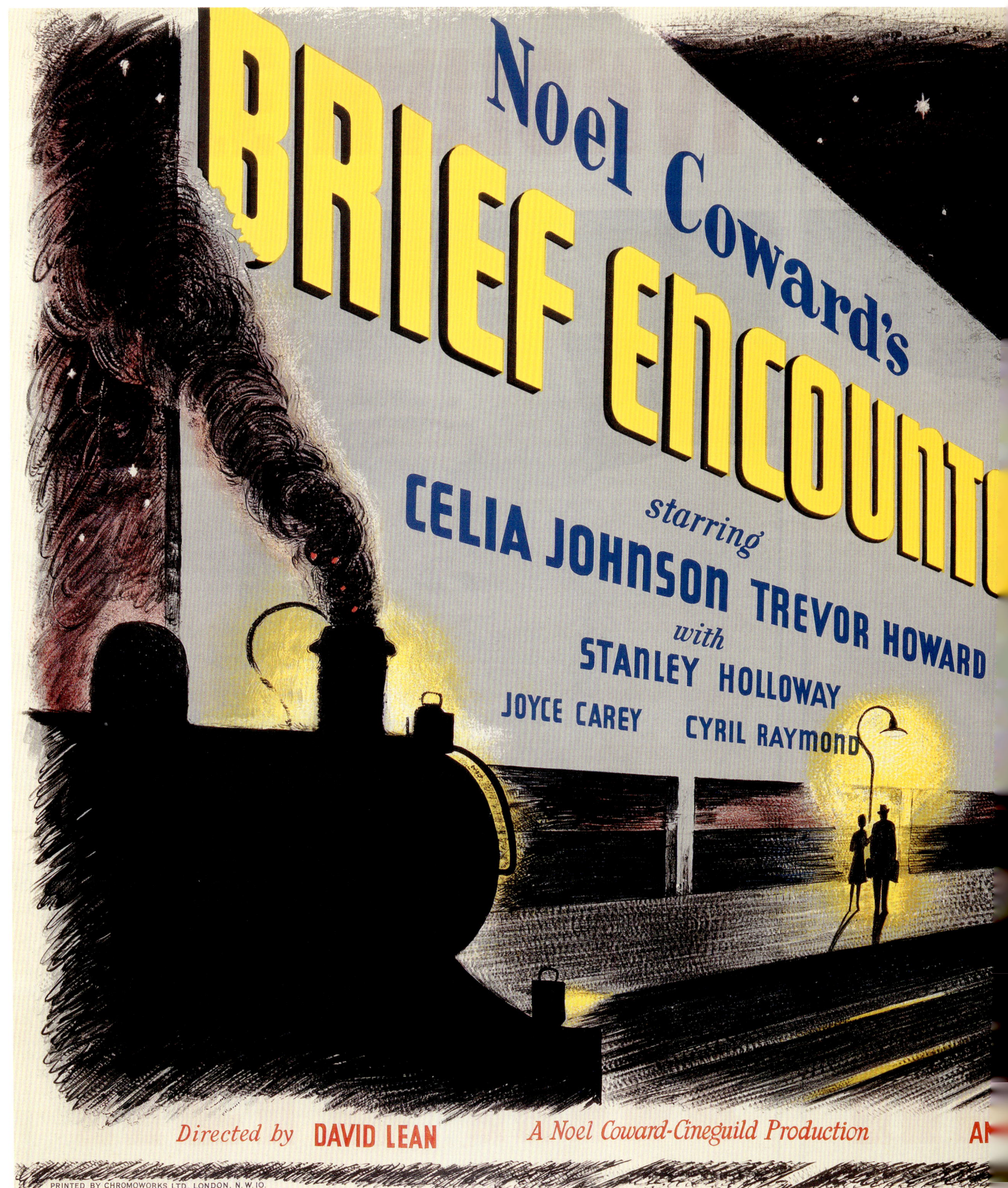

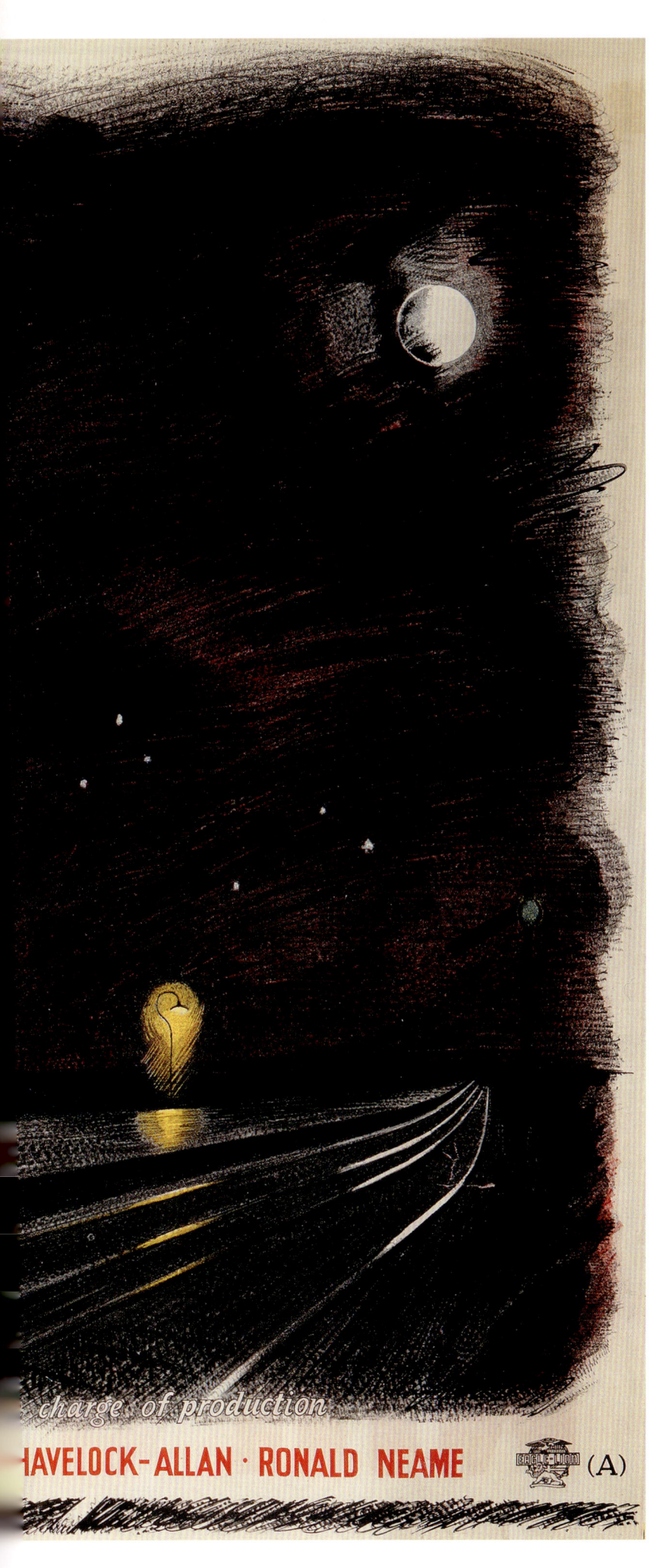

BRIEF ENCOUNTER 1945

BRITISH POSTER, ARTIST UNKNOWN

Brief Encounter is my favourite David Lean film and one of my all time favourite British films. Lean made only 16 feature films in his 40-year career, yet many are considered some of the greatest films of the twentieth century. His canon includes *The Bridge on the River Kwai* (1957), *Lawrence of Arabia* (1962) *Doctor Zhivago* (1965) and, of course, *Brief Encounter*. It was the first of Lean's films to attract international attention and it established his reputation as a ferocious talent with a distinctive style. *Brief Encounter* won a shared Palme d'Or at the Cannes Film Festival in 1946.

Based on a Noël Coward play, the film is the tale of two strangers – both married with children – who meet in a chance encounter at a train station. Despite falling deeply in love, their relationship is doomed by the weight of their own moral obligations to their families. As with the best posters, the British poster for *Brief Encounter* manages to capture the essence of the film in a single image: the two lovers are standing together in a brief pool of light, while gazing upon the inevitability of their dark future apart. The inexorable end of the relationship is further emphasized by the approaching train.

Under a handful of copies of this poster have ever surfaced. British posters from the early to mid-1940s are very rare, due to paper shortages during the war: fewer posters were printed and, following their use, they would be recycled or destroyed. The poster has only been seen on the open market twice. Both times, it was printed on the back of a 'Re-elect Winston Churchill' campaign poster.

As a rather unrelated but interesting aside, Billy Wilder said he first got the germ of the idea for *The Apartment* from *Brief Encounter*, wondering about the man who lends the couple his apartment. Wilder commented, 'I think that the interesting character is the friend who returns to his home and finds the bed still warm, he who has no mistress.'

The Lost Weekend 1945

French poster, art by Boris Grinsson

Billy Wilder's harrowing noir masterpiece, *The Lost Weekend*, was one of the bleakest films to emerge from Hollywood in the 1940s. In keeping with much of Wilder's work from this period, it focused on the darker recesses of the American psyche. Made several years before addiction became a common theme in the movies, *The Lost Weekend* is a grim and realistic look at the life of an alcoholic. It starred matinee-idol Ray Milland acting against type in a career-defining performance.

This expressionist and immersive film was a box-office success, especially among battle-weary GIs returning from the Second World War, turning to drink in their struggle to re-adjust to civilian life. It also achieved critical acclaim and was nominated for seven Academy Awards, winning four for Best Picture, Best Director, Best Actor and Best Screenplay.

The French 'style B' poster for *The Lost Weekend* by Boris Grinsson is by far the best poster on the title and embodies the mood of the film and the haunted soul of its protagonist. (For Grinsson biography, see p.80.)

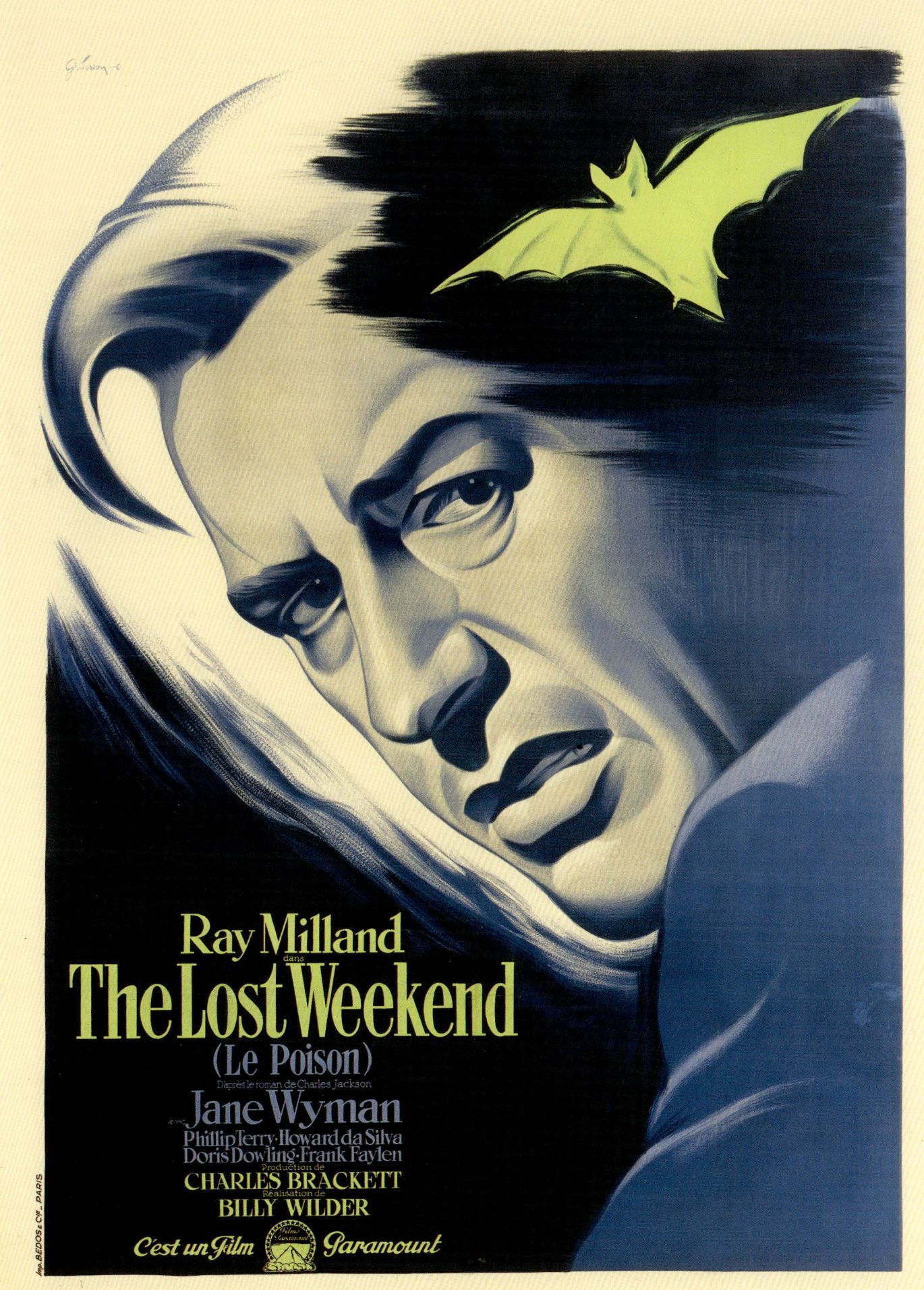

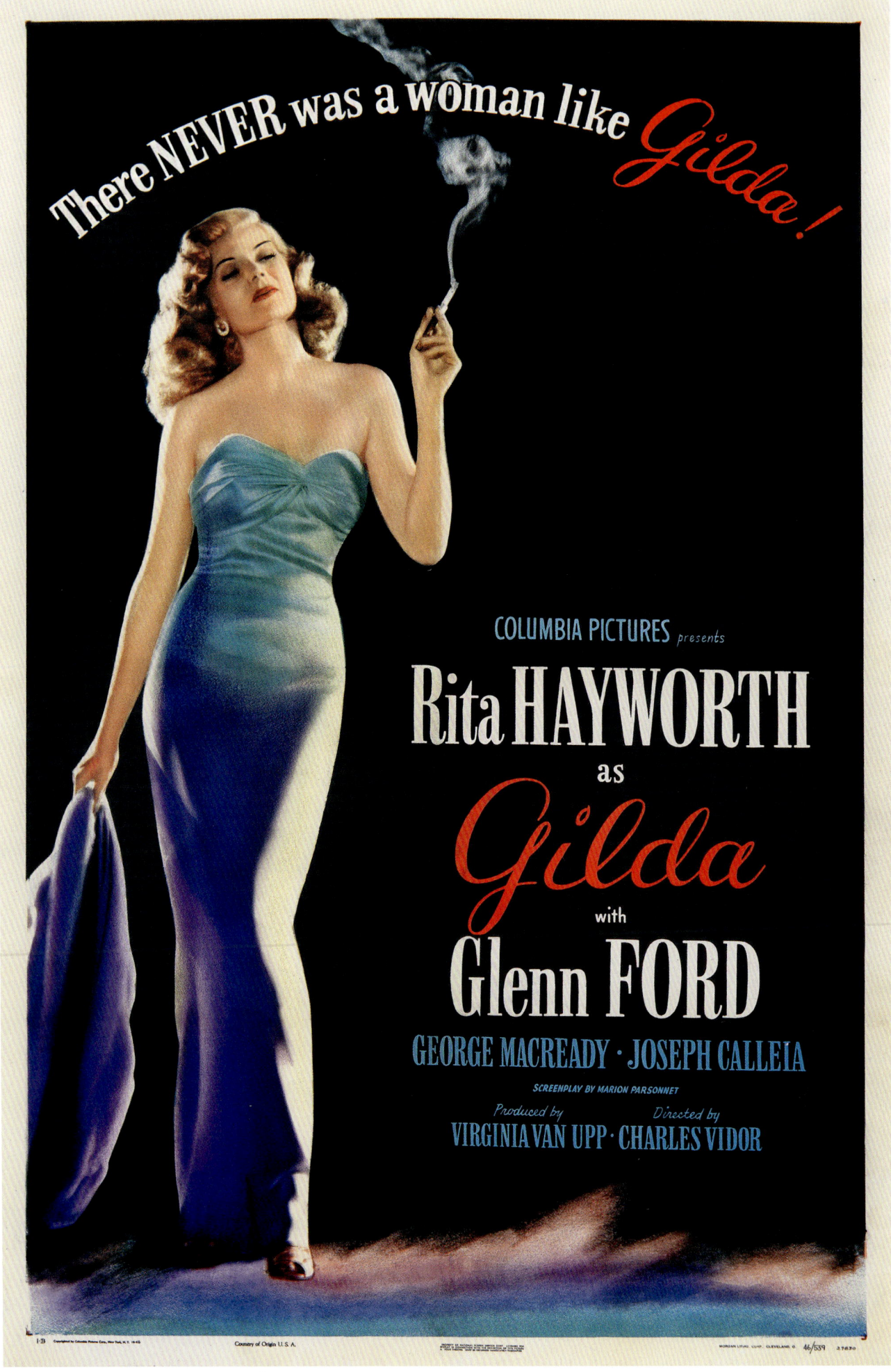

GILDA 1946

AMERICAN POSTER, ART DIRECTION BY JACK KERNESS, PHOTO BY ROBERT COBURN

Rita Hayworth embodied Golden Age Hollywood glamour and was the defining bombshell of the 1940s. Her alluring sexuality and box-office power hit their peak in *Gilda*, which includes the renowned 'striptease' scene in which the only item of clothing Gilda removes is a single glove. It was so arousing that it caused a scandal at the time and created several problems with the censors. The film solidified Hayworth's reputation as a screen icon and earned her the nickname, 'The Love Goddess'. Hayworth famously remarked that, 'Every man I've ever known has fallen in love with Gilda and awakened with me.'

The American poster for *Gilda* manages to reflect Hayworth's seductive appeal, tempting audiences into cinemas. It was created by art director Jack Kerness (1911-2010), using a Robert Coburn photograph in reverse on the poster. Robert Coburn (1900-1990) was the chief portrait photographer at Columbia Pictures at this time – a role he held for over 20 years. His work is synonymous with Hollywood's Golden Age and his star portraits included Rita Hayworth, Joan Crawford, Carole Lombard and Kim Novak. He was twice the winner of the Academy of Motion Picture Arts and Sciences' Still Photography Exhibition Award in 1941 and 1943. He is also renowned as the stills photographer on Alfred Hitchcock's *The Birds* (1963).

THE BIG SLEEP 1946
FRENCH POSTER, ART BY VICENTE CRISTELLYS

The Big Sleep was directed by Howard Hawks and was based on hardboiled writer Raymond Chandler's first novel. This classic film noir starred Bogie as cynical detective Philip Marlowe opposite Lauren Bacall's female lead. This unusual French design by artist Vicente Cristellys (d.1970) remains my favourite original release poster on the title (for my favourite re-release poster, see p.206).

Cristellys's artwork combined a colourful, almost Cubist, design with black and white photomontage. It is one of the earliest examples of the use of this approach in French poster design. Photomontage continued to grow in popularity within the country and by the 1960s it was the favourite technique employed by the poster artists of the 'Nouvelle Vague' and a distinguishing characteristic of their approach (see p.157).

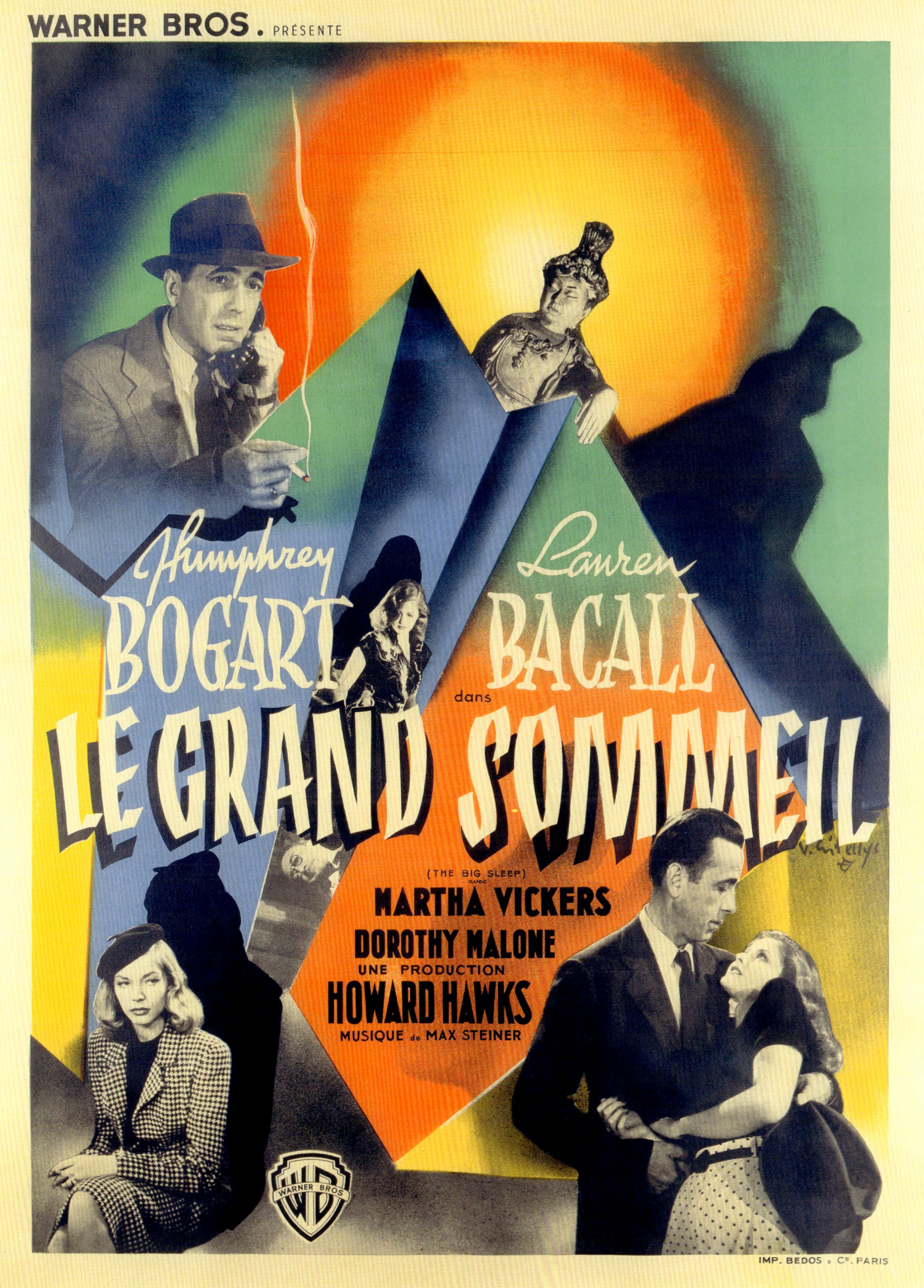

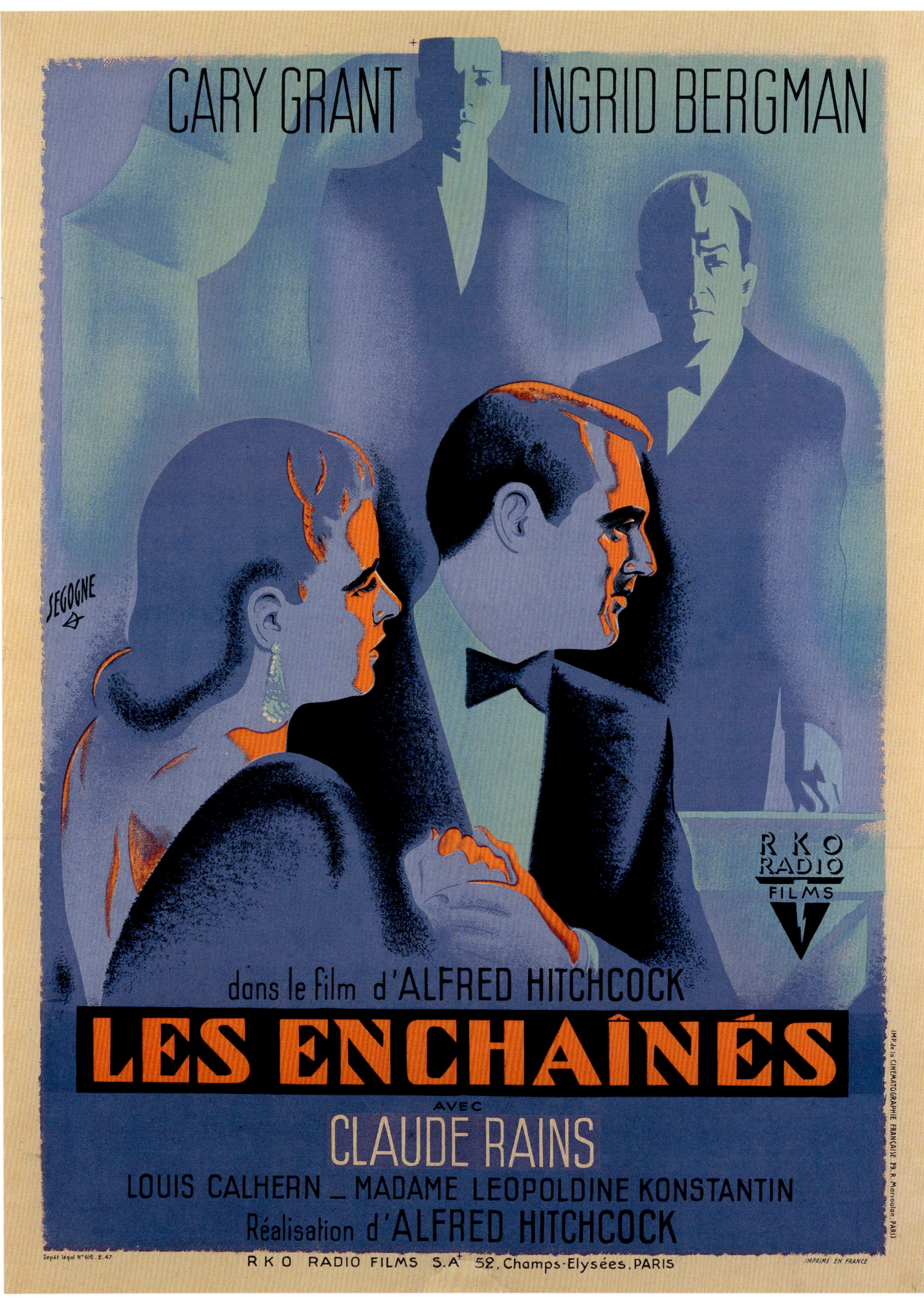

NOTORIOUS 1946
FRENCH POSTER, ART BY PIERRE SEGOGNE

Artist Pierre Segogne's French poster for *Notorious* remains one of the most sought-after posters on any Hitchcock title, and with good reason. It is one of the most beautiful posters of the 1940s and captures the sophistication and elegance of the film better than any other poster in the worldwide campaign.

One of Hitchcock's first 'love stories', the notorious titular character was played by Ingrid Bergman – notorious for the 'loose morals' of her sexual past that threaten her burgeoning romance with Cary Grant's secret agent. The film includes one of the most erotic and intimate on-screen kisses in cinema. At this time, the Hays Code insisted that a kiss could last no longer than three seconds. Hitchcock got around this by having the actors interrupt their two and a half minutes passionate embrace with brief 'nuzzling' interludes – technically never breaking the three-second rule.

OUT OF THE PAST 1947
AMERICAN POSTER, ART BY WILLIAM ROSE

Jacques Tourneur's *Out of the Past* is quintessential film noir, with atmospheric black and white cinematography, a doomed anti-hero and a seductive femme fatale. Artist William Rose's American poster is also a textbook piece and one of the most collectable in the genre.

This was one of Robert Mitchum's first big roles. He was only 29 at the time but managed to convey the world-weary cool of a man twice his age, who has seen it all and more. His co-star was Jane Greer in one of the most convincing and wicked portrayals of a femme fatale ever seen on screen. Many actresses in the 1940s were very talented stars but never quite understood the subtle combination of dark and light temperament that such a character required. Greer's performance was utterly credible and an audience could easily accept that men would do anything for her. The actress summed it up best herself when she commented, 'I was believable ... because although my character Kathie was a bitch, a liar and a killer, she looked soft and innocent.'

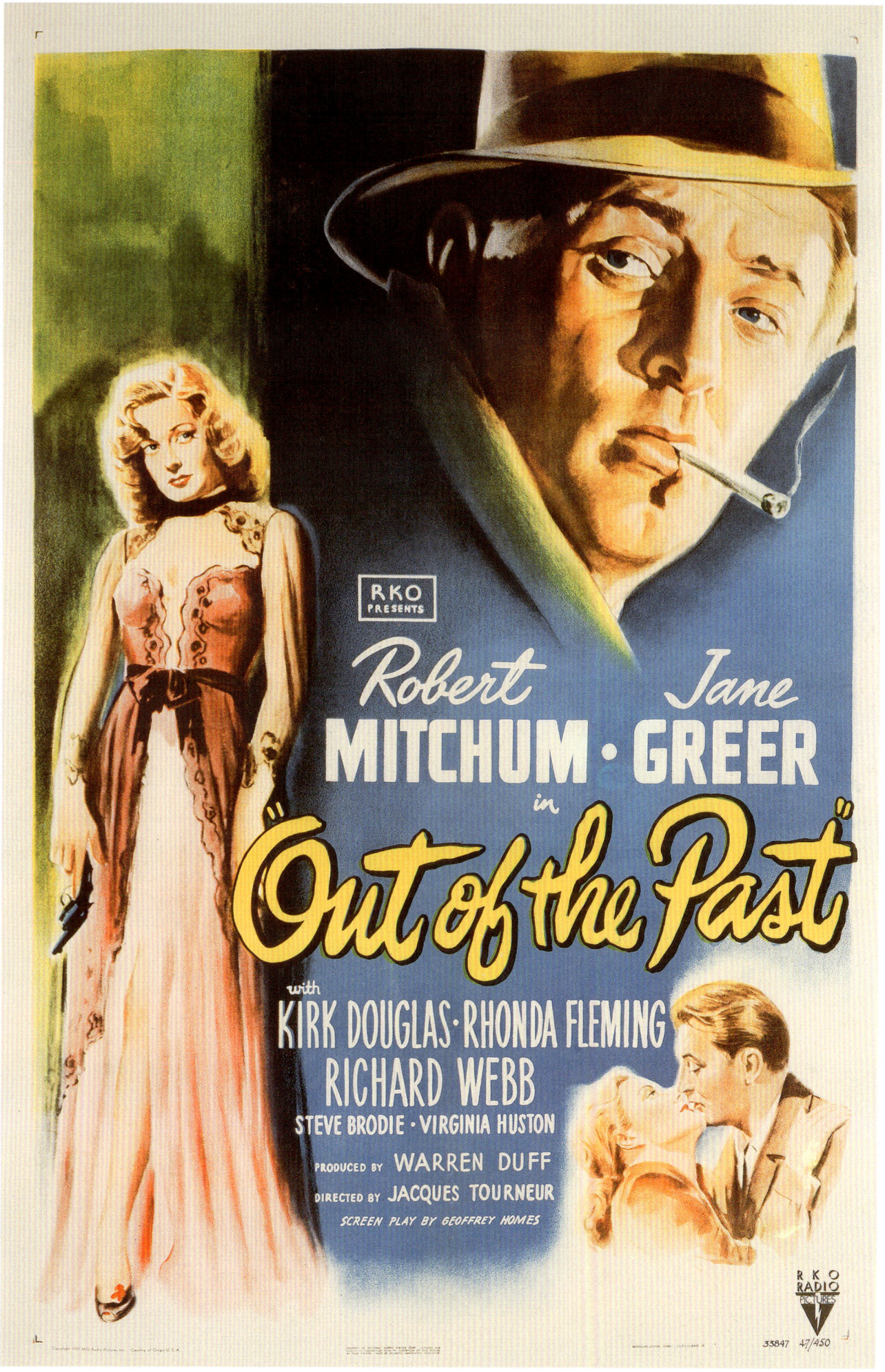

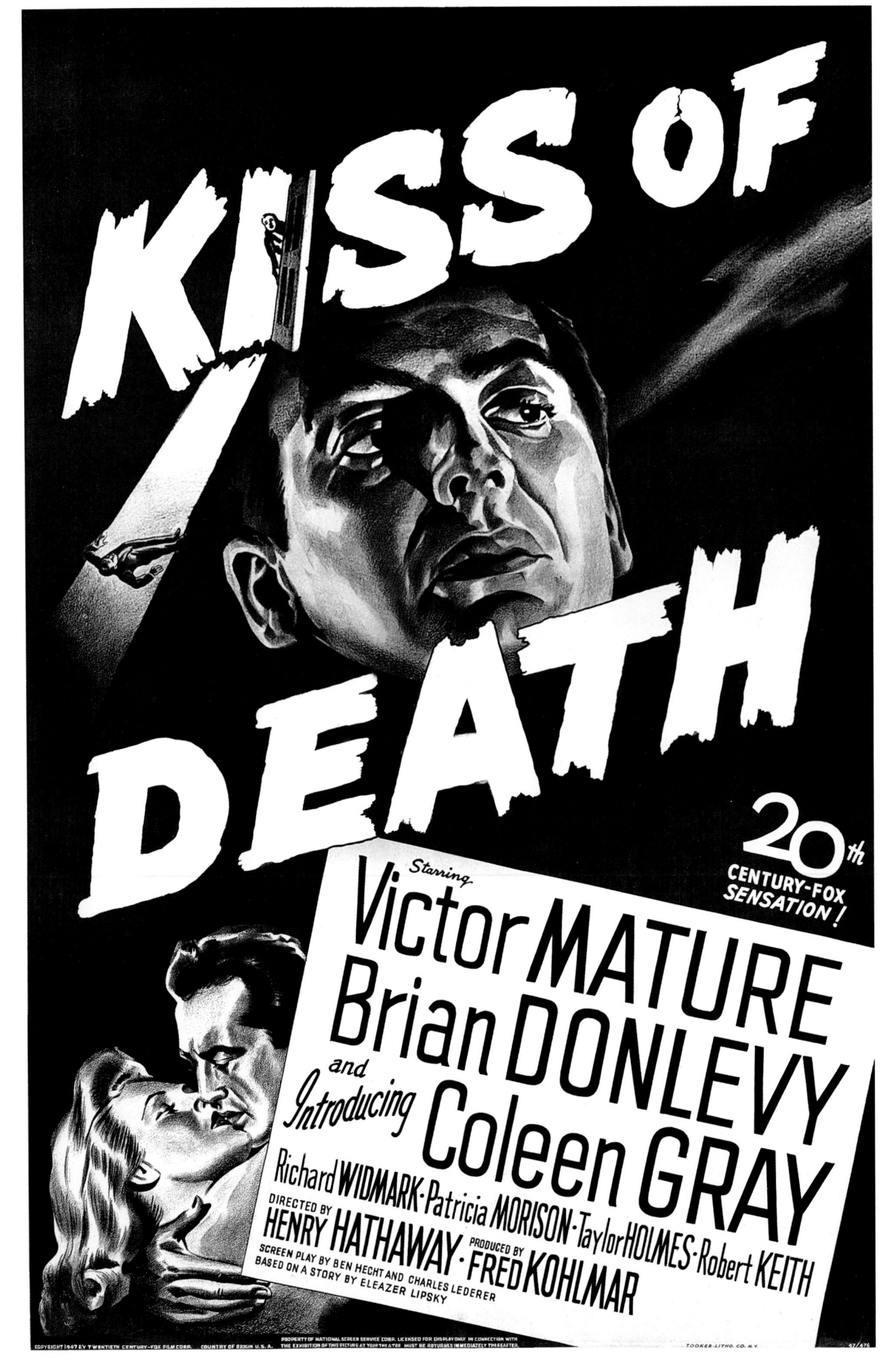

KISS OF DEATH 1947
AMERICAN POSTER, ART DIRECTION BY JEROME NOVAK

In contrast to the crisp chiaroscuro that typifies film noir, the accompanying posters were usually a riot of colour. The monochrome poster for Henry Hathaway's *Kiss of Death* is a rare exception, with art director Jerome Novak choosing to deliberately emphasize the film's use of sharp shadows. It remains one of the only posters from the period printed in black and white and the result is a poster that embodies the film noir genre.

Over 99 per cent of the posters from Twentieth Century Fox in this period were printed with borders, and *Kiss of Death* is one of only a handful of borderless exceptions. In the early days of movie poster collecting, buyers would often assume that the poster had been trimmed and was thus worth much less than it really was. This was only cleared up when it was published for the first time in *Reel Art: Great Posters from the Golden Age of the Silver Screen* (Abbeville, 1988).

THE LADY FROM SHANGHAI 1947
ITALIAN POSTER, ART BY ANSELMO BALLESTER

In the late 1940s, Orson Welles was working at the top of his game in theatre and film, and was given complete artistic freedom for his new project, *The Lady from Shanghai*. When Columbia boss, Harry Cohn, saw Welles' final rough-cut, however, he was aghast, and demanded that it be heavily re-edited, re-dubbed and re-scored. The final release was a box-office failure – whether as a result of Cohn's heavy-handed interference or perhaps due to the public's outrage at Welles' decision to crop his then-wife Rita Hayworth's legendary red locks and dye them blonde. The film's bad reception significantly damaged Welles' reputation. In recent years, however, it has been reappraised and is credited as an important work in his canon – a visually luminous noir that is superbly acted and creatively styled.

Italian artist Anselmo Ballester is renowned for the posters he created for Columbia's releases, especially his posters of 1940s bombshell, Rita Hayworth. Of all the posters available on Hayworth worldwide, Ballester art remains the most collectible, and this poster for *The Lady from Shanghai* is one of his greatest examples. (For Ballester biography, see p.123.)

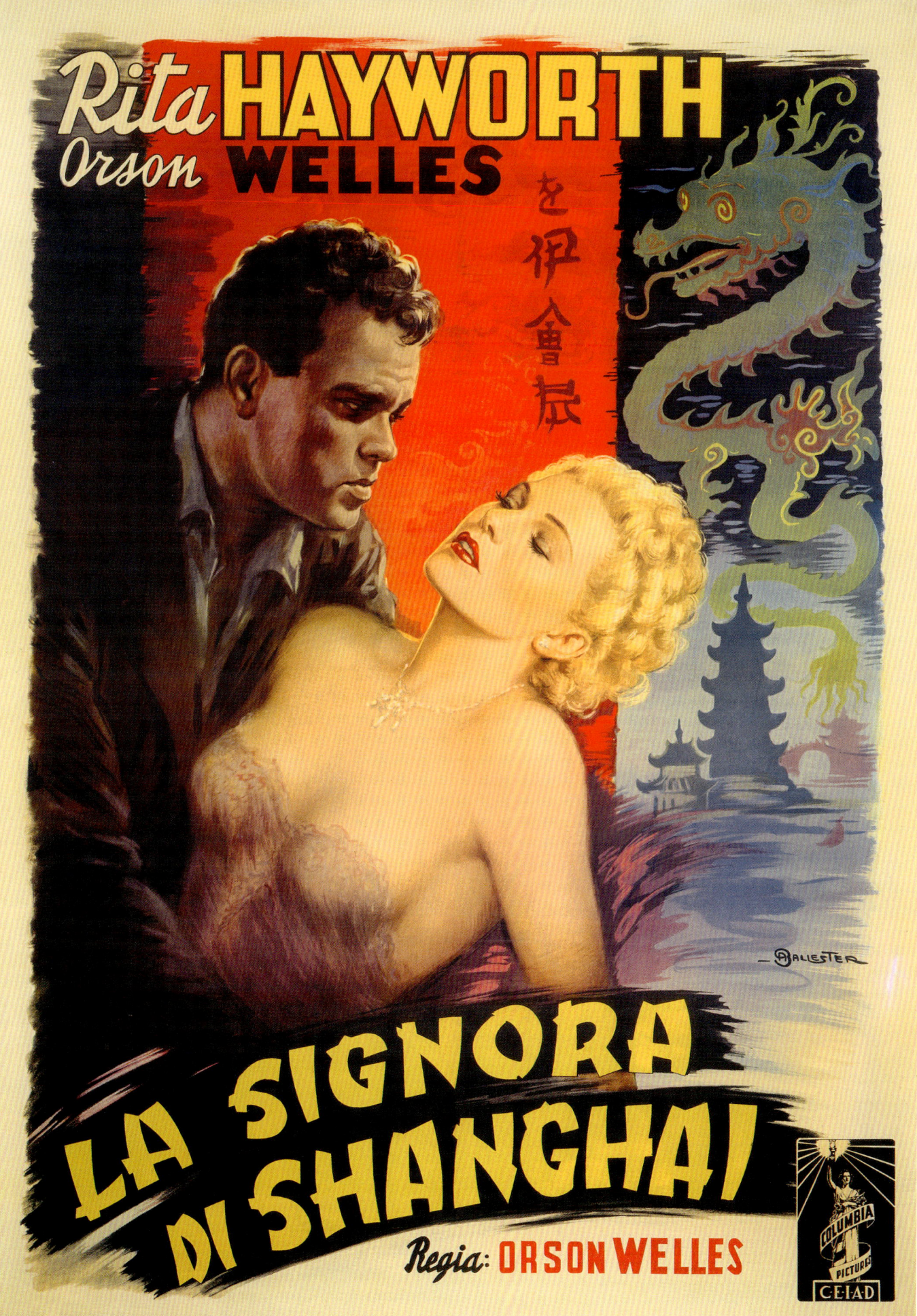

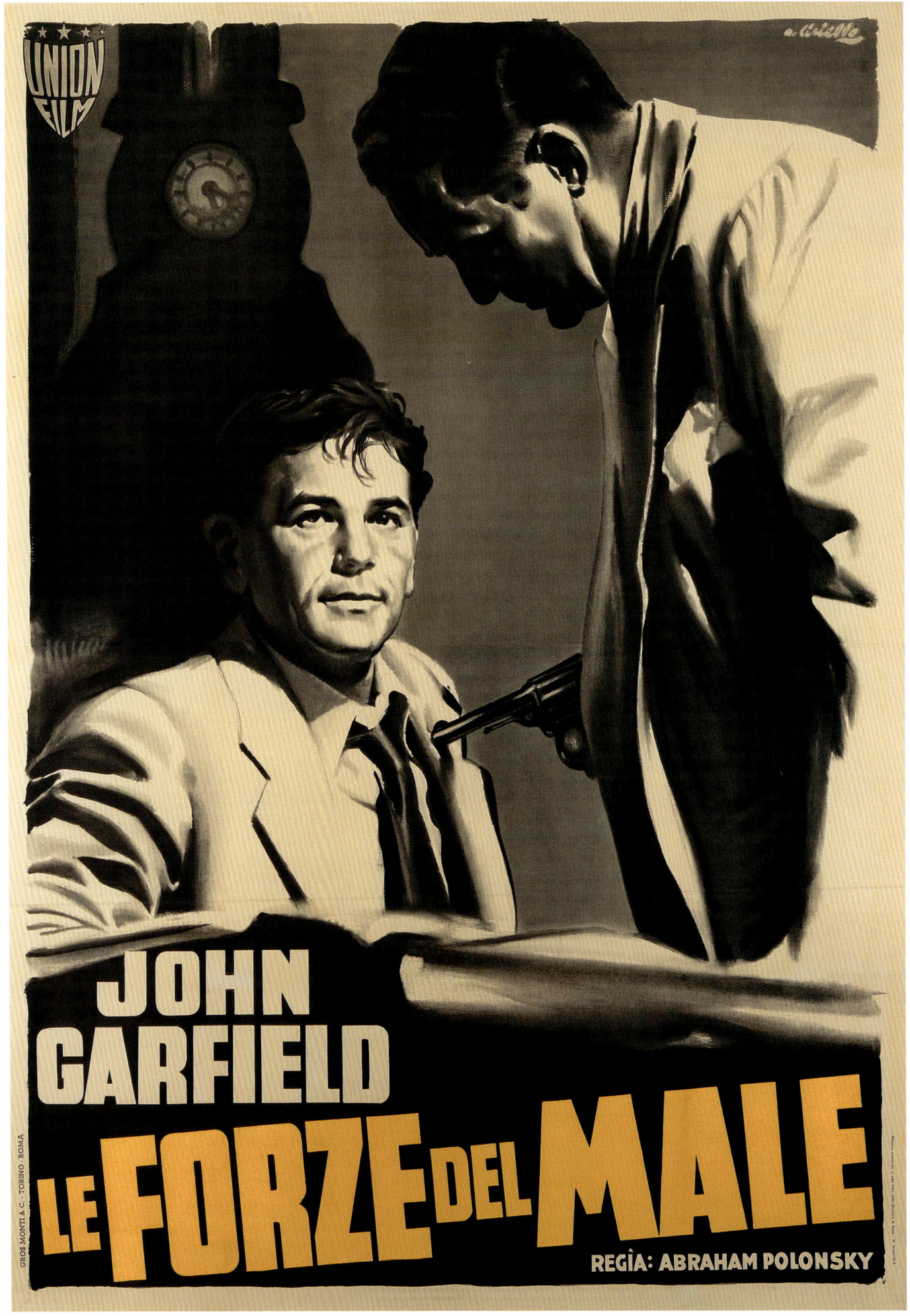

FORCE OF EVIL 1948
ITALIAN POSTER, ART BY AVERARDO CIRIELLO

Averardo Ciriello (1918-?d.) was known for his comic and poster art. He started out in magazine illustration before moving into film poster design after the Second World War. In addition to *Force of Evil*, he is particularly remembered for his posters for *Spellbound*, *The Apartment*, *From Russia with Love* and *Thunderball*. In the 1970s, he also became known for his paintings in the field of erotic comic art.

Alongside the American poster for *Kiss of Death* (see p.106), Ciriello's poster for the Italian release of *Force of Evil* is one of the few examples of black and white design being used to such deliberate and striking effect on a film poster. It is highly effective. With the clock on the wall, the gun to the chest and the expression of frozen panic, the poster also perfectly captures the tense pressure on John Garfield's character: time is running out and there is nowhere left to go.

Force of Evil sank at the box office on its release in 1948. However, in the 1960s, the film began to be reappraised and it is now recognised as an atmospheric and gritty noir. It features a superb performance from John Garfield – one of my favourite actors – incisive direction from Abraham Polonsky and stunning cinematography by George Barnes. Martin Scorsese has cited the film as a formative influence on him as a director.

Just a few months after *Force of Evil* was released, Garfield and Polonsky found themselves two of the most badly affected victims of the McCarthy blacklistings. Both men were called separately before the US Congressional House Committee on Un-American Activities, accused of Communist affiliation. It ended Polonsky's career and he had to write under a pseudonym for several years. When Garfield was called, he famously refused to 'name names', effectively destroying his career. The stress of being barred from the industry has been cited as the major contributing factor in Garfield's death of a heart attack at the age of just 39. As Polonsky has said, 'He defended his streetboy's honor and they killed him for it.' Garfield's funeral was attended by thousands of people crowding the streets of New York, desperate to pay tribute to his extraordinary talent. It was the biggest funeral in the city since the death of Rudolph Valentino.

LADRI DI BICICLETTE 1948

ITALIAN POSTER, ART BY ERCOLE BRINI

Ladri di biciclette (*Bicycle Thieves*) is a masterpiece of Italian neo-realism and one of the greatest films of the twentieth century. Set against the backdrop of post-war poverty in Rome, director Vittorio de Sica's bleak tale follows a poor father who has his indispensable bicycle stolen on the first day of a much-needed job. He sets off on a desperate search across the city to find it, with his young son in tow. Ercole Brini's beautiful Italian poster for the film captures something of the father's anguish, and also depicts the relationship between the father and son – one of the central themes of the film.

Ercole Brini (1913-1989) studied at Rome's Academy of Fine Arts. From the early 1940s, he focussed on cinematographic art and developed a reputation as one of the best in his field. Brini was predominantly known for his distinctive watercolour style that often revealed the delicate emotions that lay behind the surface of his characters' faces. *Ladri di biciclette* remains one of his most famous poster campaigns of the 1940s. During the 1950s, he was the principle artist for Paramount studio's releases in Italy. He designed posters for their five Audrey Hepburn titles, which remain among some of the most sought-after film posters today.

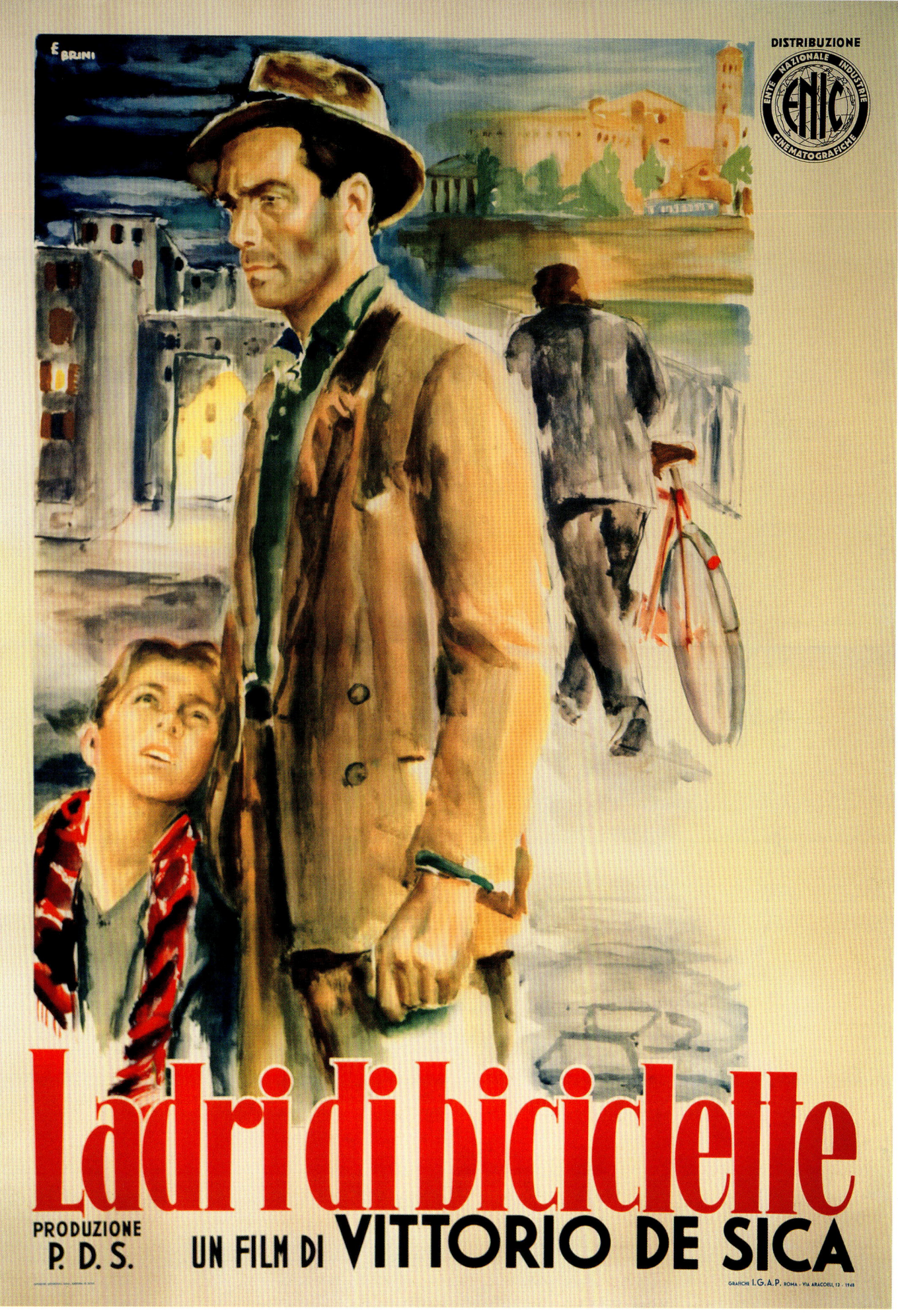

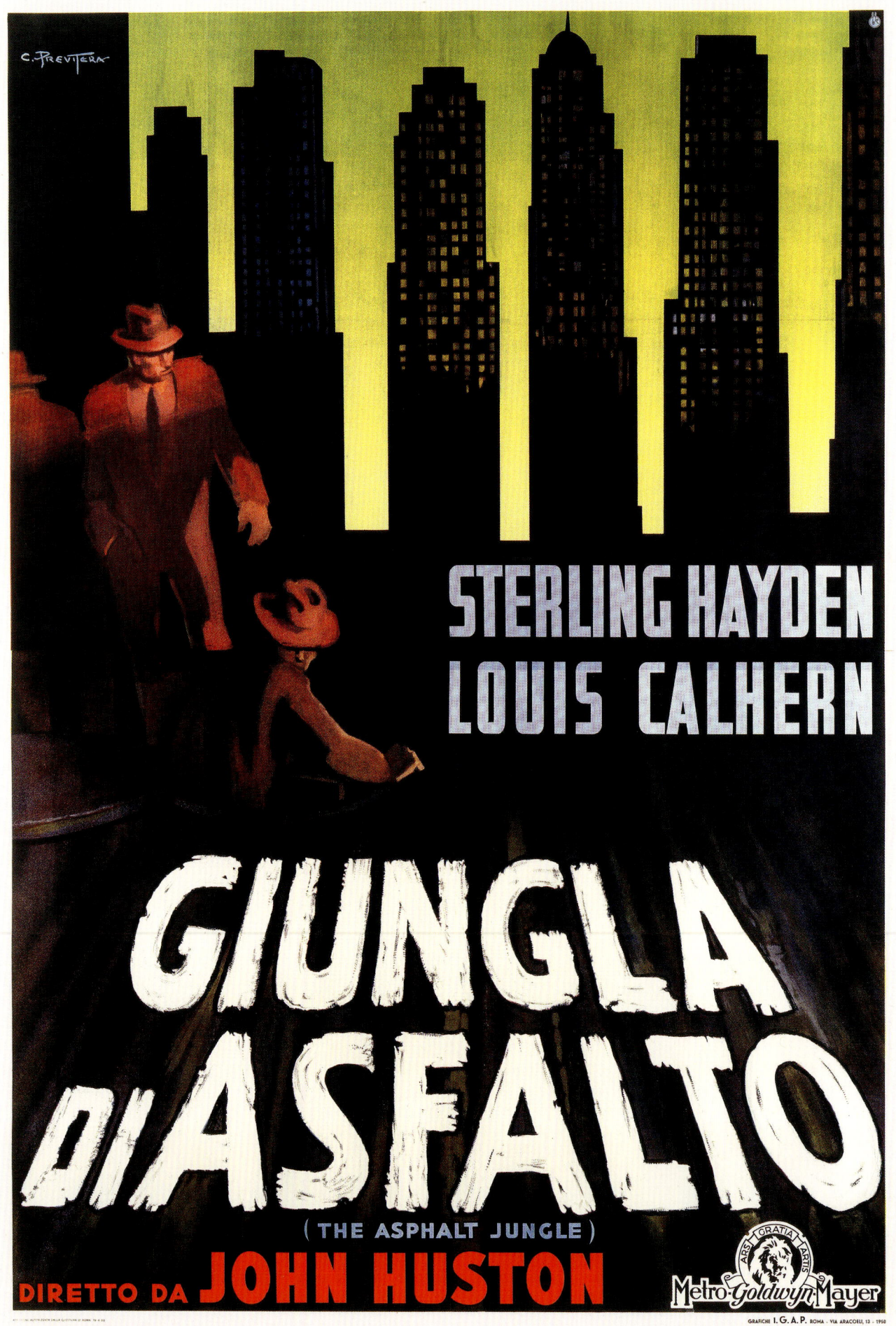

THE ASPHALT JUNGLE 1950
ITALIAN POSTER, ART BY C. PREVITERA

MGM was a studio known for its breezy musicals and wholesome family values. *The Asphalt Jungle* was a marked deviation from form and it remains one of the studio's most interesting films of the decade. Directed by John Huston, this tight, low-budget noir was a hugely influential heist movie. Along with Stanley Kubrick's *The Killing* made six years later, it defined the heist genre. (Sterling Hayden starred in both films, and they are often confused for each other.)

The Asphalt Jungle's gritty tale won plaudits on its release and was nominated for four Academy Awards. Archer Winsten of the *New York Post* wrote that it, 'Has the authority of a blow in your solar plexus. It leaves you physically tired with sheer tension, participation and belief. It is the crime picture of the decade, and it may be the best one ever made. This picture drives home the corollary thought that criminals are also human beings.' Such a sympathetic portrayal of the criminal mind was too much for studio boss Louis B. Mayer's straight-laced morals and he dismissed it as, 'Full of nasty, ugly people doing nasty, ugly things. I wouldn't walk across the room to see something like that.' This was towards the end of Mayer's reign and less than a year after the film's release, he would be out of the job.

American film posters from MGM at this time were amongst the worst of all the studios – dull and uninspiring. The American poster for *The Asphalt Jungle* was simply the title of the film in large letters with the movie's tagline, *The City Under the City*, underneath. In contrast, the Italian poster, by artist C. Previtera, took this tagline as its visual inspiration – creating a raw and atmospheric design that embodied the mood of the film. It is the best poster on the film. Many collectors look for posters that depict Marilyn Monroe on them – despite it being one of her earliest films and her only appearing on screen for around five minutes. When the film was re-released in Italy a few years later and Monroe's star had risen, it was promoted, in true Italian style, as a Marilyn picture. She was given first billing ahead of Sterling Hayden and a huge portrait shot dominated the artwork.

No Way Out 1950
American poster, Design by Paul Rand

The brilliant and bold American poster for *No Way Out* was created by design legend Paul Rand (1914-1996). The foremost American graphic Modernist of the twentieth century, Rand introduced the 'Swiss Style' of design to the States. Over the course of a career that spanned six decades, he had a profound impact on the profession and redefined the language of design.

Rand studied at Pratt Institute, Parsons School of Design and the Art Students League and by his early twenties was already making an impression on the design landscape, creating covers for *Direction* magazine, *Apparel Arts* and *Esquire*. By the early 1940s, he was an art director for the prestigious William H. Weintraub agency in New York and in 1946 he published his seminal work, *Thoughts on Design*; the single most influential graphic design book of the twentieth century. In the 1950s and 1960s, Rand became renowned for his corporate logo work, crafting iconic logos for brands such as IBM, UPS and ABC television. He also taught at Yale for several years and was inducted into the New York Art Directors Club Hall of Fame in 1972.

Rand's phenomenal influence was borne from an ability to think innovatively, without constraint from tradition, and to think simply. The greatest of the Bauhaus artists, László Moholy-Nagy, said of him, 'He thinks in terms of need and function. He is able to analyze his problems but his fantasy is boundless.' Rand himself explained that, 'Simplicity is not the goal. It is the by-product of a good idea and modest expectations.'

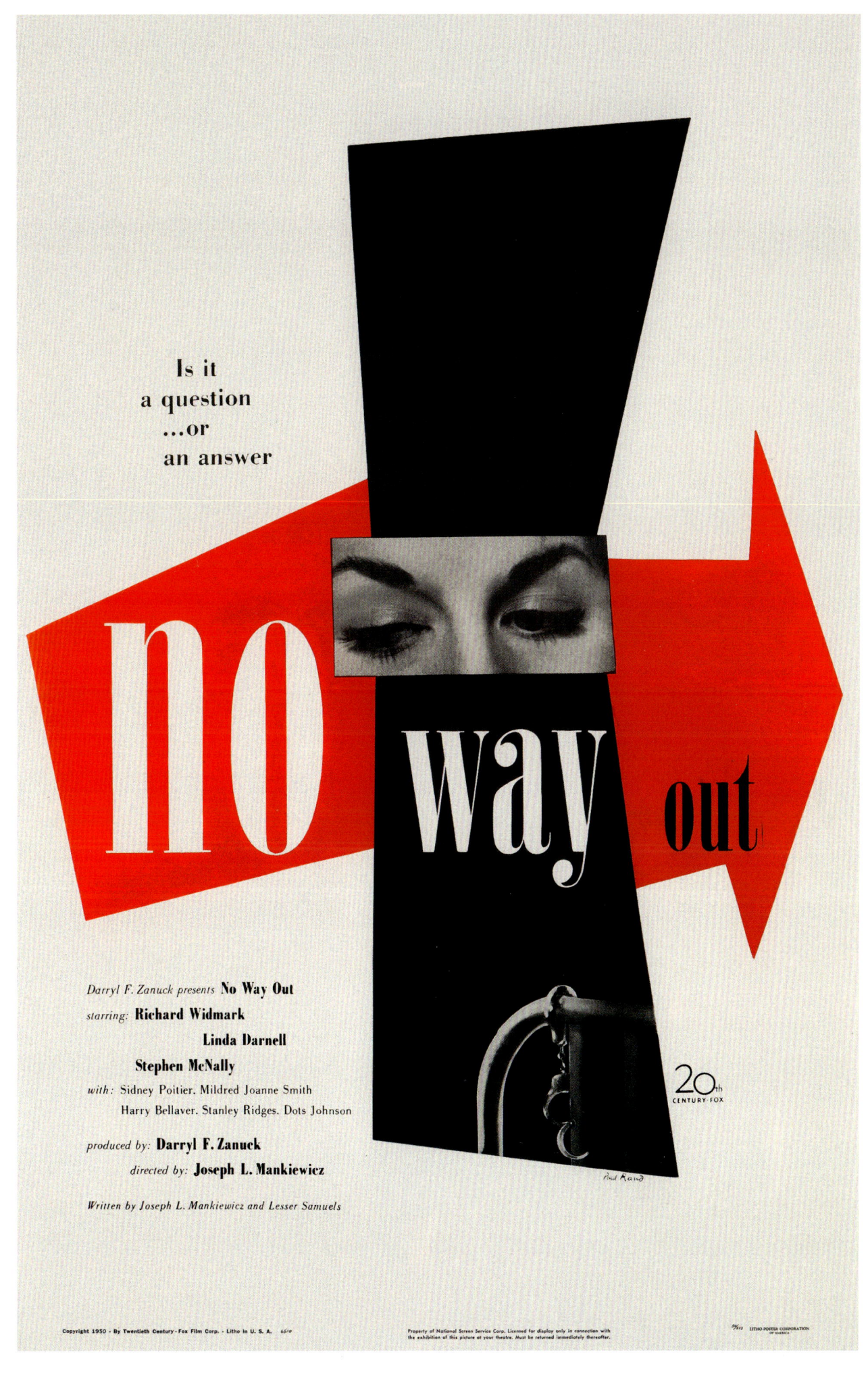

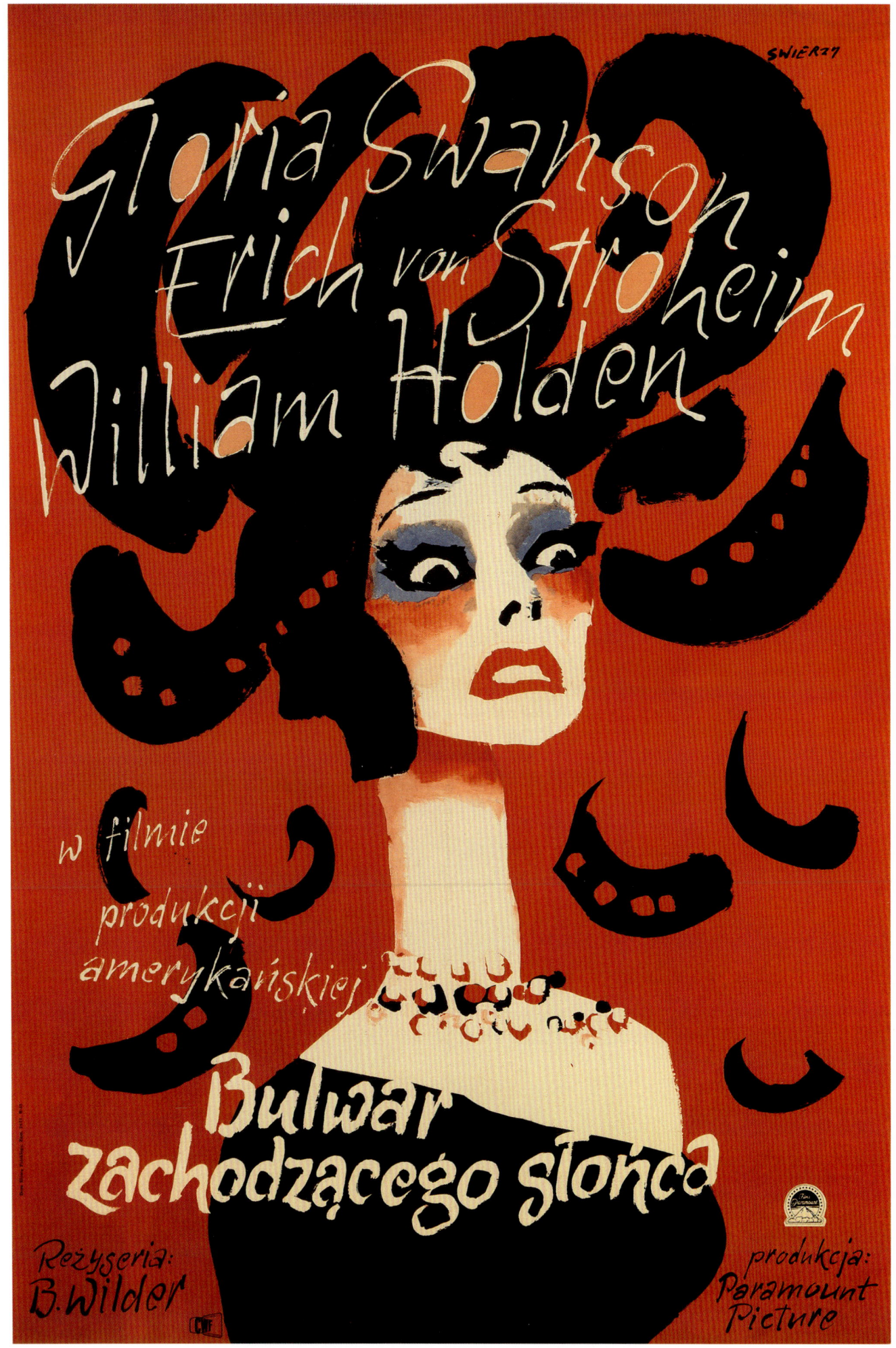

SUNSET BOULEVARD 1950
POLISH POSTER, ART BY WALDEMAR ŚWIERZY

Directed by Billy Wilder, *Sunset Boulevard* is a glorious black and white masterpiece and a Hollywood classic. It was nominated for 11 Academy Awards (winning three), and was one of the first films chosen by the US Library of Congress to be preserved under the National Film Registry for its historical and cultural significance.

Gloria Swanson had been one of the leading actresses of the silent era, receiving thousands of fan letters a day while living in an elegant mansion on Sunset Boulevard in its heyday. She was beautiful, talented and extravagant. When Wilder approached her to play the leading lady in his new film – about a silent-era star who lives in decaying grandeur on Sunset Boulevard and fantasises about a glorious comeback – the actress had not made a film in over ten years. She gave the performance of her career as her distorted alter-ego, Norma Desmond. The powerful Polish poster by Waldemar Świerzy brilliantly depicts her unstable and possessive madness. The use of just a head shot was also a fitting reflection of the film's most famous line, 'I'm ready for my close-up'.

Waldemar Świerzy (b.1931) is one of the most important poster artists of post-war Poland. He began designing posters in the early 1950s and has produced a vast body of award-winning work. As with his design for *Sunset Boulevard*, Świerzy often consciously limits his palette of colours and keeps elements to a minimum. In doing so, he intensifies the psychological content and effect of his work.

Gun Crazy 1950
American poster, Artist unknown

Gun Crazy remains one of the most iconic 'B' film noirs of all time, directed by poverty row maestro, Joseph H. Lewis. The film was based on a script by the talented screenwriter Dalton Trumbo, who the studio could only afford because he had been blacklisted. Lewis created an amazing piece of cinema from an almost non-existent budget. The film explodes with pace and innovation and is particularly noted for its real-time bank robbery sequence shot in one take from the backseat of a car. It influenced everything from *Bonnie and Clyde* to the films of the French New Wave.

Originally released as *Deadly is the Female*, the film was re-released less than a year later under the much more profitable title of *Gun Crazy*. It starred Welsh-born Irish actress Peggy Cummins, one of the most renowned 'bad girls' of 1950s cinema. The American poster for the film sees her in full seductive mode. The poster reflected a style of 'trash' pulp advertising that became extremely popular in the 1950s.

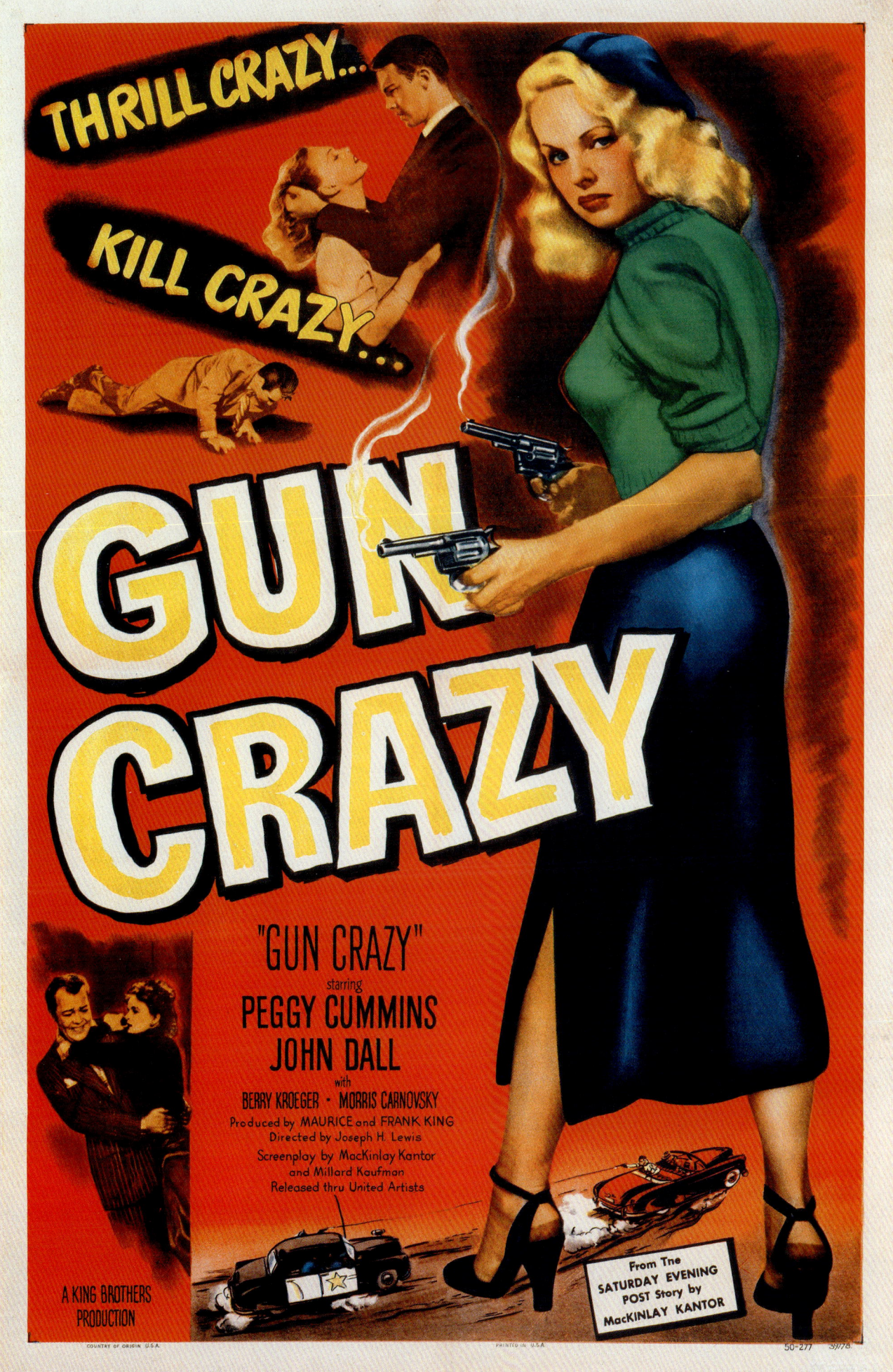

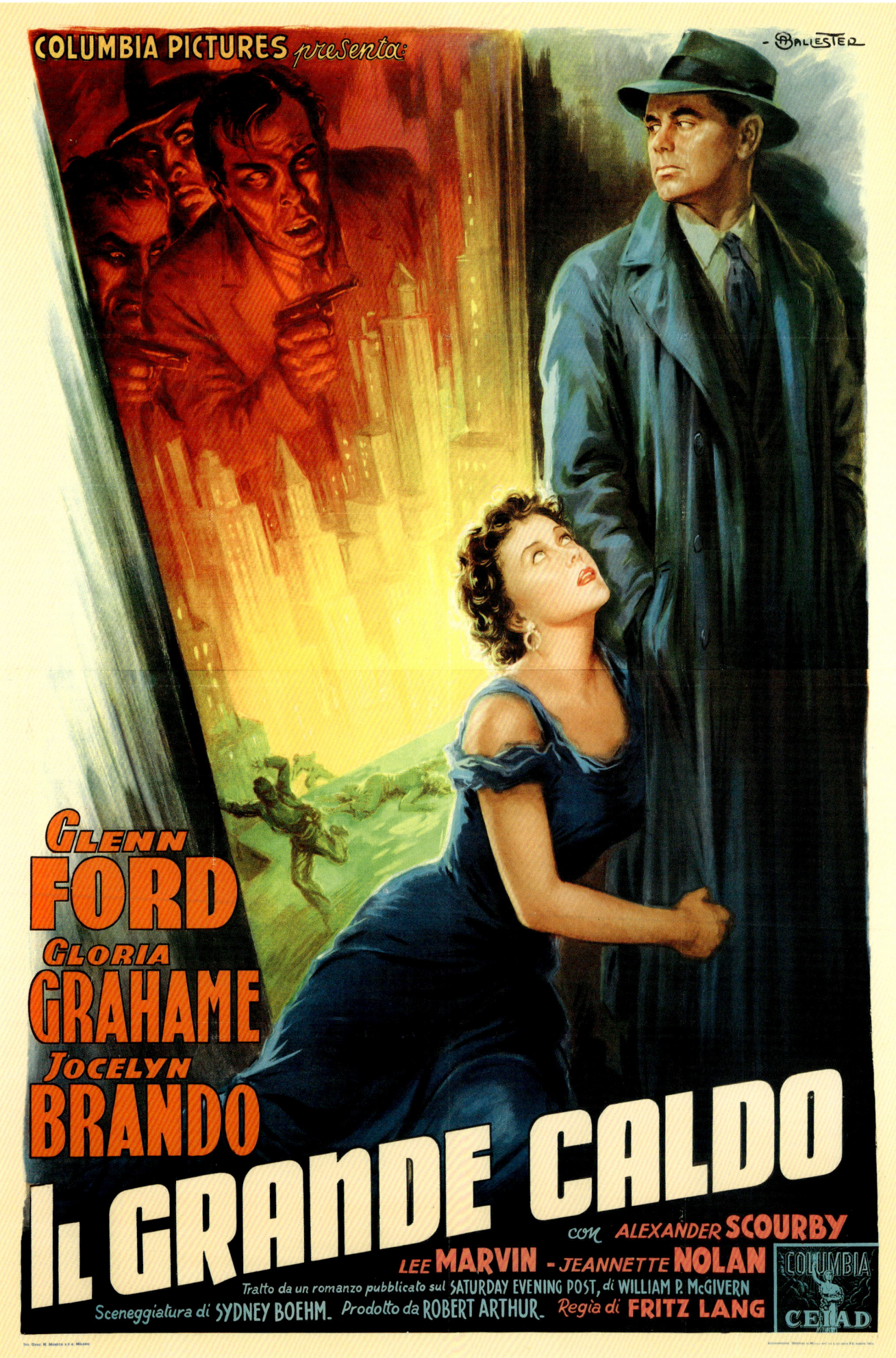

THE BIG HEAT 1953
ITALIAN POSTER, ART BY ANSELMO BALLESTER

The Big Heat is one of my favourite noirs. Made by director Fritz Lang in the latter part of his career, it is widely acknowledged as his finest American work. It is a harsh and vicious masterpiece, unflinchingly filmed in Lang's definitive style. The best artwork is, without a doubt, Anselmo Ballester's stunning large Italian poster, which captures the bleak atmosphere and ferocity of the film.

Anselmo Ballester (1897-1974) was one of the most respected – and remains one of the most collected – Italian film poster artists of the twentieth century. He produced over 500 film posters during his 45-year career.

Ballester's artistic talent was encouraged from a young age by his father Federico, himself a well-known painter. After studying at the Academy of Fine Arts in Rome, Anselmo began illustrating movie posters in the silent era and continued working for all of the major studios up until his retirement in the 1970s. He remains most renowned for the work he produced as chief artist at Minerva Films (the Italian production company) and through BCM, a company he established with fellow poster artists Luigi Martinati and Alfredo Capitani and which specialised in the production of film posters (BCM stood for Ballester-Capitani-Martinati). At BCM, Ballester worked almost exclusively on posters for Columbia Studios' productions, such as this poster for *The Big Heat*.

Ballester understood the importance of balancing a beautiful aesthetic with a commercial sensibility – an insight that perhaps explains his extraordinary longevity in the industry. As he wrote in his own diary, 'To become a creator of film posters ... it is necessary to study passionately, to always draw and paint everything from the truth. Then you can let your imagination run free. Whether you are creating a work of art, or a more humble advertising poster, you must be able to attract the interest of the public, to satisfy both the most refined people and the roughest, who are the majority.'

LE SALAIRE DE LA PEUR 1953
FRENCH POSTER, ART BY ROBERT LEVEQUE

Henri Georges Clouzot was a maestro of the suspense thriller. Made a year before his iconic horror, *Les Diaboliques*, his *Le salaire de la peur* (*The Wages of Fear*) is a revered masterpiece of heart-stopping tension. It won the Grand Prix at the 1953 Cannes Film Festival and the BAFTA for Best Film of 1954.

In a stinging satire of American capitalism, the plot involved four men hired by an oil company at $2000 a head to transport two trucks of highly dangerous nitroglycerine across the country along rickety roads. The dramatic journey ultimately results in the death of all four men. Artist Robert Leveque's French poster portrays one of the film's most nerve-wracking moments. It also manages to encapsulate the desperate dread that flows through the film.

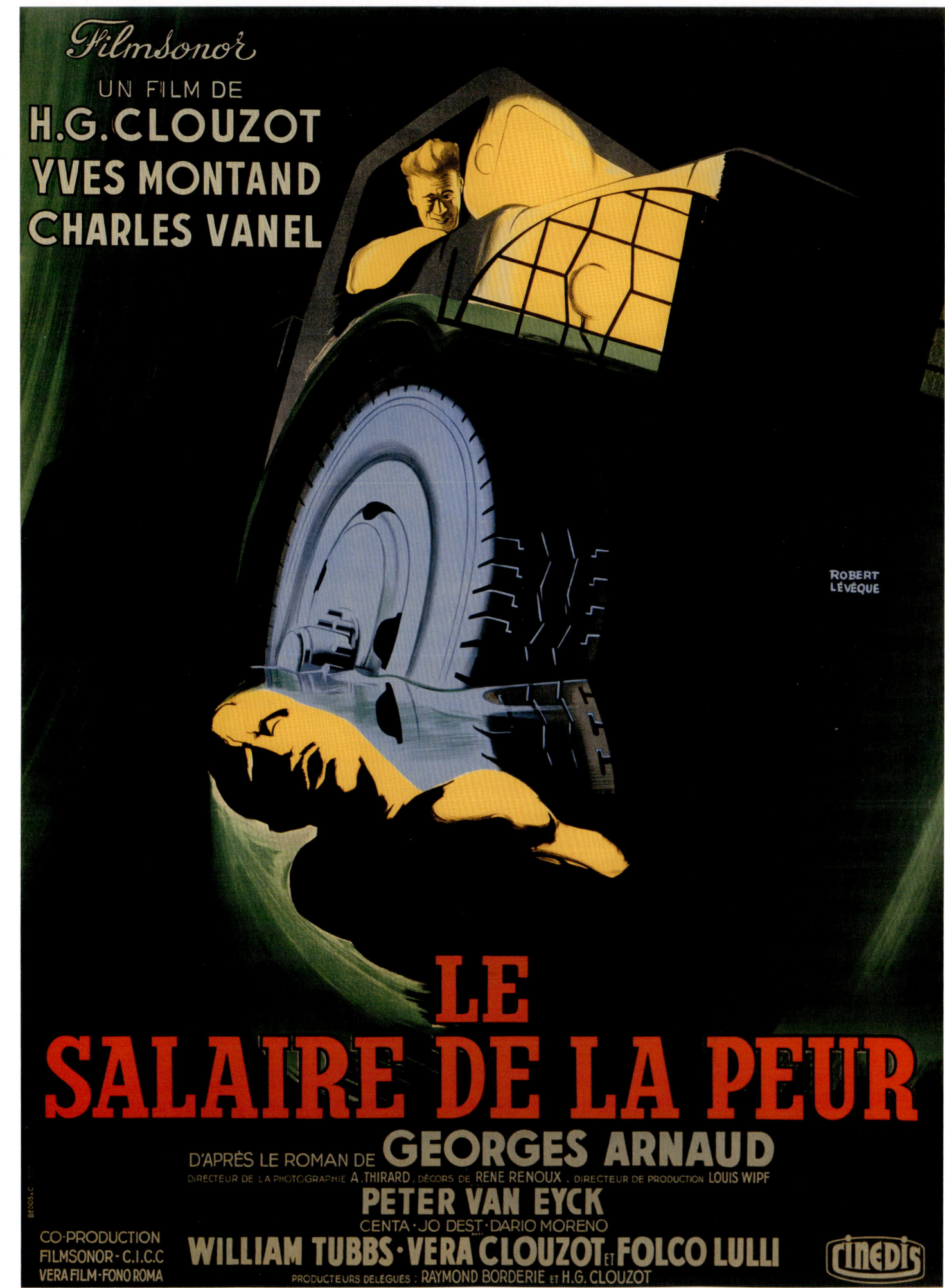

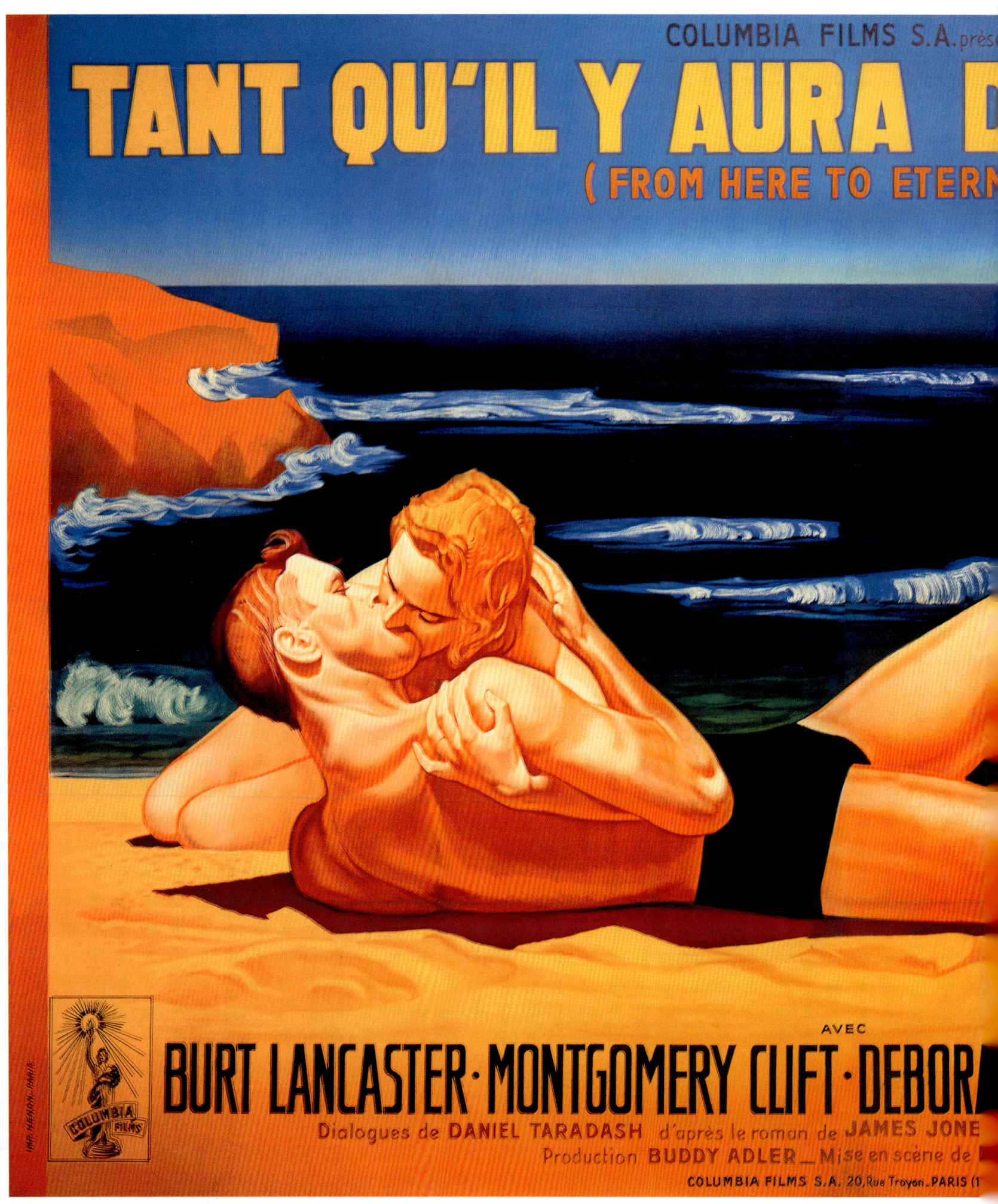

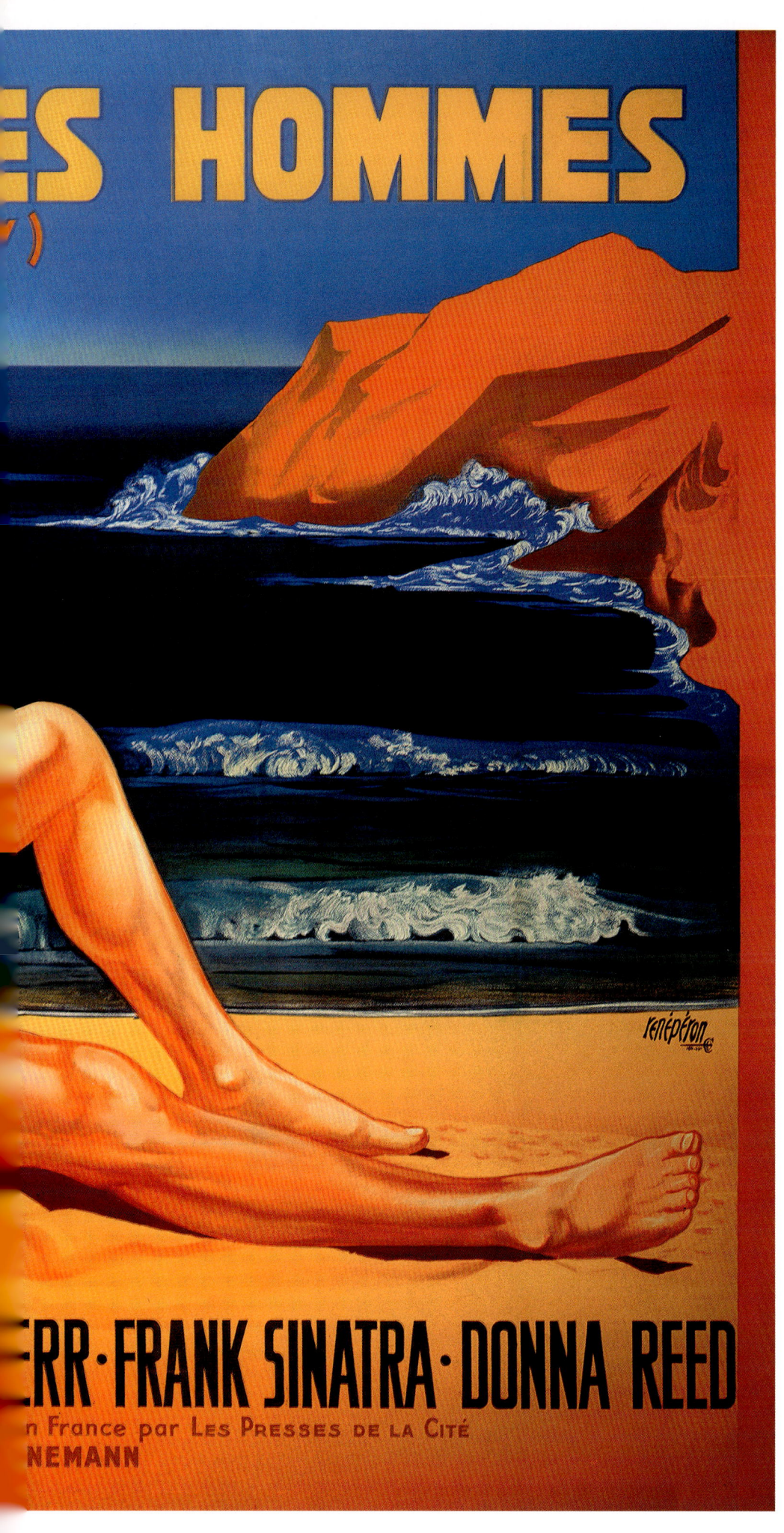

FROM HERE TO ETERNITY 1953
FRENCH POSTER, ART BY RENÉ PÉRON

René Péron (1904-1972) was renowned as one of the masters of French poster art and his eye-catching designs, which displayed a preference for strong and contrasting colours, were perfect for attracting potential cinemagoers. His poster for *From Here to Eternity* is one of the most impressive posters I have had the privilege of handling – its large size only adding to its impact. It is rare for a movie poster to feature the key scene from a film and this is one of the few posters in the worldwide campaign to feature the iconic kiss between Burt Lancaster and Deborah Kerr.

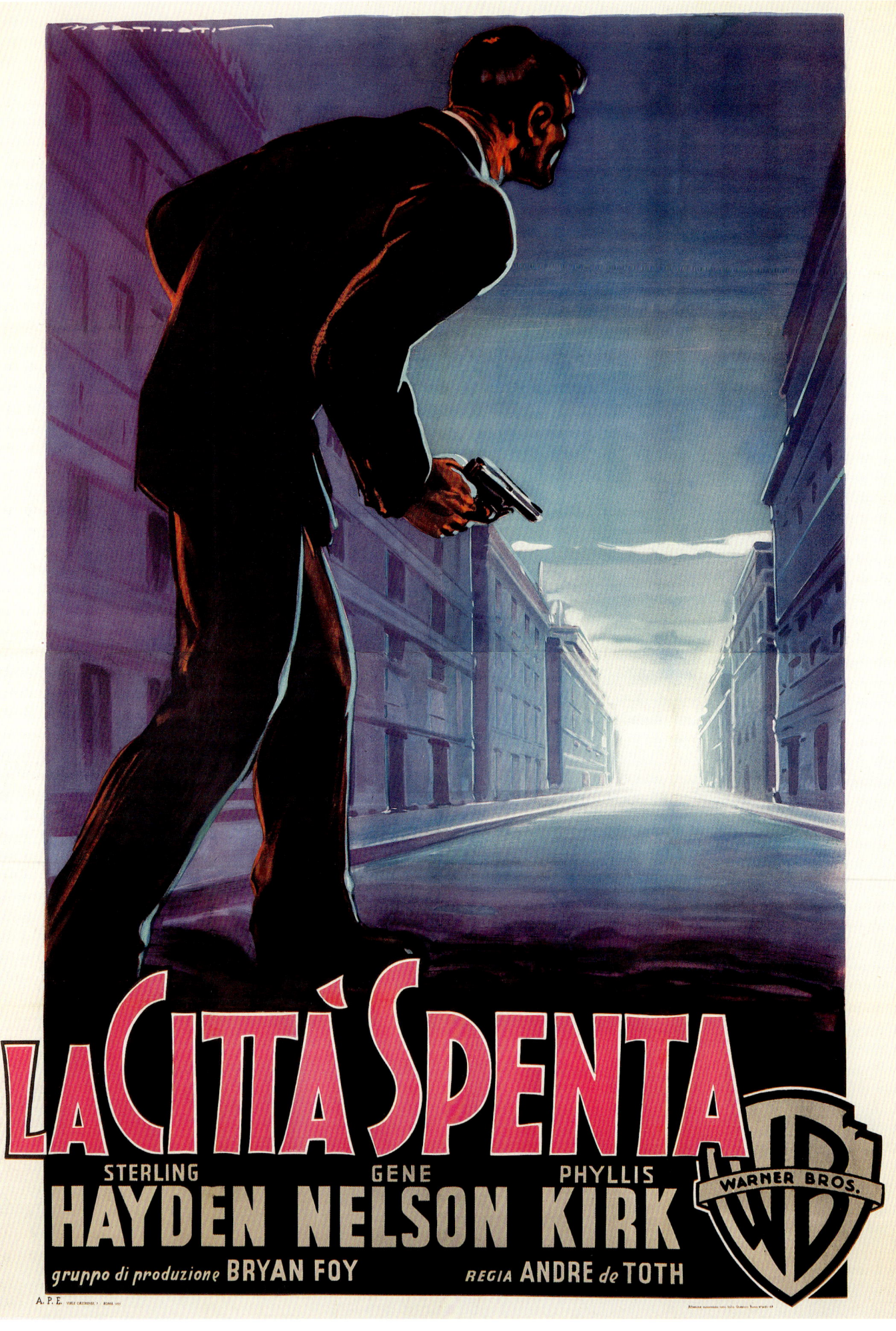

CRIME WAVE 1954
ITALIAN POSTER, ART BY LUIGI MARTINATI

I have always loved this Italian poster for *Crime Wave* by artist Luigi Martinati. He managed to capture the dark and hardboiled feel of this uncompromising film, which is also known by its alternative title, *The City is Dark*. Shot entirely on location on the streets of Los Angeles, Martinati captured the central importance of the urban landscape in his artwork. The shadowy figure stepping into the unknown is also particularly noiresque.

Luigi Martinati (1893-1984) had a prolific career in film poster art. Born in Florence, he moved to Rome in 1911 and trained as an artist's apprentice. He became the manager of one of the leading advertising agencies in Rome, where he worked on the poster campaigns for a number of film companies, notably Warner Bros. In the mid-1940s, he joined forces with two other giants of Italian film poster design, Anselmo Ballester and Alfredo Capitani, to form a company devoted exclusively to the production of film posters and which was responsible for an endless stream of striking, memorable images. Martinati's personal style was often characterized by one or more large portrait shots that dominated the poster, frequently with a smaller scene in the foreground (see p.91). His poster for *Crime Wave* was unusual in that it portrayed an almost faceless character.

THE BIG KNIFE 1955

ITALIAN POSTER, ART BY NICOLA SIMBARI

Based on a 1949 play by Clifford Odets, *The Big Knife* was a harsh and cynical look at the ugly underbelly of Hollywood. Robert Aldrich's bitter tone and raw lighting created a jarring study of fame and film industry politics. It remains one of the most celebrated movies ever made on the subject and a personal favourite. It is perhaps strange that three posters from the film feature in this 'essentials' list, however, the artwork is remarkably different on each and appreciated for different reasons. It is also a good example of how one film was marketed in many different ways.

The striking large Italian poster, by artist Nicola Simbari, depicts Jack Palance's central character being – literally – strangled by film. It is a fitting reflection of his increasing suffocation at being blackmailed by the studio. The dark tones of his torment contrast against the alluring red of the femme fatale, who leads him closer to his inevitable and tragic demise.

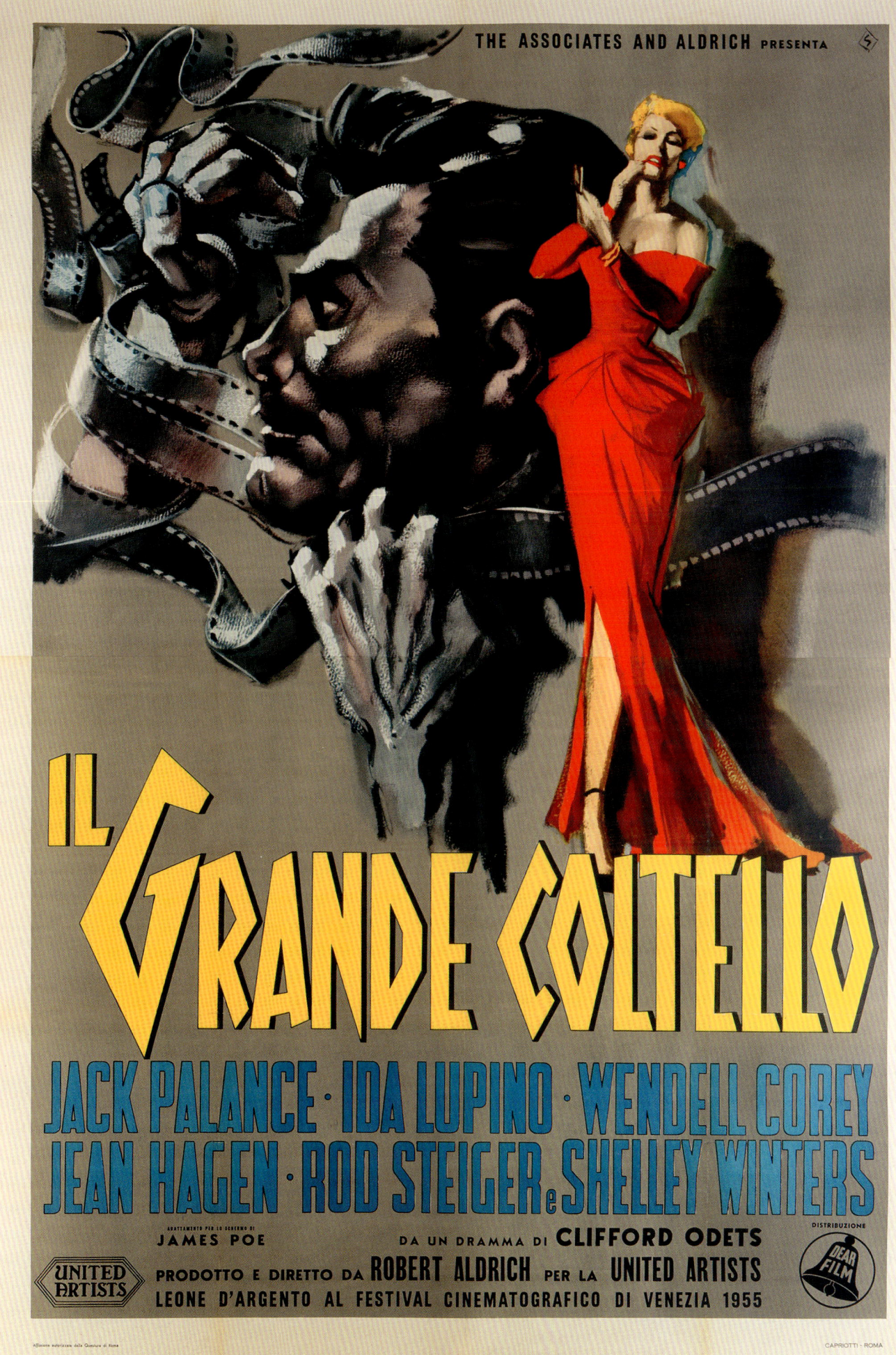

THE BIG KNIFE 1955

GERMAN POSTER, ART BY HANS BRAUN

When *The Big Knife* was released in Germany, it was aptly named *Hollywood Story*. Hans Braun's design is one of the best German posters of this period, featuring a fantastic portrait of Palance's troubled soul. He is haunted by the studio's anger and the female temptress forever at his back.

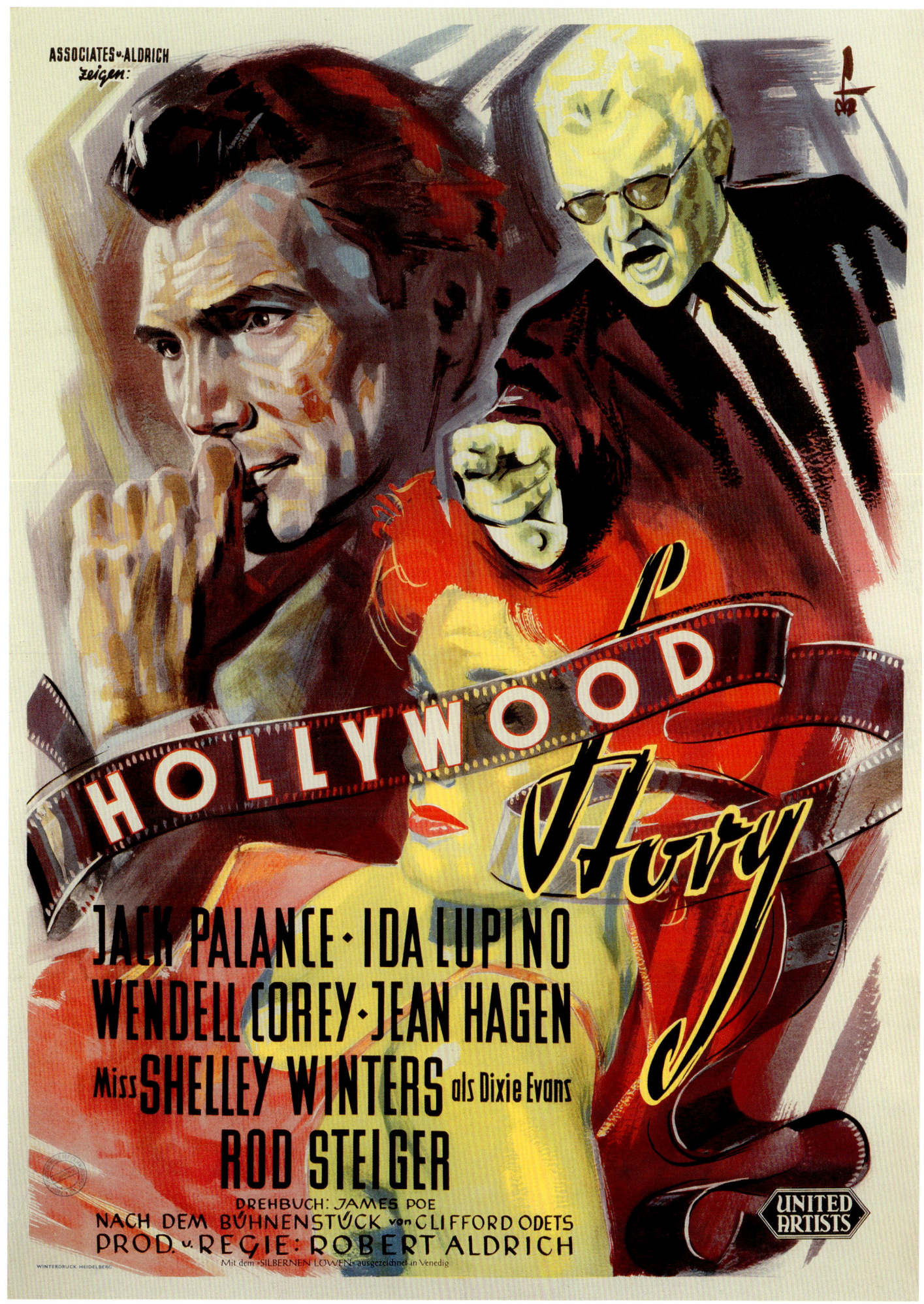

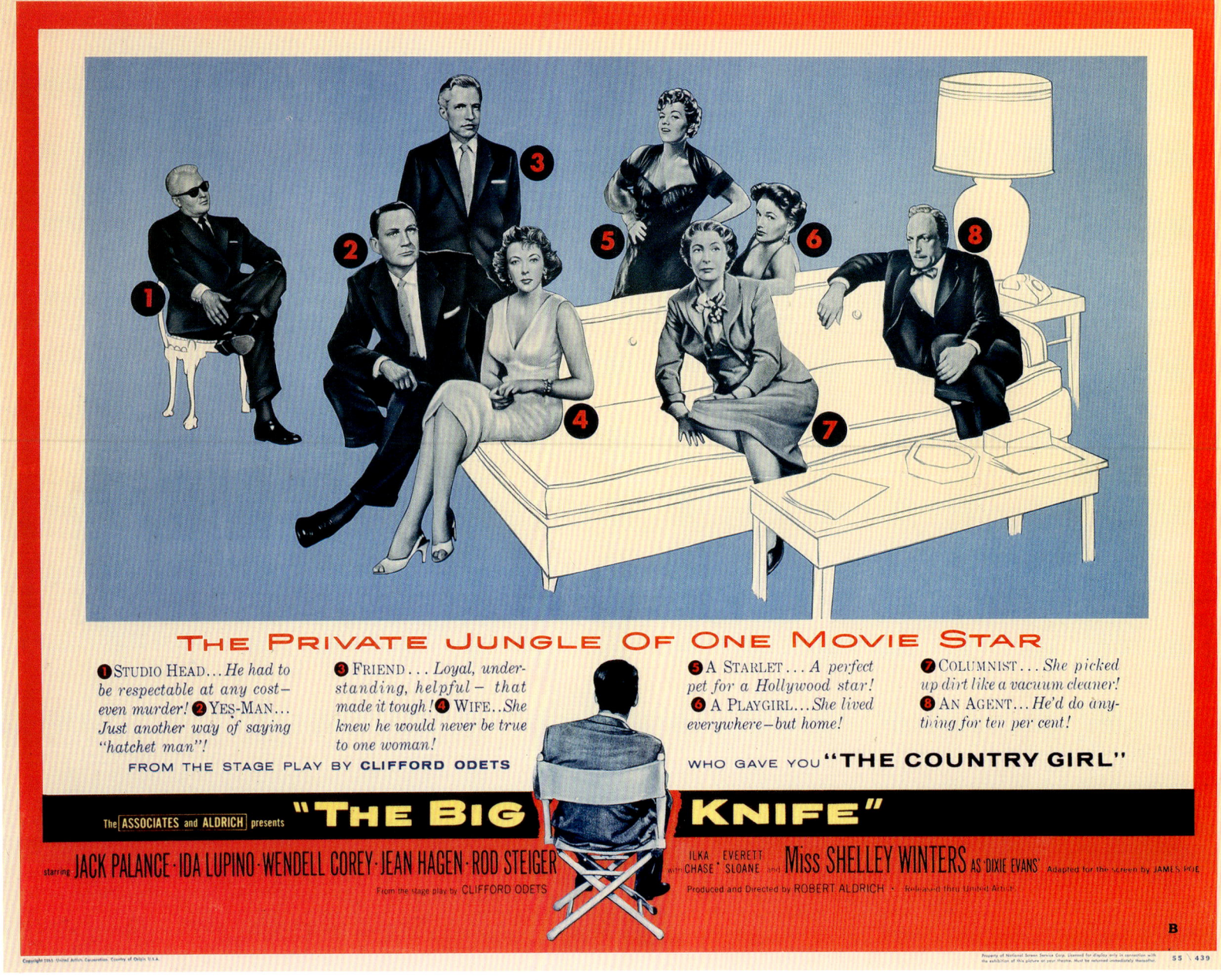

THE BIG KNIFE 1955

AMERICAN POSTER, ARTIST UNKNOWN

The 'style B' American half sheet poster for *The Big Knife* is such an intriguing premise for a film poster design – the cast are arranged in a tableau with one-line zingers describing the role they play in the twisted plot. It is a great example of the different approach taken by United Artists on their 'style B' half sheet posters (see p.136).

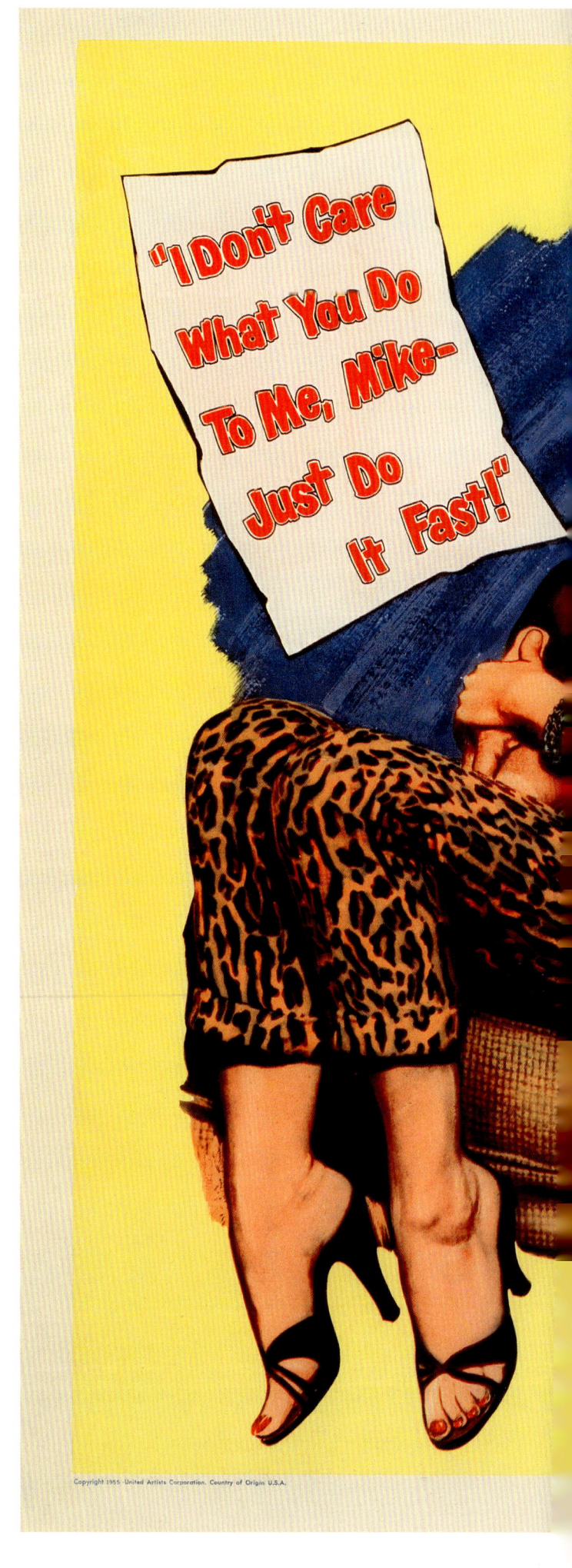

KISS ME DEADLY 1955

AMERICAN POSTER, ARTIST UNKNOWN

During a brief period in the 1950s, United Artists made alternative, 'style B' half sheet posters for a number of films they distributed. The designs were characterized by a highly imaginative and atypical style compared with other American posters of the time. Due to their unusual nature, they were printed in smaller qualities. Three of my favourite 'style B' half sheets are for *The Big Knife* (see previous page), *12 Angry Men* (see following page) and *Kiss Me Deadly*, which features one of the best taglines of the decade, *I Don't Care What You Do To Me, Mike – Just Do It Fast!*

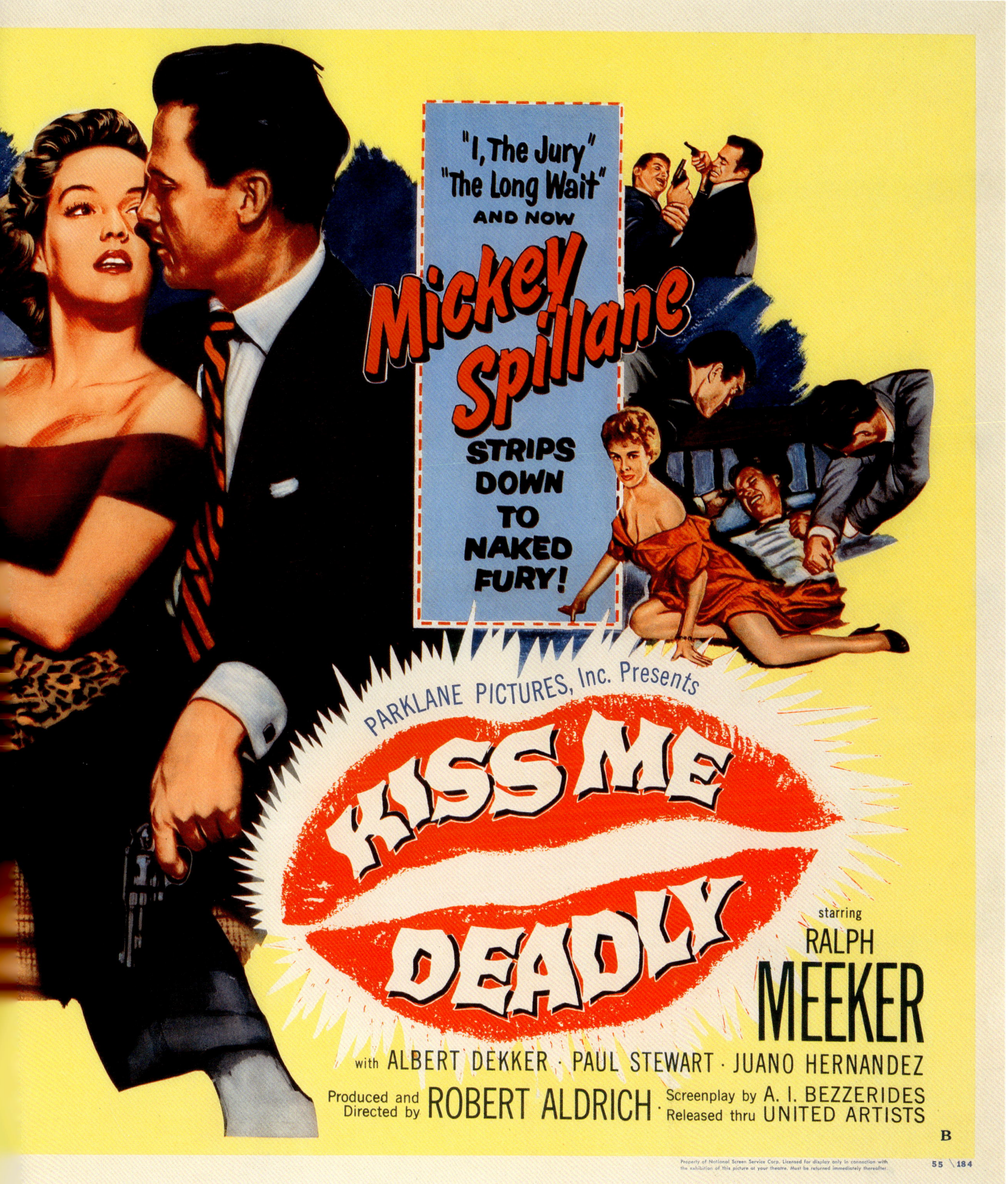

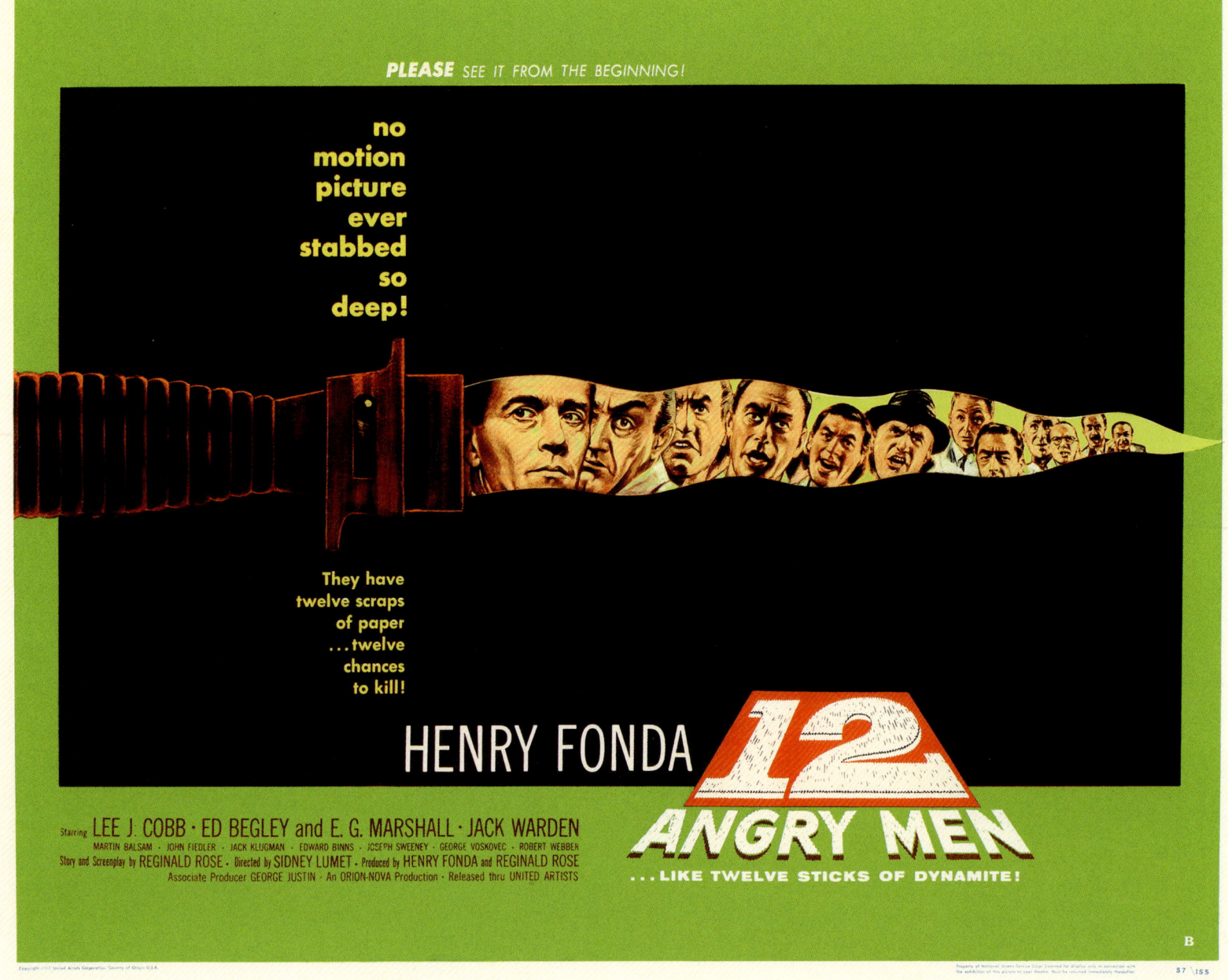

12 Angry Men 1957

American poster, Artist unknown

This 'style B' half sheet poster for *12 Angry Men* uses the knife graphic to great effect. The tagline also hammered home the imagery, *No motion picture ever stabbed so deep ... twelve scraps of paper ... twelve chances to kill!* When the film opened in 1957, A. H. Weiler of *The New York Times* also enjoyed using knife imagery in his review, writing that the film was, 'A penetrating, sensitive and sometimes shocking dissection of the hearts and minds of men who obviously are something less than gods.'

Les Diaboliques 1955
French poster, Art by Raymond Gid

Made just a year after *The Wages of Fear* (see p.125), *Les Diaboliques* is Clouzot's horror masterpiece, a suspense thriller that mounts with paranoia to an almost unbearably tense conclusion. The French poster was the work of artist Raymond Gid and is one of the most outstanding and abstract French posters of the period.

Raymond Gid (1905-2000) was a French designer and typographer, renowned for his commercial posters and his published books. His style was very free and conceptual and he had an ability to evoke an atmosphere through simple lines. *Les Diaboliques* is his most famous film poster. He is also known for *Vampyr* (1932) and *Le silence de la mer* (1949) and his advertising work with Bally shoes and Amnesty International. In addition, he illustrated several well-known liturgical texts.

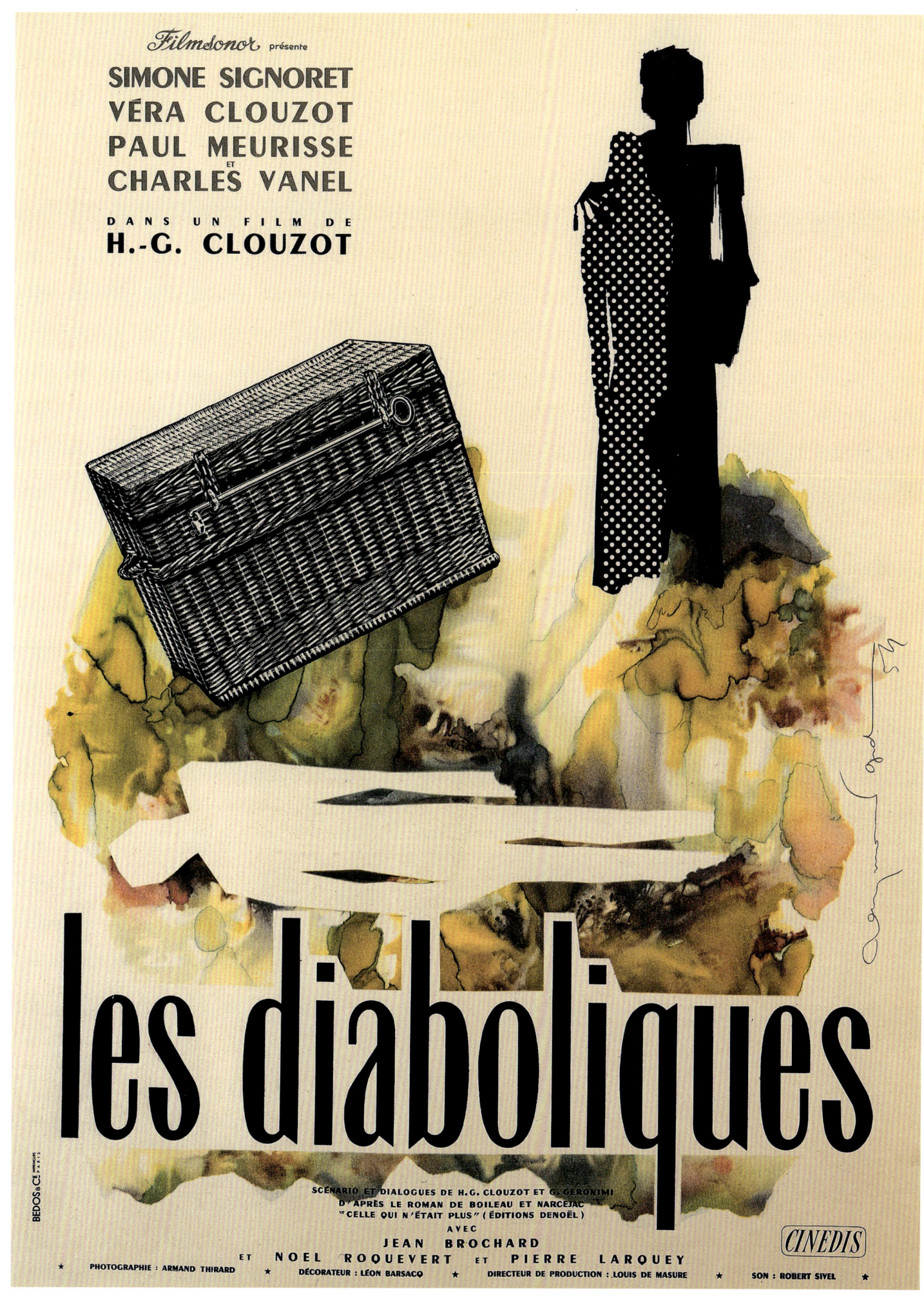

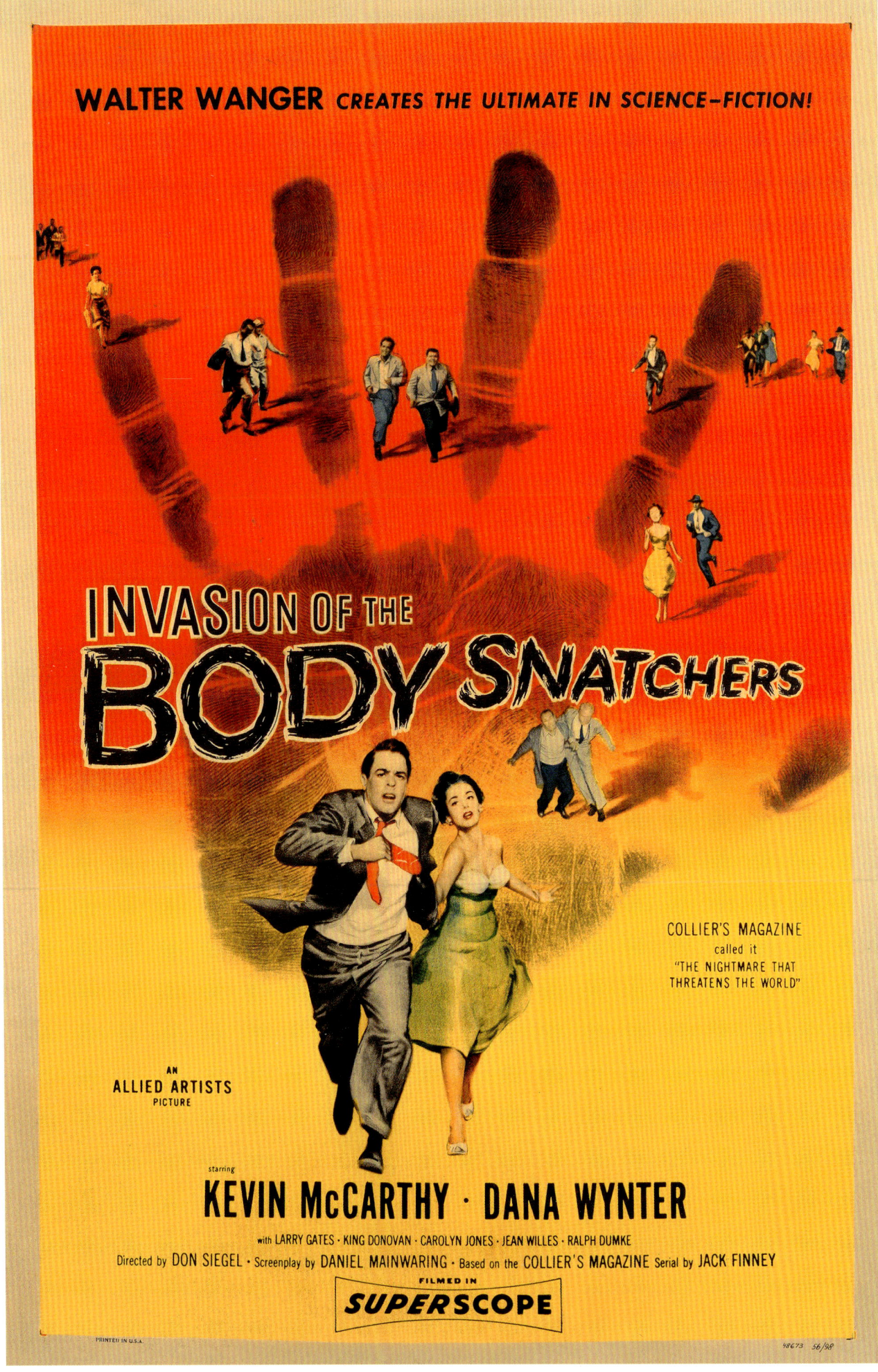

Invasion of the Body Snatchers 1956
American poster, Artist unknown

Shot in just 19 days on a tiny budget, *Invasion of the Body Snatchers* is one of the most enduring and influential films of the 1950s, projecting a sophistication and subtlety missing in the more Gung-Ho Gore science fiction films of the period. Using Jack Finney's 1954 novel as its basis, *Invasion of the Body Snatchers* was an astute commentary on the bland conformity of American suburbia during the time of ruthless McCarthyism.

Watching the film, the growing paranoia and sense of menace are palpable as the central protagonists – played by Kevin McCarthy and Dana Wynter – desperately try to escape an unseen and omnipresent enemy. It is this sense of prescient danger and looming horror that are conveyed to such winning effect on the American poster for the film.

THE MAN WITH THE GOLDEN ARM 1955

AMERICAN POSTER, DESIGN BY SAUL BASS

Saul Bass (1920-1996) was one of the greatest graphic designers of the twentieth century and a pioneer in developing a bold and arresting new style of design. He is famous for his album covers and corporate logos, but it was his innovative movie title sequences and film poster campaigns that cemented his 'legendary' status. His genius perhaps lies in the compelling simplicity of his approach. As Martin Scorsese remarked in the foreword to *Saul Bass: A Life in Film & Design* (Laurence King, 2011), 'It has something to do with the economical beauty and elegance of the design, and the range of feeling it contains.'

In 1954, Bass was commissioned by the director Otto Preminger to design the logo for his new film, *Carmen Jones*. Preminger was so impressed with Bass's simple flame and rose concept that he asked the artist to film the title sequence. A year later, the director invited Bass to work on *The Man with the Golden Arm*, for which Bass created his celebrated title sequence and poster campaign, featuring a jagged arm suggestive of the jarring and disjointed existence of a drug addict. The poster graphics were greatly acclaimed by everyone except the studio heads at United Artists, who were nervous about using such an abstract approach as the heart of the advertising campaign. They insisted that Bass superimpose photographs of Frank Sinatra, Kim Novak and Eleanor Parker onto the posters. The 'pure' version of Bass's design, free of photographic add-ons, was not used for the main campaign and only featured on a handful of posters, including this version which was used for the New York premiere. I have only ever seen two copies of this poster.

Bass went on to work with Preminger on a further 12 films, including his iconic work on the title sequence and poster campaign for *Anatomy of a Murder*.

Another director who Bass enjoyed a close relationship with was Alfred Hitchcock, including working on the title design for *North by Northwest* and *Psycho* (and storyboarding the famous shower scene). Bass's visionary poster for *Vertigo* remains one of his most popular and striking designs.

FRANK SINATRA · ELEANOR PARKER · KIM NOVAK

THE MAN WITH THE GOLDEN ARM

A FILM BY OTTO PREMINGER · FROM THE NOVEL BY NELSON ALGREN · MUSIC BY ELMER BERNSTEIN · PRODUCED & DIRECTED BY OTTO PREMINGER

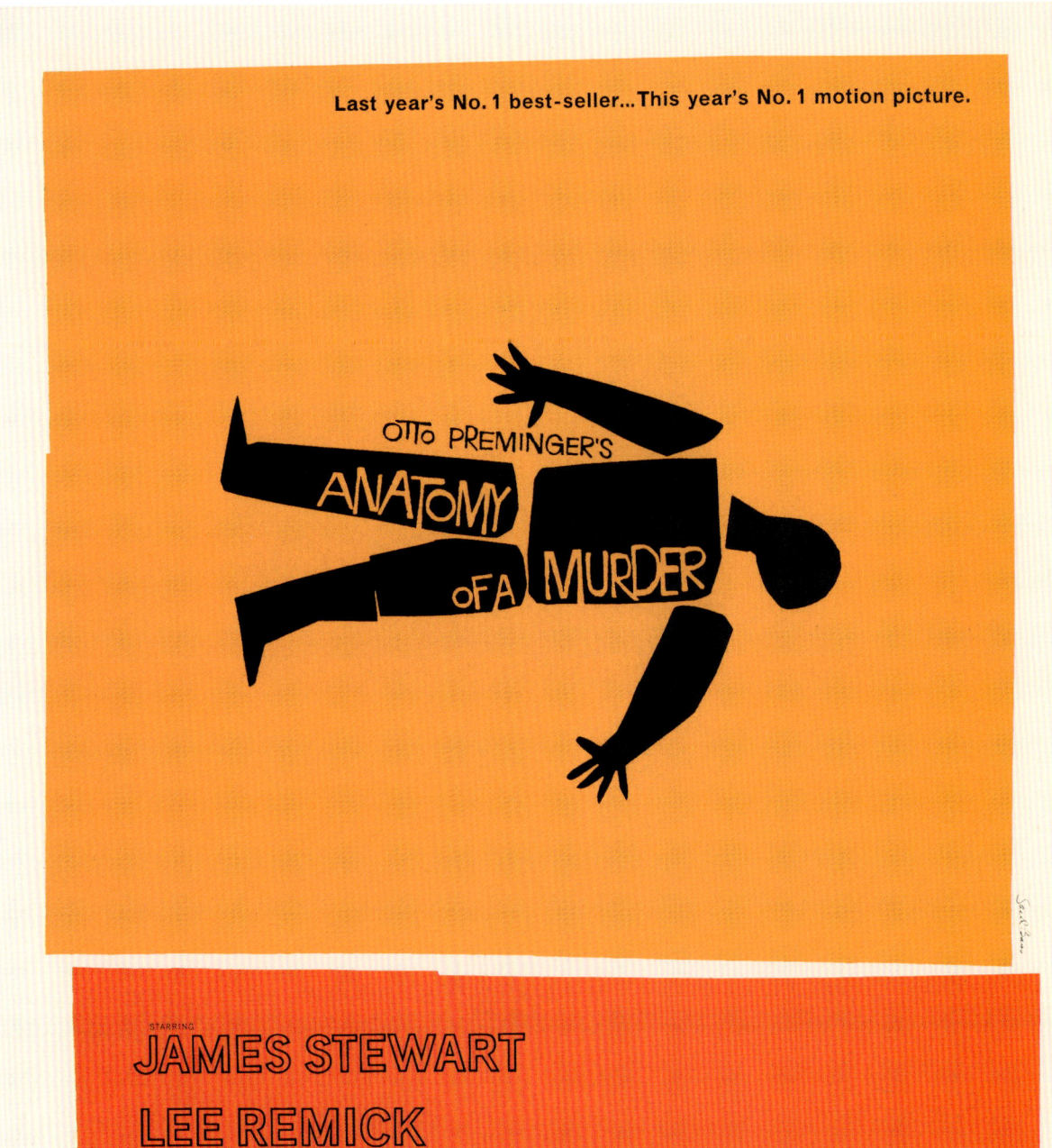

ANATOMY OF A MURDER 1959
AMERICAN POSTER, DESIGN BY SAUL BASS

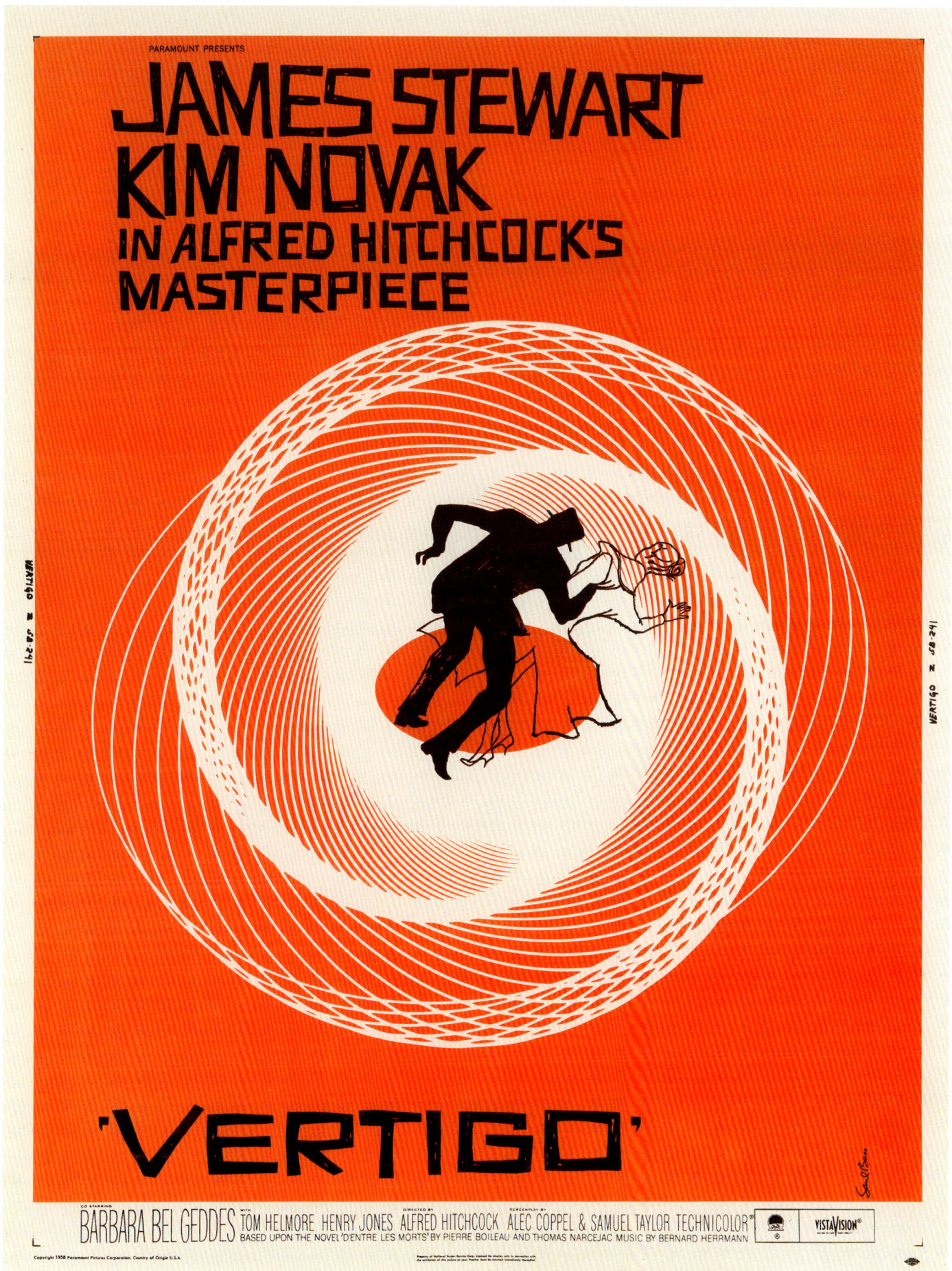

Vertigo 1958
American poster, Design by Saul Bass

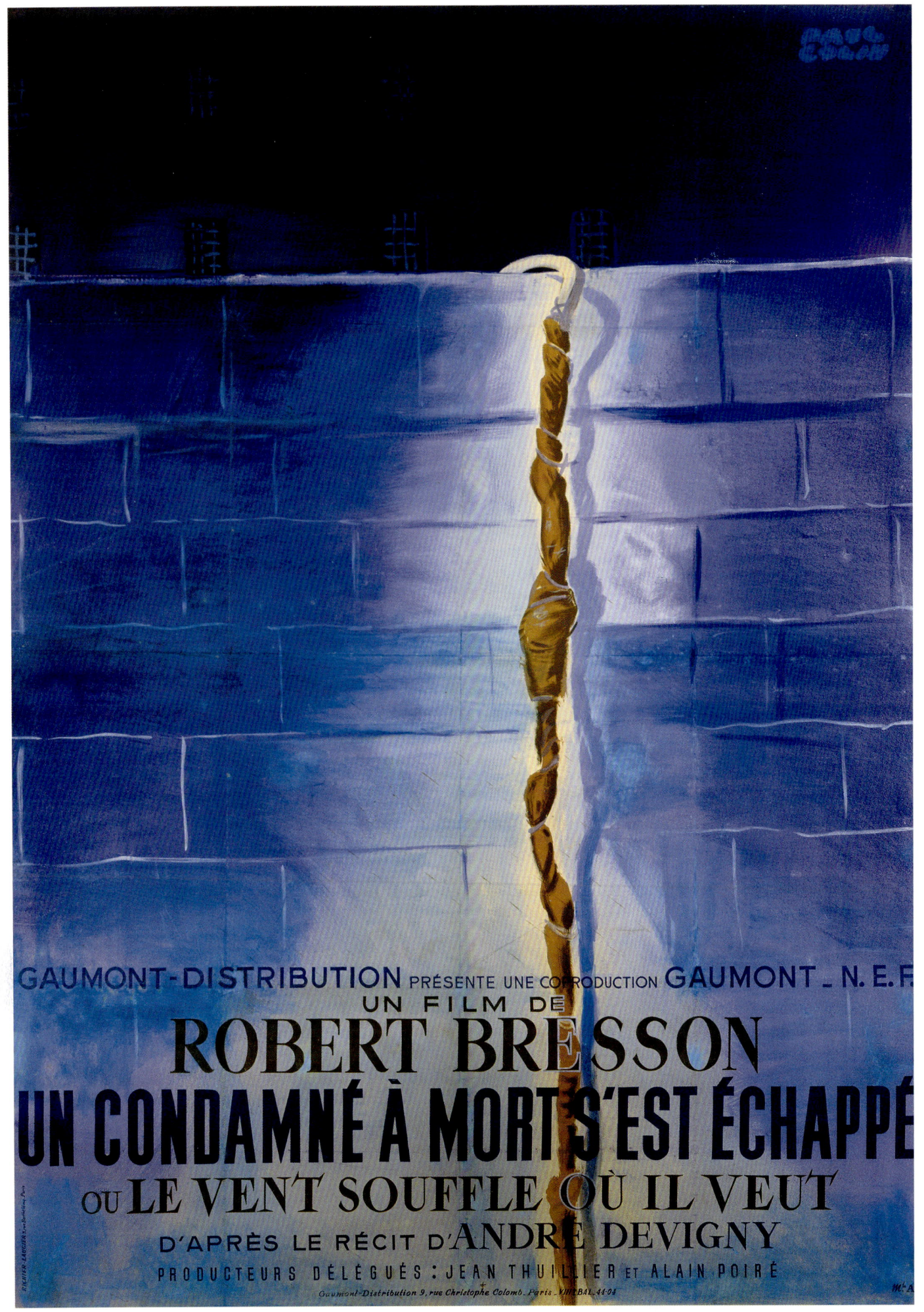

Un condamné à mort s'est échappé 1956
French poster, Art by Paul Colin

André Devigny was a member of the French Resistance who was imprisoned by the Gestapo during the Second World War at Fort Montluc prison in Lyon. The story of his dramatic escape was immortalised in Robert Bresson's film, *Un condamné à mort s'est échappé* (*A Man Escaped*). With a uniquely Bresson approach to pacing, aesthetic and sound, it is regarded as one of the most accomplished and suspenseful 'jailbreak' films ever made. Bresson had an unparalleled insight into the mind of his central character as had himself been imprisoned by the Nazis during the war. The scrupulous authenticity of his portrayal was backed by Devigny's statement at the start of the film that, 'This story is true. I give it as it is, without embellishment.'

    Bresson brought his meticulous attention to detail to the production. It was filmed on location in Fort Montluc itself, and the escape rope – rags tied to hand-fashioned metal hooks – was an exact replica of that used by Devigny in his original escape. For the alternative 'style B' poster for the French release, artist Paul Colin made the unusual decision to use the rope as the focus of his design, thus emphasising its central importance. (For Colin biography, see p.62.)

ATTACK OF THE 50 FOOT WOMAN 1958
AMERICAN POSTER, ART BY REYNOLD BROWN

Size is a common theme in the *what if?* world of science fiction and the genre has often explored scenarios in which the scale of the everyday world becomes distorted. *Attack of the 50 Foot Woman* is one such offering, which sees Allison Hayes grow into a terrorising giantess after an unfortunate encounter with an alien. The film is a second rate B-movie at best, however, Reynold Brown's American poster for the film is one of the best examples of 1950s science fiction poster art, depicting a magnificent Hayes in risqué garb and with avenging talons.

Reynold Brown (1917-1991) won a scholarship to attend art school in the early 1930s. He embarked on a career in comic book art until a providential meeting with artist Norman Rockwell convinced him to leave cartoons in pursuit of his dreams of becoming an illustrator. He illustrated technical service manuals during the Second World War, before moving to New York in 1945 and beginning his career in commercial illustration – designing magazine and book covers for *Life*, *Saturday Evening Post*, *Popular Science* and the paperback editions of the Perry Mason series for Pocket Books.

Between 1952 and 1970, Brown designed over 250 movie posters and is one of the most acclaimed artists from this period. He worked on campaigns for *Ben-Hur* (1959), *Spartacus* (1960), *The Alamo* (1960) and *Doctor Zhivago* (1965). He is most renowned for his work on science fiction and horror B-movies from the 1950s, including *Creature from the Black Lagoon* (1954), *The Incredible Shrinking Man* (1957) and, most famously, *Attack of the 50 Foot Woman*. Reynold had a talent for creating detailed scenes of epic grandeur and mass panic that appropriately reflected the suspicion and paranoia of the age.

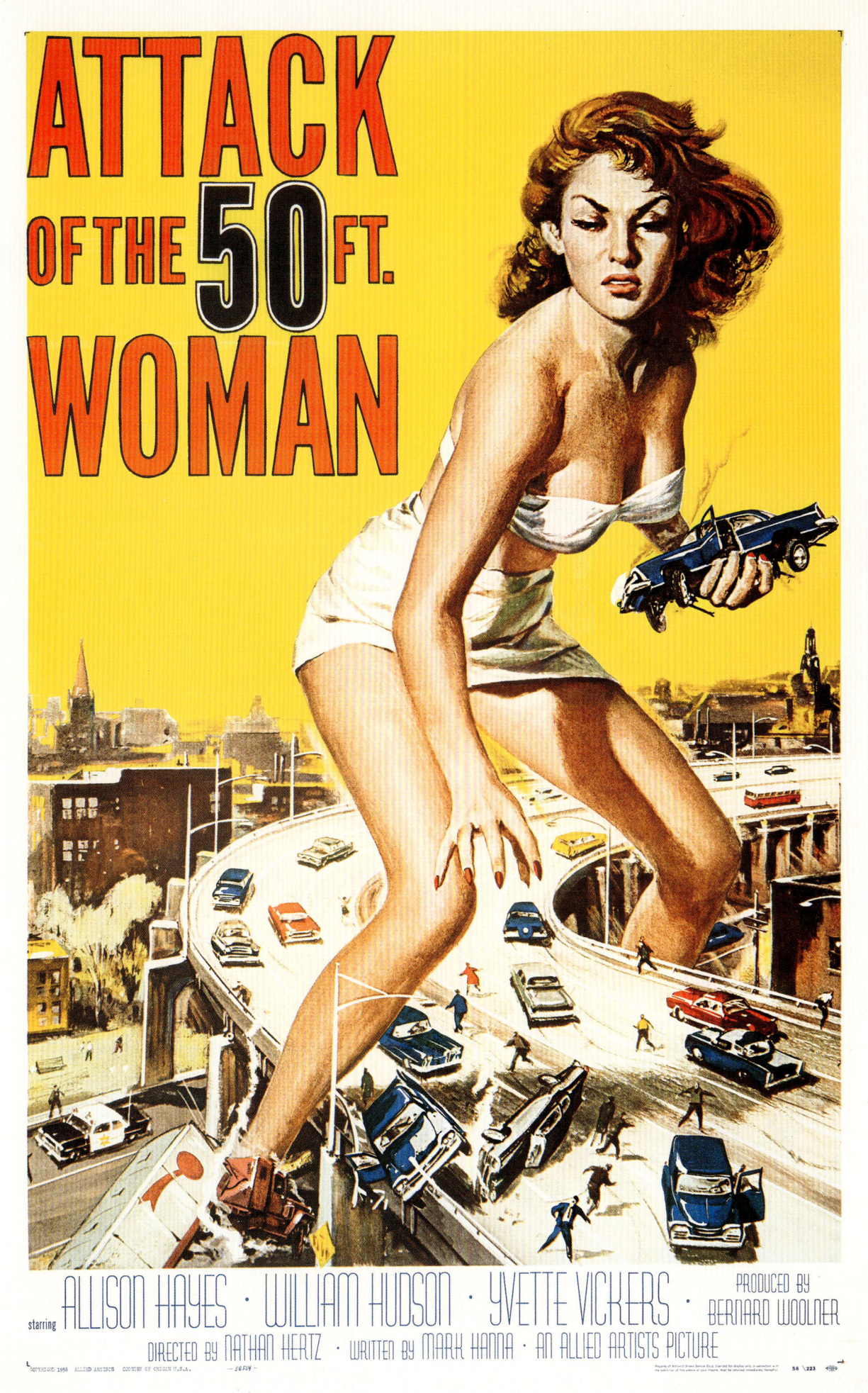

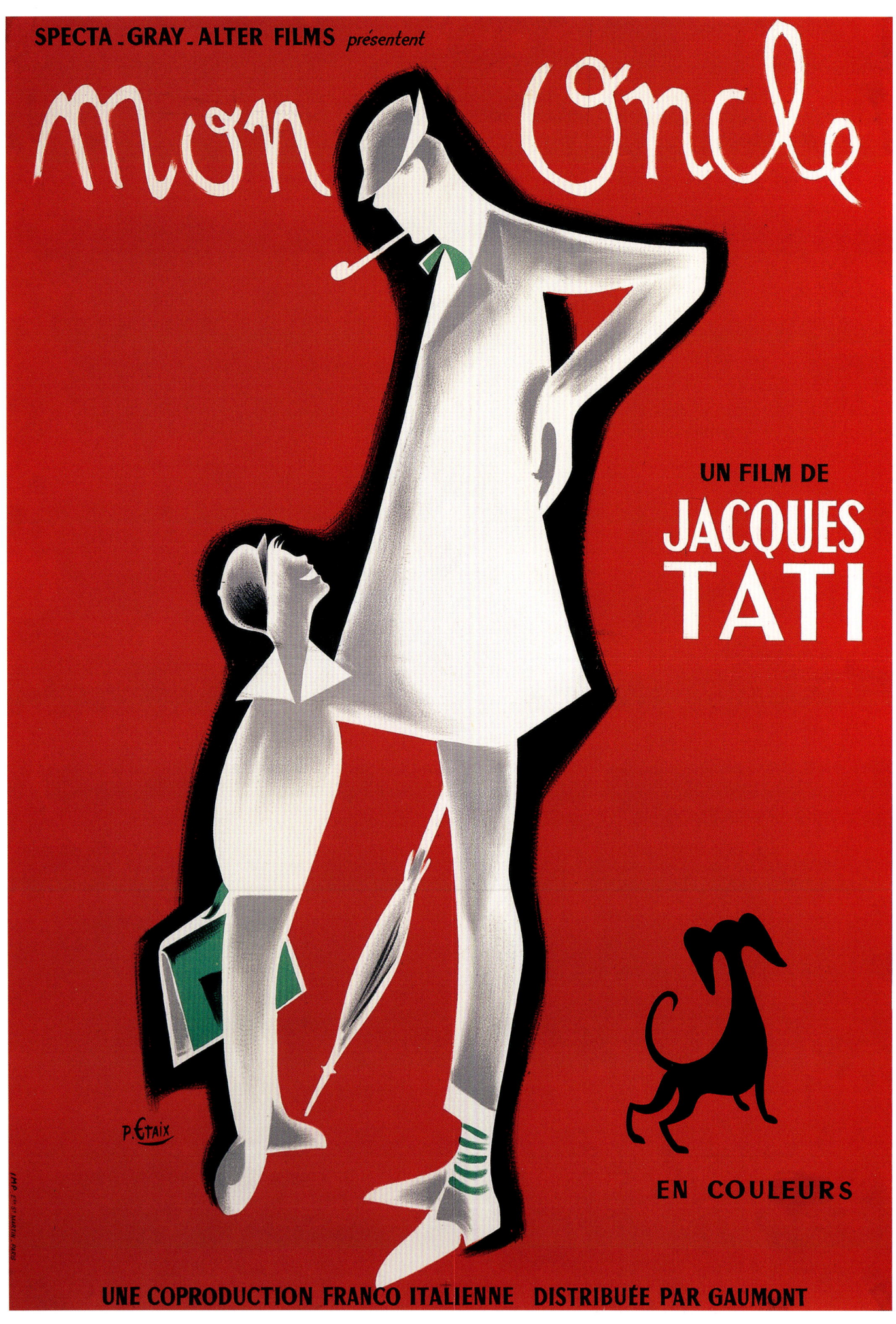

Mon Oncle 1958

French poster, Art by Pierre Étaix

Pierre Étaix (b.1928) is a renowned artist, designer, filmmaker and clown. A fan of the intelligent slapstick comedy of the silent screen, Étaix has frequently been called 'the French Buster Keaton'.

Born in the Loire region of France, Étaix moved to Paris in his mid-twenties and worked as an illustrator while also performing in cabaret and as a circus clown with the renowned Nino Fabri. In 1954, a chance meeting with Jacques Tati resulted in Étaix collaborating on Tati's tour de force, *Mon Oncle*, as assistant director, gagman and designer. Étaix was also responsible for the striking French poster campaign for the film. The stripped-down graphics and bold colour scheme were very modern for the time and it has since become one of the most famous French posters of the 1950s.

Étaix's work on *Mon Oncle* gave him a taste for filmmaking and in 1961 he made his first short film, *Rupture*. This was followed two years later by *Heureux anniversaire*, which won him an Academy Award for Best Short Film. Between 1963 and 1970, he made five feature films, including *Le Soupirant* (1962) and *Yoyo* (1964). In 1973, he formed the National Circus School in France with his wife Annie Fratellini, and the couple also toured as a clowning double-act.

Ascenseur pour l'échafaud 1958
Polish poster, Art by Jan Lenica

With its raw energy, fresh outlook, new methods and unquestionable style, the *Nouvelle Vague* arguably changed the cinematic landscape more than any other movement. In the same vein, the poster artists who accompanied this movement adopted their own unique and influential style. As a visual device designed to promote the films of the French New Wave, the film poster art embodied the essence of the movement. A great example is Jan Lenica's Polish poster for Louis Malle's *Ascenseur pour l'échafaud* (*Lift to the Scaffold*); a film about a murderer stuck in a broken lift while the police accuse him of a crime he did not commit. Lenica's conceptual approach appropriately reflected the entrapment of the protagonist.

Jan Lenica (1928-2001) was a respected cartoonist, graphic designer and animated filmmaker. He was allegedly the first to coin the phrase, 'Polish School of Poster' to describe the group of artists in post-war Poland striving to combine an appreciation of painting and illustration with the simplicity of graphic design.

Lenica originally studied music and architecture before beginning a career in illustration drawing cartoons for satirical magazines. He began designing movie posters in the early 1950s and won the state award for lithography while he was still in his twenties. He designed over 150 posters which, along with his innovative animated films, have been exhibited and won awards around the world. His style was often characterised by an abstract simplicity that used colour and satirical metaphor in an almost childlike approach. A distorted human figure or head was a recurrent motif.

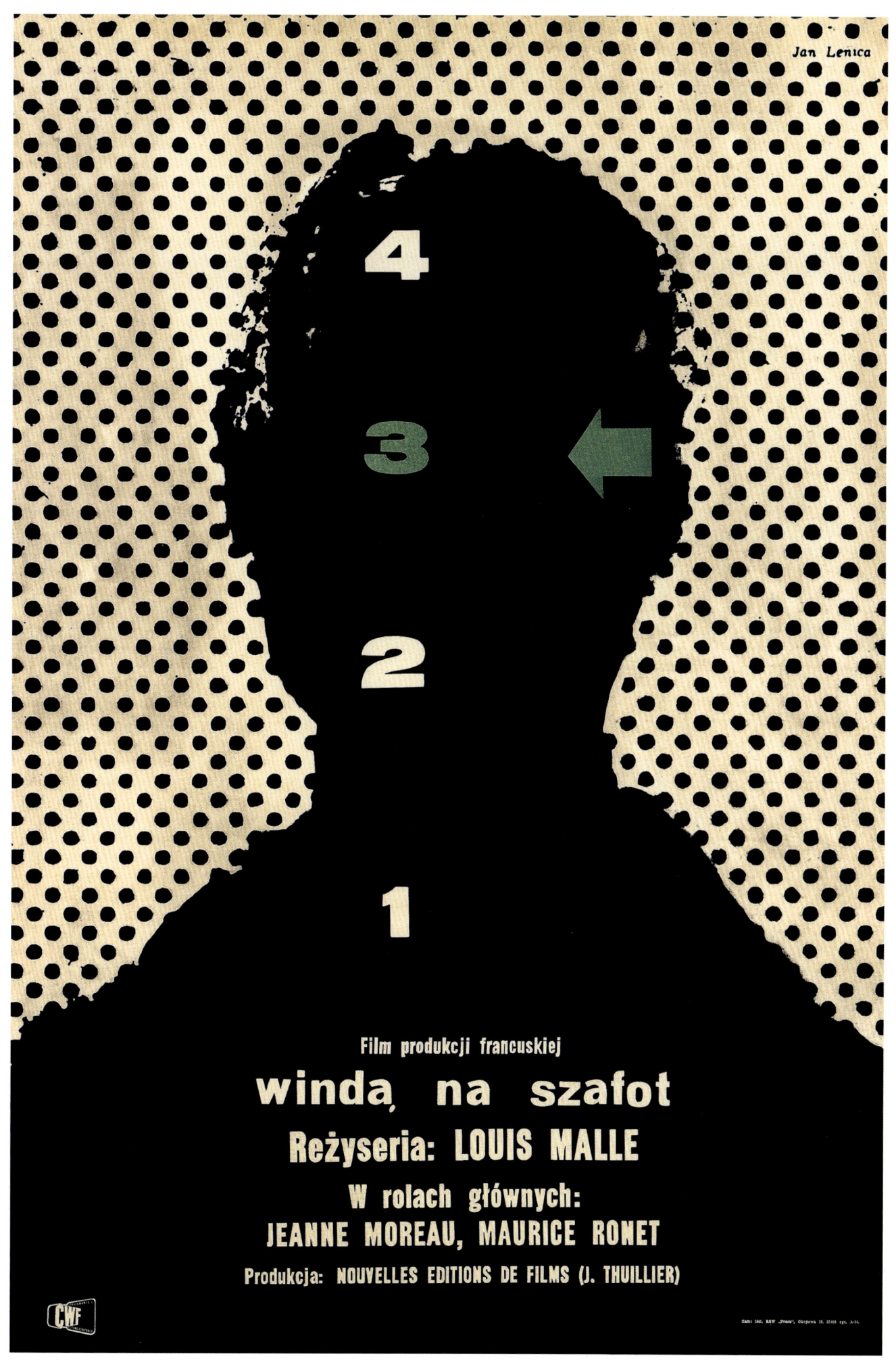

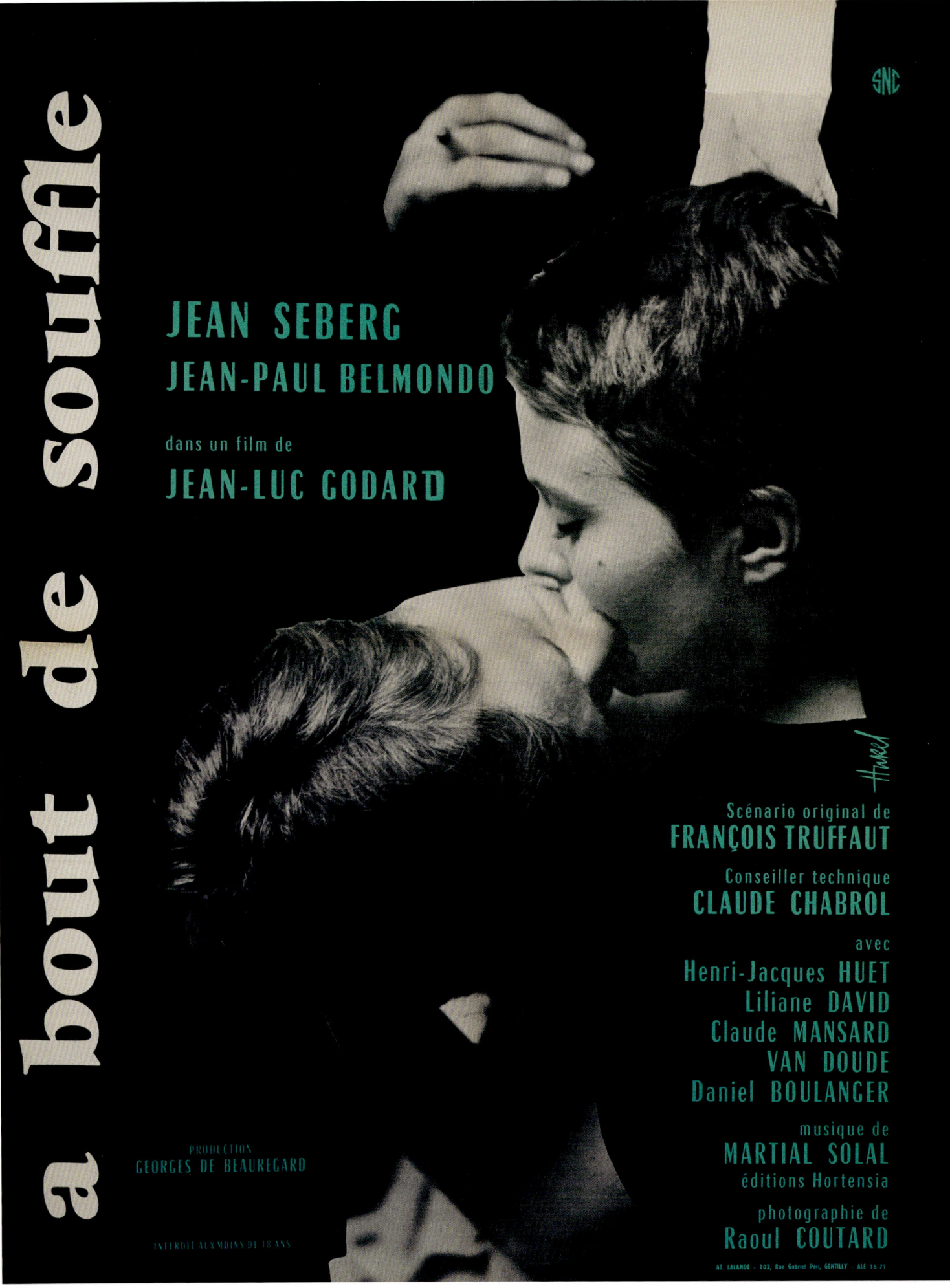

À BOUT DE SOUFFLE 1959

FRENCH POSTER, ART BY CLÉMENT HUREL

The French poster for Jean-Luc Godard's *À bout de souffle* (*Breathless*) is one of the best examples of the use of photomontage in poster design – a technique favoured by the poster artists of the French New Wave. The artwork was by Clément Hurel (1927-2008), one of the most prolific poster artists in France, responsible for over 1500 posters throughout his career. His poster for *À bout de souffle* is one of his most famous works. It used a seemingly simple stylistic devise – rotating the photo of Belmondo and Seberg kissing and the film's title counterclockwise – to great effect. Hurel was also a passionate advocate of the rights of poster designers, fighting for years against the abuse of intellectual copyright and the uncredited use of artists' work.

PICKPOCKET 1959

FRENCH POSTER, ART BY CHRISTIAN BROUTIN

This poster for *Pickpocket* was designed by Christian Broutin (b.1933), a French artist best known for his work in movie posters (particularly during the French New Wave period), advertising and book illustration. Broutin graduated from the National School of Applied Arts and Crafts in 1951. He began working in cinema advertising under the artist René Ferraci and designed his first movie poster at the age of 21 for *Fair Wind to Java* (1954). Between 1954 and 1966, he designed over 100 movie posters, most famously for François Truffaut's *Jules et Jim*, which won the Toulouse-Lautrec poster prize in 1962. This design for *Pickpocket* was not used for the main campaign and is only seen on this small French size. It is one of my favourite French New Wave posters and is also Broutin's personal favourite of all of his movie posters.

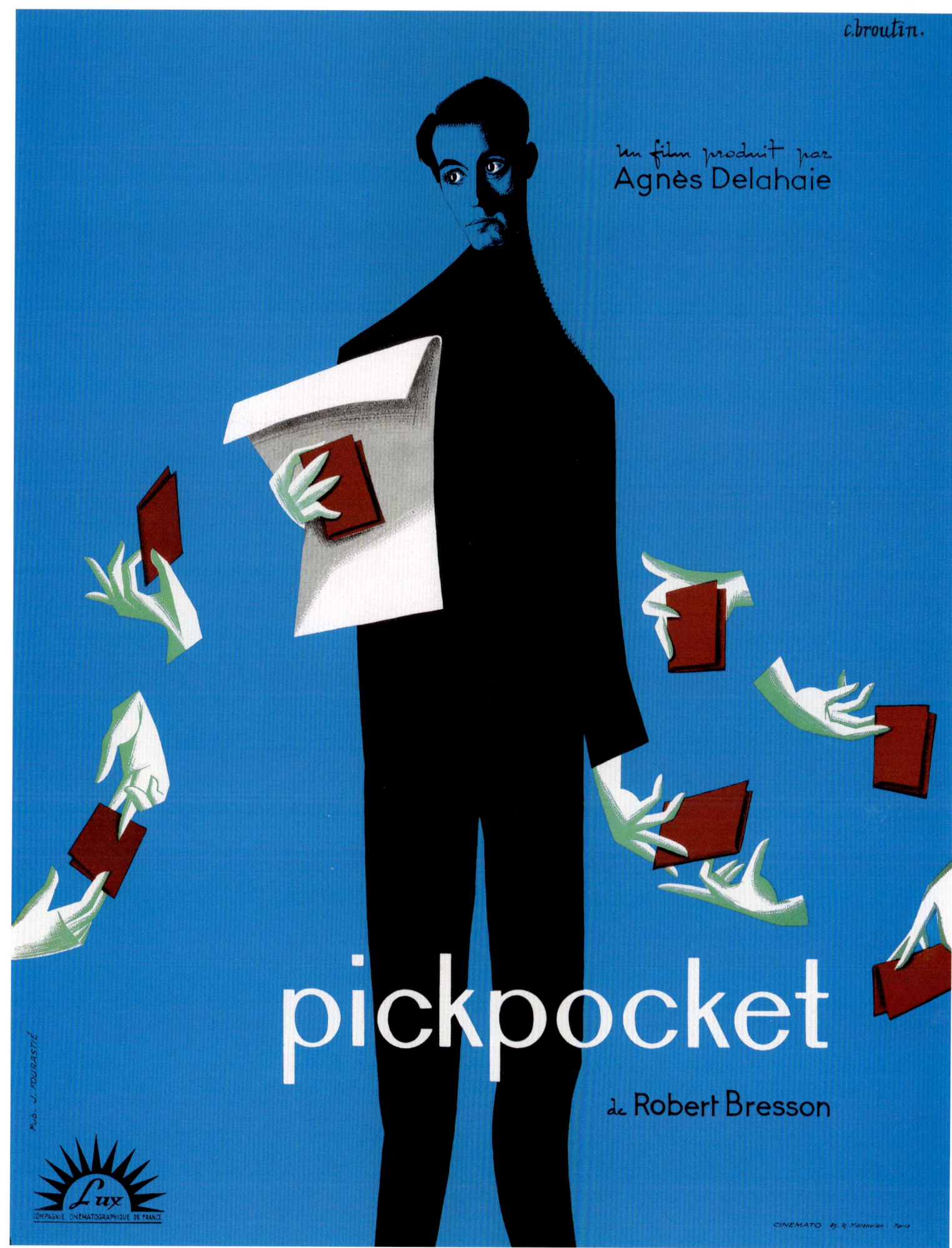

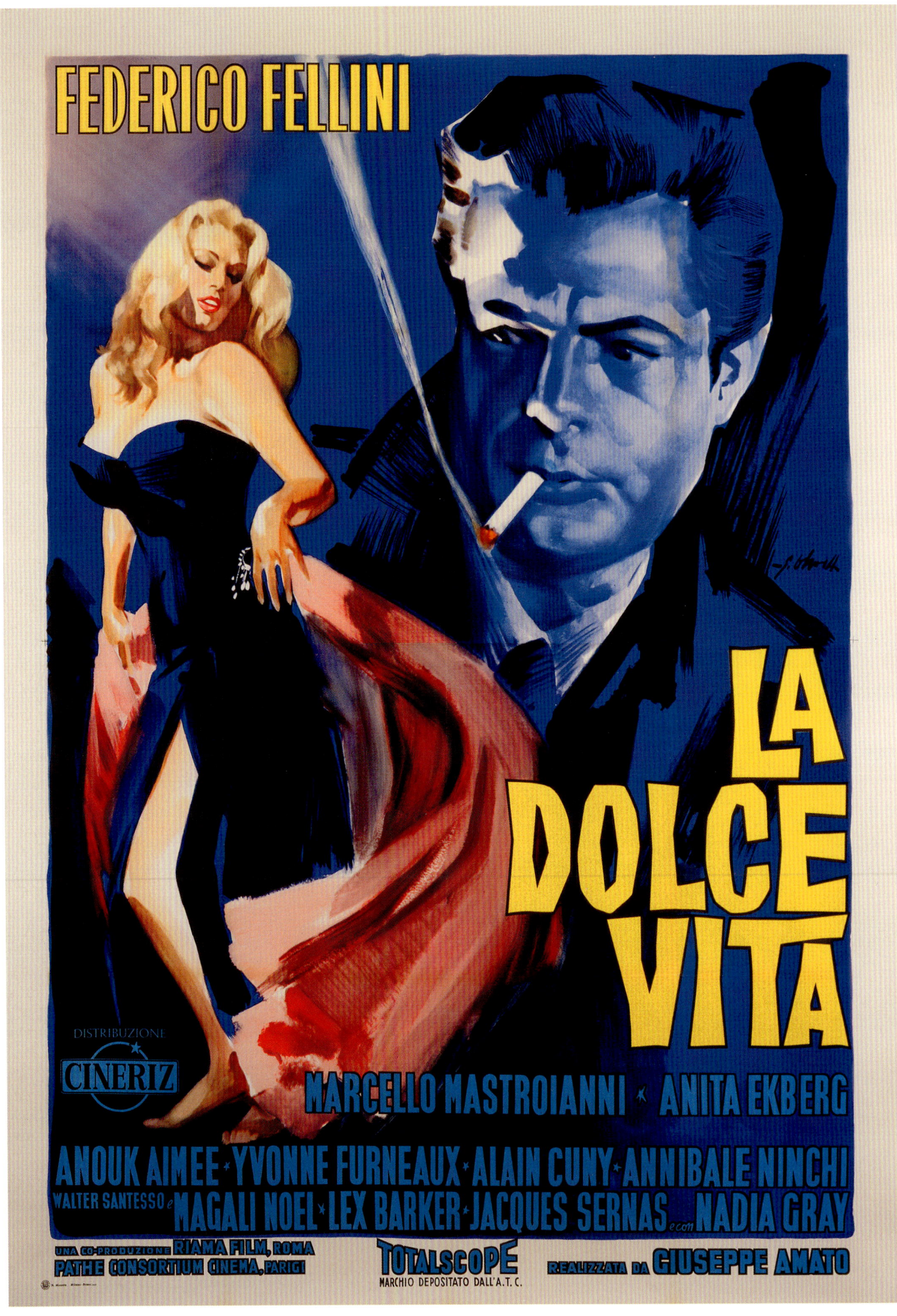

LA DOLCE VITA 1959
ITALIAN POSTER, ART BY GIORGIO OLIVETTI

Federico Fellini's *La Dolce Vita* is a landmark film. It was nominated for four Academy Awards and won the Palme d'Or at Cannes in 1960. It is a flawless balance between Fellini's neo-realist roots and the extravagant surrealism of his later films.

    The film premiered at the Venice Film Festival in 1959, where artist Giorgio Olivetti's poster was used to promote it. His design was also used as the main poster when the film went on general release a few months later in 1960. Giorgi Olivetti (1908-?d.) depicted Mastroianni as a tabloid reporter, and temptation in the form of Anita Ekberg, the statuesque blond, dancing in the Trevi Fountain. It has become one of cinema's most iconic images, the embodiment of the Italian 'sweet life'.

LA DOLCE VITA 1960

ITALIAN POSTER, ART BY SANDRO SIMEONI

La Dolce Vita was shot in 1959 and captured the atmosphere in Rome at the end of the 1950s. It immortalized Rome's most famous street, La Via Veneto, with its pavement cafes and nightclubs populated by the rich and famous, surrounded by the new phenomena of the 'paparazzi'. Via Veneto's atmosphere is captured to great effect on Sandro Simeoni's alternative (and lesser-known) poster for the Italian release.

Sandro Simeoni (1928-2007) studied art in Ferrara before moving to Rome in the 1950s and establishing himself as a successful poster artist. Over the course of his long career, he designed hundreds of Italian posters, for both American and Italian films. In addition to *La Dolce Vita*, some of his most famous posters include *Vertigo* (1958), *L'Avventura* (1960), *Accattone* (1961) and *A Fistful of Dollars* (1964).

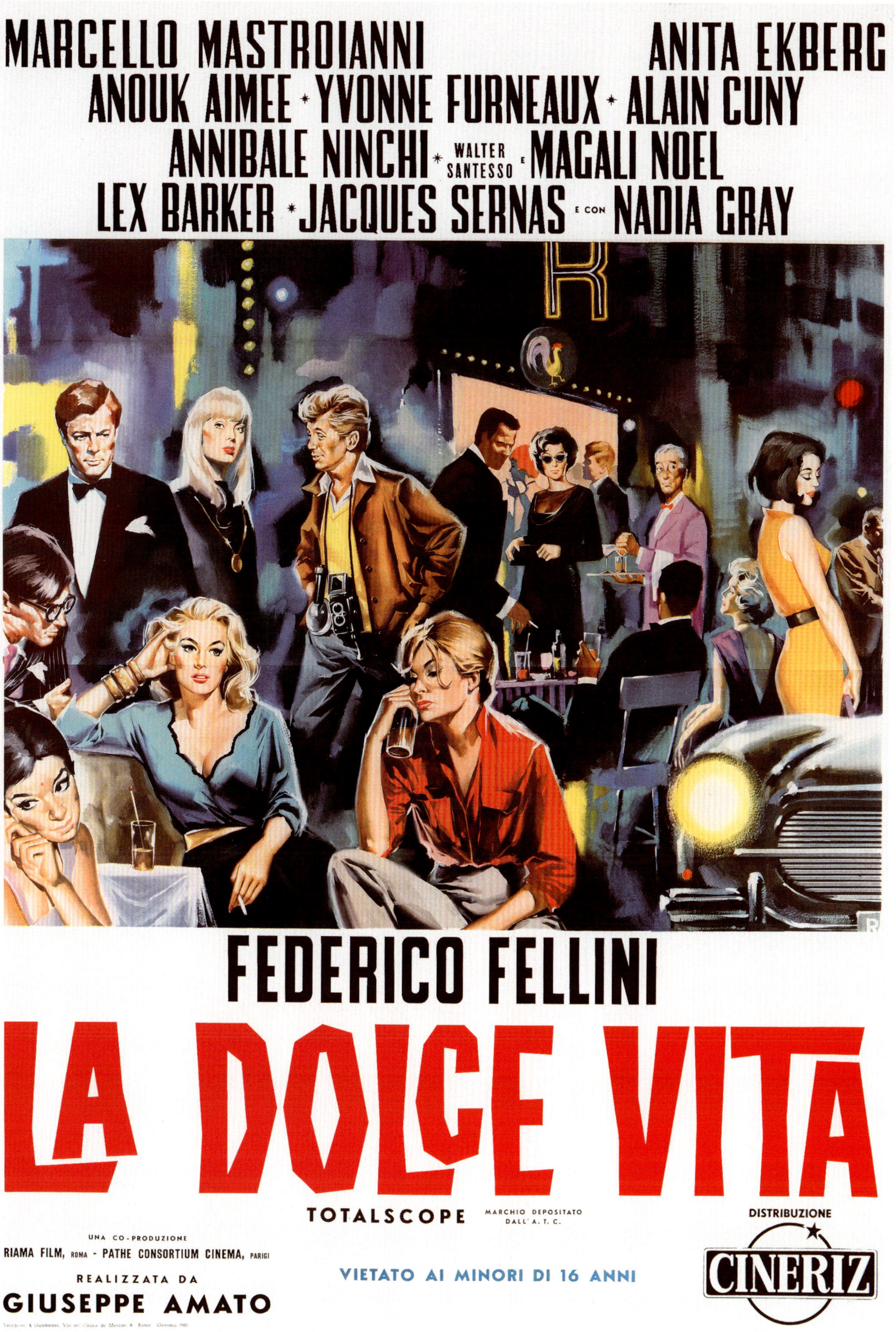

MARCELLO MASTROIANNI · ANITA EKBERG
ANOUK AIMEE · YVONNE FURNEAUX · ALAIN CUNY
ANNIBALE NINCHI · WALTER SANTESSO E MAGALI NOEL
LEX BARKER · JACQUES SERNAS E CON NADIA GRAY

FEDERICO FELLINI
LA DOLCE VITA

TOTALSCOPE MARCHIO DEPOSITATO DALL' A.T.C.

DISTRIBUZIONE

UNA CO-PRODUZIONE
RIAMA FILM, ROMA - PATHE CONSORTIUM CINEMA, PARIGI

REALIZZATA DA
GIUSEPPE AMATO

VIETATO AI MINORI DI 16 ANNI

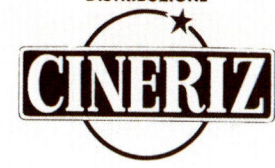

PSYCHO 1960

BRITISH POSTER, ARTIST UNKNOWN

A magnum opus of the horror genre, Hitchcock's *Psycho* was a revolution on its release. There were frenzied reports of the public screaming, fainting and having heart attacks in the aisles at the sense-assaulting shock of seeing the film's heroine killed off after just 30 minutes. This shower scene is one of the most analysed and influential sequences in cinema history: 70 cameras were used to create the 45 seconds of footage and Bernard Herrmann's shrieking score was accompanied by stabbing sound effects created by puncturing a melon with a knife.

Hitchcock masterminded the marketing of the film – going to great lengths to keep the plot a secret. The press were not given any advance screenings (with allegedly even screenwriter Joseph Stefano seeing it for the first time in a movie theatre) and the trailer danced around the horror without ever revealing crucial plot details. At this time, cinema patrons could generally enter the theatre at any point during a film. Hitchcock insisted that entrance to *Psycho* only be allowed before the start of the movie and that, 'No one … but no one will be admitted to the theatre after the start of each performance', a point emphasised to great effect on this 'style B' British poster, featuring Hitchcock himself in admonishing pose. Hitchcock was famous for making a cameo appearance in each of his films but this is the only time he also made a cameo on an original release poster.

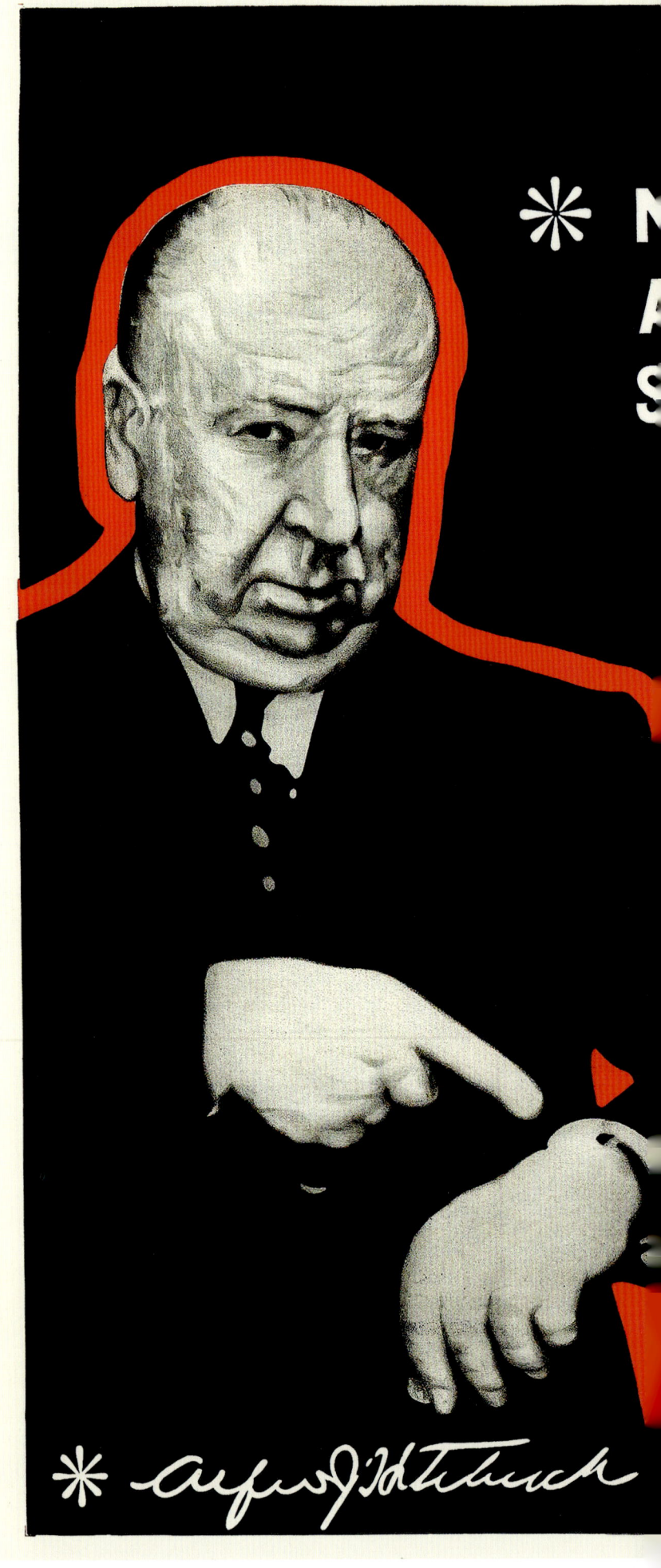

ONE ... BUT NO ONE ... WILL BE
MITTED TO THE THEATRE AFTER THE
RT OF EACH PERFORMANCE OF

ALFRED HITCHCOCK'S

PSYCHO

CERT X

STARRING

ANTHONY PERKINS · **VERA MILES** · **JOHN GAVIN**

and **JANET LEIGH** as **MARION CRANE**

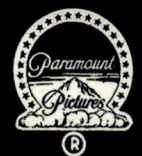

PRINTED IN ENGLAND BY W. E. BERRY, LTD., BRADFORD.

Peeping Tom 1960
British poster, Artist unknown

A groundbreaking work by director Michael Powell, *Peeping Tom* is recognised as one of the definitive films of the horror genre. Its initial reception, however, was far from positive. Powell's exploration of sex, obsession and violence was rejected by hysterical critics dismissing it as a base exploitation movie. Powell's career was effectively destroyed in the wake of its release and it was only years later that the film began to receive overdue critical praise.

The central theme of *Peeping Tom* is voyeurism, which is conveyed with terrifying effect on the poster for the film's British release. Not only was the central character a 'peeping Tom', but Powell was asking greater questions of the audience's own complicity in reacting to the film's title and marketing. 'The most frightening thing in the world' to the audience was, perhaps, acknowledging their own inner voyeur.

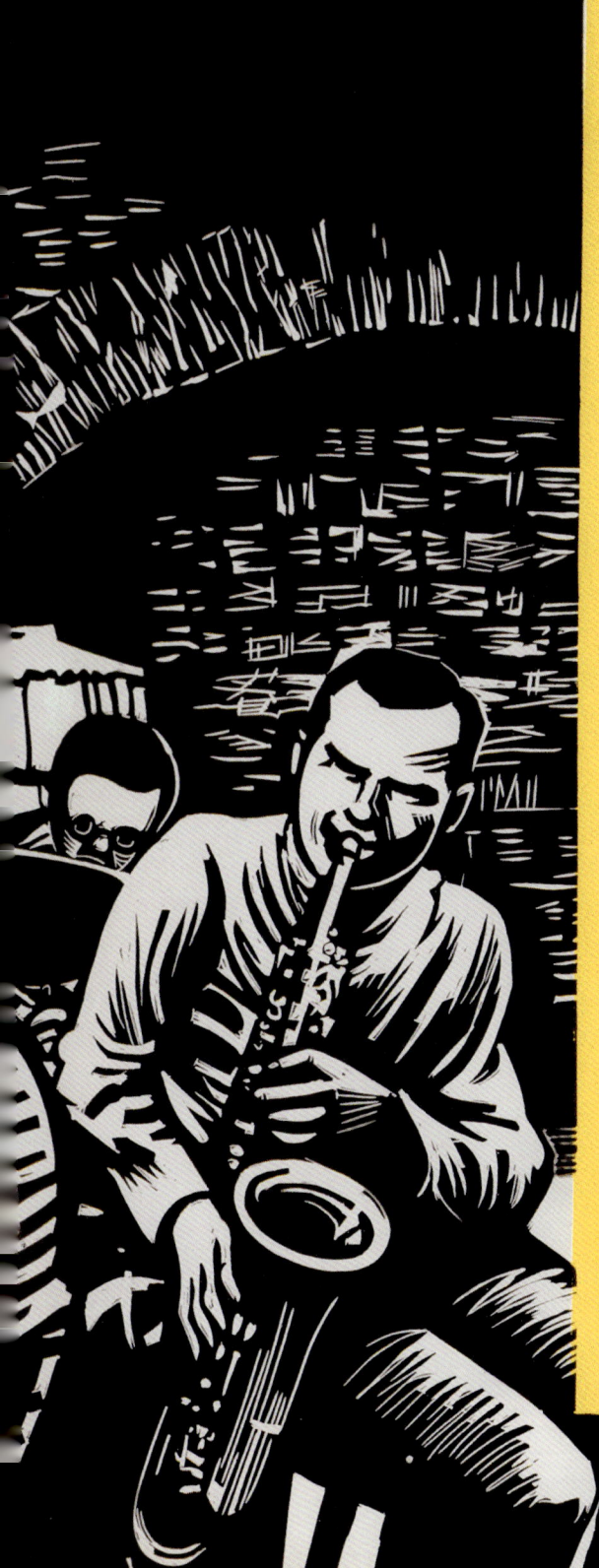

8½ 1963
Czechoslovakian poster, Art by Bedřich Dlouhý

This stunning Czechoslovakian poster for *8½* was designed by the renowned artist Bedrich Dlouhý (b.1932). Dlouhý studied at the Specialised Ceramics School in Prague (1949-1952) and Academy of Fine Arts in Prague (1953-1959) and has held several celebrated exhibitions of his posters and paintings worldwide. Although Dlouhý did not produce as many posters as some of his contemporaries, he is considered one of the greatest talents in Czech poster design of the 1960s and 1970s. He adopted a minimalist and imaginative approach, often using a combination of painting and photography. His poster for *8½* features a cracking photograph of Marcello Mastroianni, reflecting the increasing disintegration of the character's line between reality and fantasy.

CERTIFICATE X ADULTS ONLY

Distribution by ANGLO AMALGAMATED FILM DISTRIBUTORS LIMITED

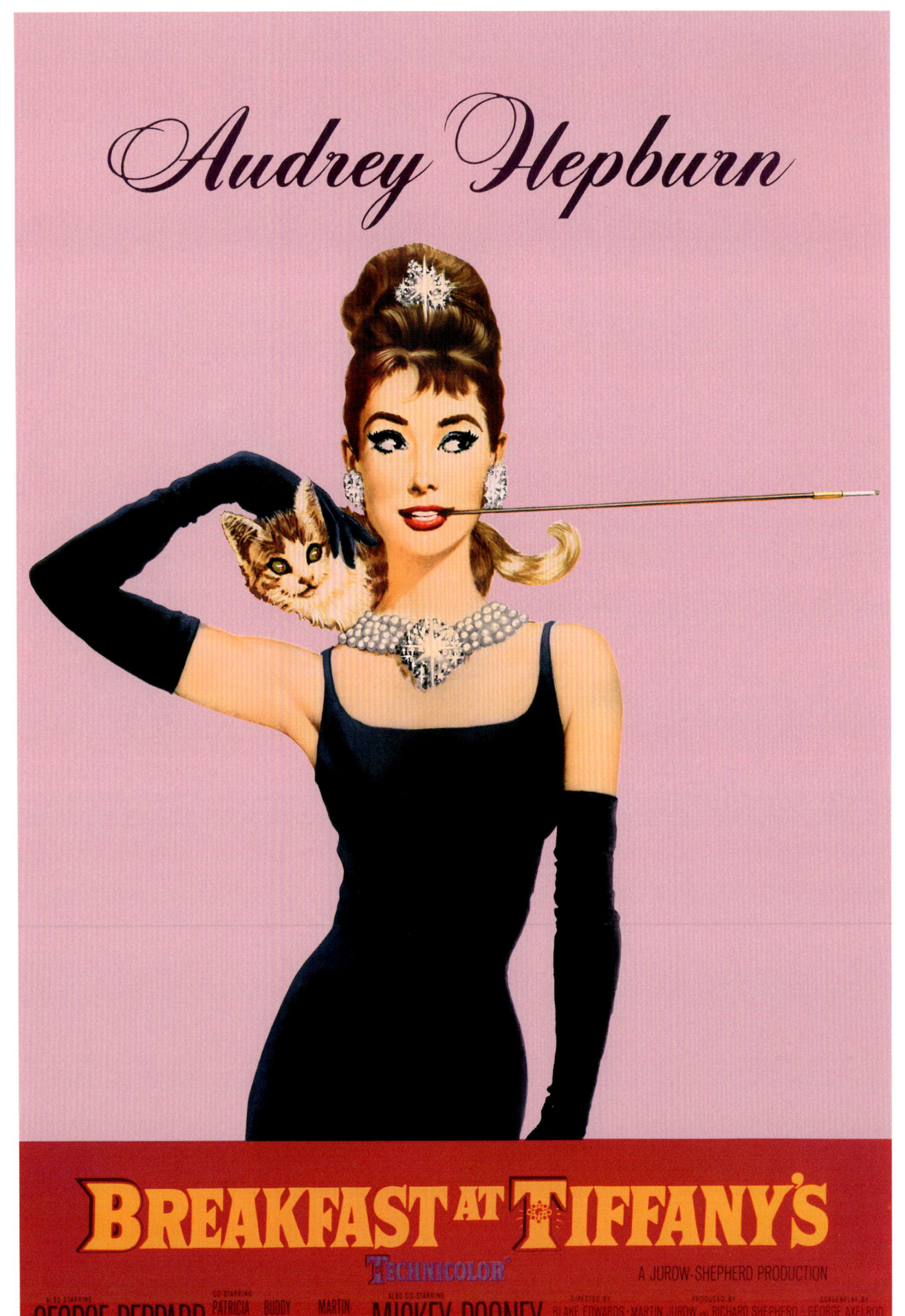

Breakfast at Tiffany's 1961
American poster, art by Robert E. McGinnis

Robert E. McGinnis (b.1926) is a respected illustrator, famous for hundreds of paperback covers and as many movie posters. He has an innate understanding of the female form and his ability to convey a sensual elegance has made him a continued favourite with art directors.

McGinnis apprenticed at Disney Studios and studied fine art at Ohio State University. After serving as a Merchant Marine during the Second World War, he began a successful career in commercial illustration. He has illustrated covers for major American publishing houses, such as Dell and Signet, and for magazines such as *Ladies' Home Journal*, *Time* and *Saturday Evening Post*.

One of McGinnis's first movie assignments was in 1960, tasked with illustrating the promotional campaign for Audrey Hepburn's new movie, *Breakfast at Tiffany's*. His classic illustration of Audrey in a full-length black dress, long cigarette holder, glittering jewels and cat on shoulder, posed against a white background framed by colour block borders, is one of the most iconic (and reproduced) movie poster images in the world. McGinnis also designed this seldom seen rare 'pink' poster, which was used for the film's New York premiere at Radio City Music Hall on 5 October 1961. Only two copies of this poster have ever surfaced and the copy I handled back in the early 2000s was double-sided and rolled – exceptionally rare for a poster from this time. One of the two copies sold at auction in March 2004 for over £13,000 (approx $24,000).

McGinnis went on to work on over 40 film campaigns, most notably for several James Bond films, including *Thunderball*, *You Only Live Twice* and *Diamonds Are Forever*. He was inducted into the Society of Illustrators Hall of Fame in 1993. Although officially retired, he still accepts the occasional commission – in 2009 he illustrated a widely publicized advertising campaign for Stella Artois, which harked back to the 1960s style that had made his name.

THE CONNECTION 1962
BRITISH POSTER, ART BY PETER STRAUSFELD

Shirley Clarke was a key player in developing an alternative, avant-garde approach to filmmaking in the 1950s and 1960s. With a background in dance and choreography, Clarke began directing short films in 1953. She was the only female member of a group established to advance the cause of independent film, rejecting the mainstream as corrupt, morally questionable and artistically weak. When Clarke released *The Connection* in 1962, it won a special award at the Cannes Film Festival. It was also banned by the New York State Censorship Board and became a test case for the freedom of expression.

I love this film, and likewise Peter Strausfeld's unusual woodcut artwork for the British poster. Although Strausfeld depicts a scene with movement – pianist, saxophonist and bassist mid-song – the players are also perfectly still in the moment, reflecting the atmosphere of waiting as the strung-out musicians kill time until their 'connection'.

Peter Strausfeld (1910-1980) was one of Britain's most important post-war poster designers. Born in Germany, Strausfeld came to Britain with the outbreak of the Second World War. Interned on the Isle of Man in 1940-41, he developed a friendship with Austrian film producer, George Hoellering. After the war, Hoellering became the director of the Academy Cinema on London's Oxford Street and commissioned Strausfeld to create the posters for the cinema's releases, to be displayed across the London underground network. For the next 30 years, Strausfeld designed over 300 posters for the picture house, which he produced using his trademark wood and linocuts. Because only around 200 of each design were ever printed, and most pasted onto walls, very few copies have survived.

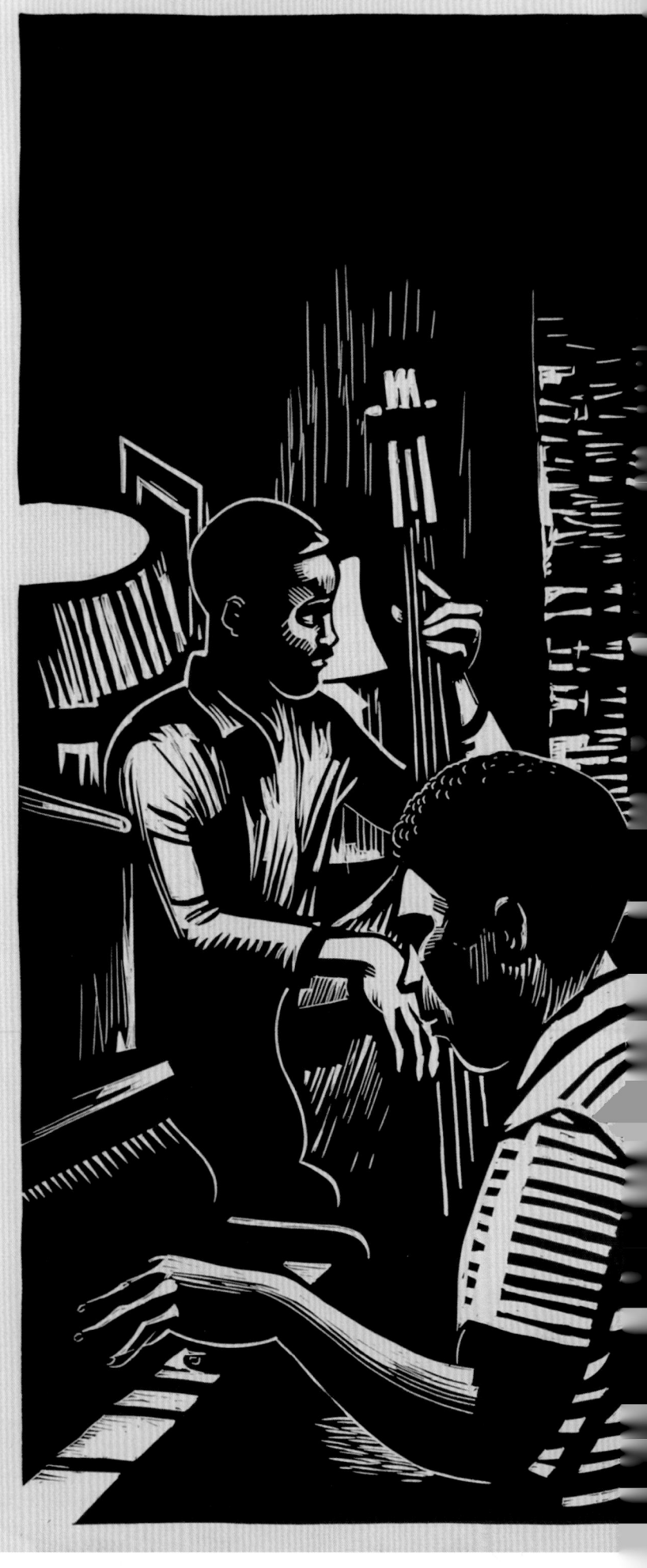

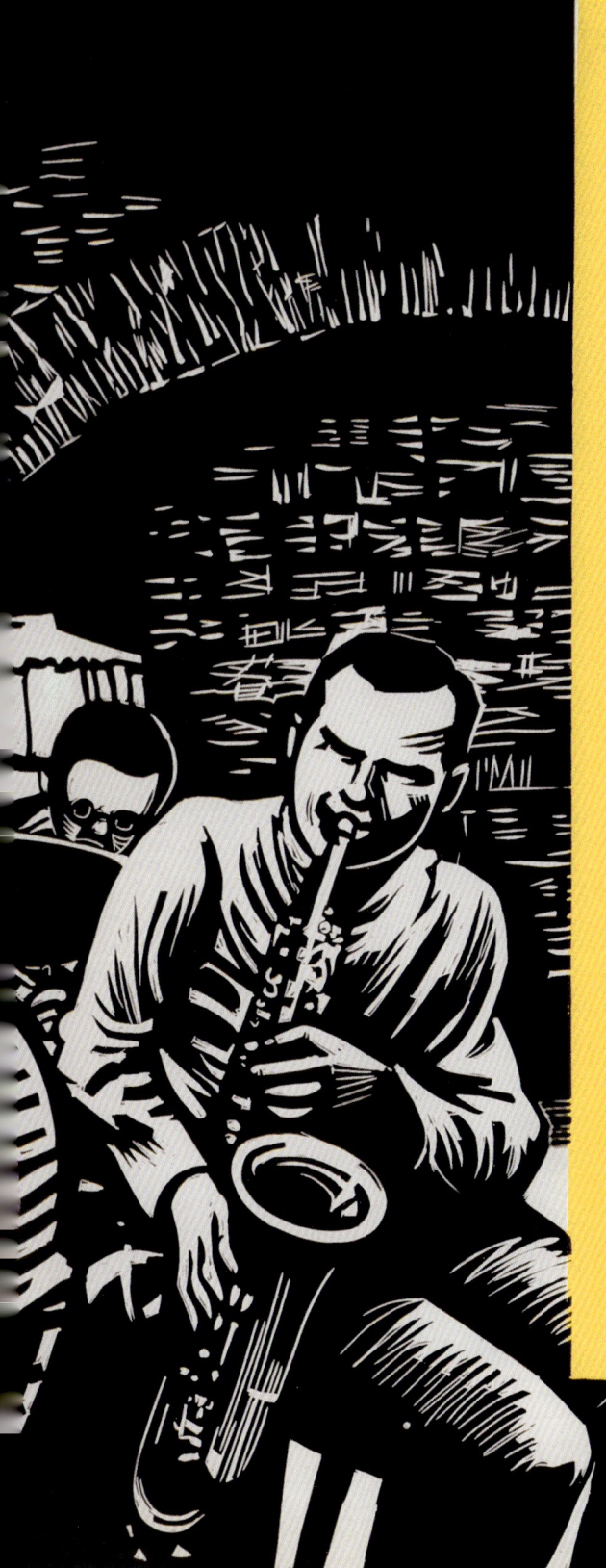

8½ 1963
CZECHOSLOVAKIAN POSTER, ART BY BEDŘICH DLOUHÝ

This stunning Czechoslovakian poster for *8½* was designed by the renowned artist Bedrich Dlouhý (b.1932). Dlouhý studied at the Specialised Ceramics School in Prague (1949-1952) and Academy of Fine Arts in Prague (1953-1959) and has held several celebrated exhibitions of his posters and paintings worldwide. Although Dlouhý did not produce as many posters as some of his contemporaries, he is considered one of the greatest talents in Czech poster design of the 1960s and 1970s. He adopted a minimalist and imaginative approach, often using a combination of painting and photography. His poster for *8½* features a cracking photograph of Marcello Mastroianni, reflecting the increasing disintegration of the character's line between reality and fantasy.

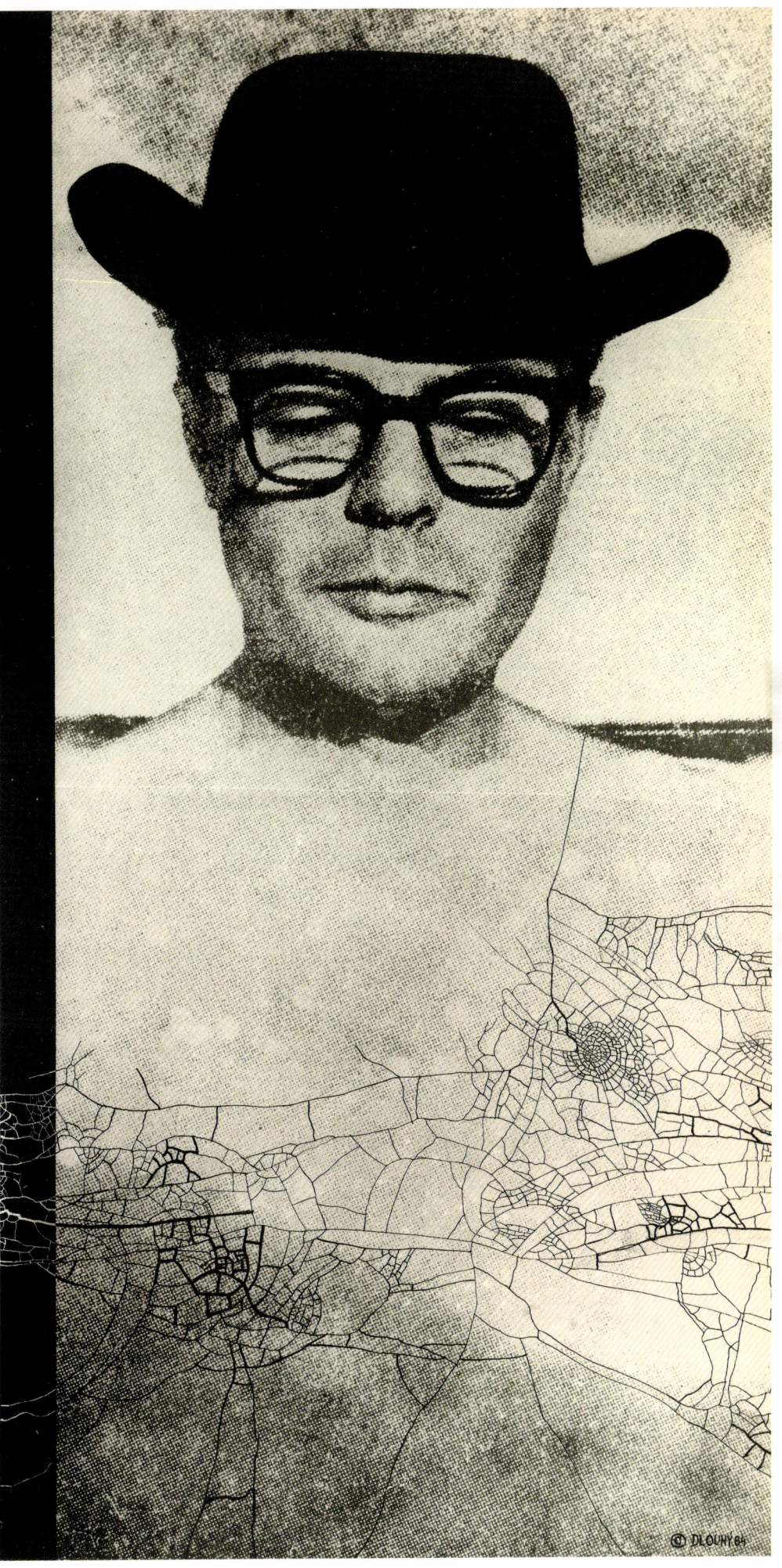

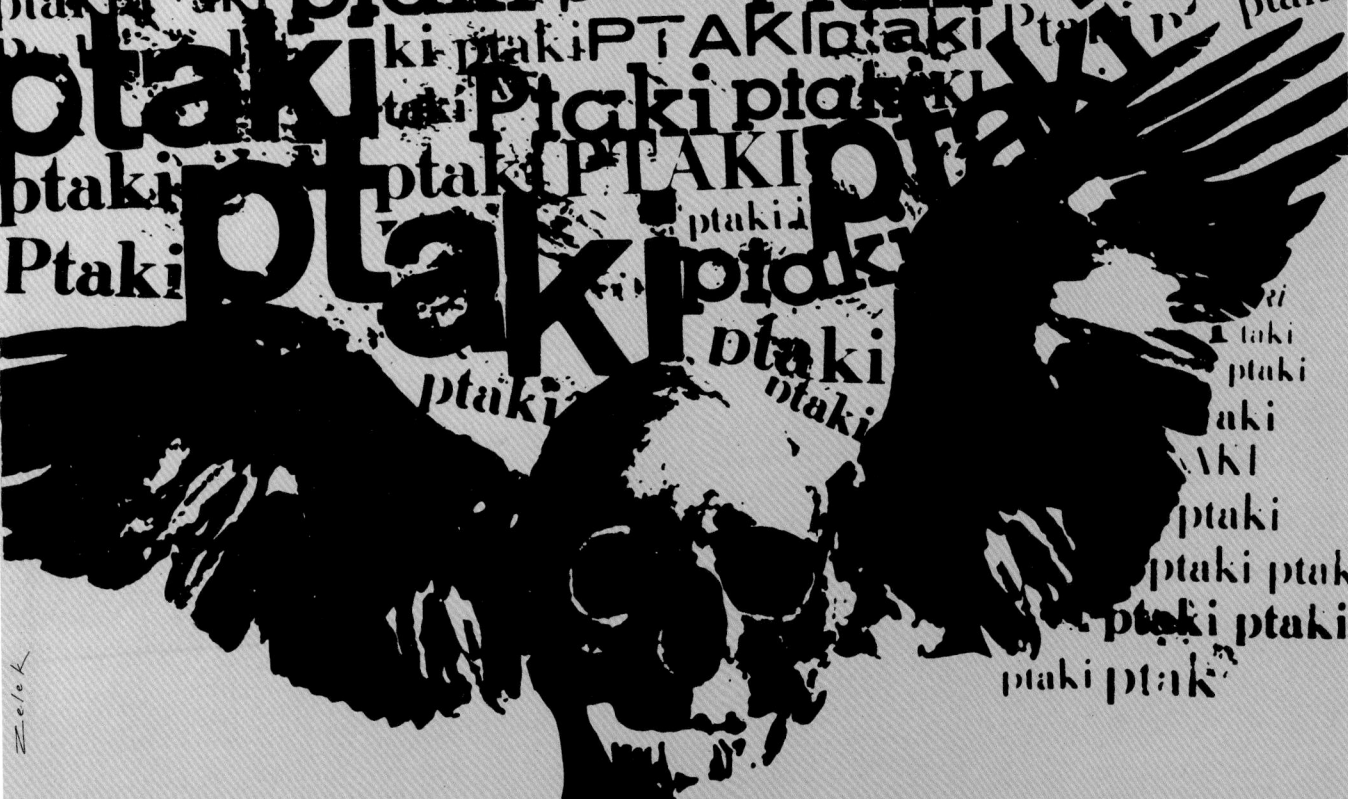

THE BIRDS 1963

POLISH POSTER, ART BY BRONISŁAW ZELEK

Under Communism, the mass media faced strict censorship. The poster art from this time, particularly from Poland and Czechoslovakia, demonstrated extraordinary creativity and artwork was powerful, poetic, surreal and often disturbing. Images of the stars, usually a big selling point in the West, were subordinated to highly original concepts. These poster artists effectively turned the street into their own gallery.

One of the most celebrated Eastern European film posters from this period is Bronisław Zelek's poster for the Polish release of *The Birds*. The monochrome design featuring a winged-skull and the Polish word for 'Birds' endlessly repeated as a flock is horrifically effective.

Bronisław Zelek (b.1935) has been an important influence on Polish poster art. After studying under Henryk Tomaszewski – seen as the father of the 'Polish School' of poster design – Zelek became part of a new group of artists that incorporated photographic elements into their work. His style is further characterised by clean, simple graphics that are frequently composed of just two colours.

GOLDFINGER 1964
BRITISH POSTER, DESIGN BY ROBERT BROWNJOHN

Robert Brownjohn (1925-1970) was an influential American graphic designer, who remains most famous for his work on James Bond films and for the *Let It Bleed* album for The Rolling Stones. Brownjohn studied at the Chicago Institute of Design, before moving to New York in the 1950s and establishing himself as part of the thriving arts and music scene. He freelanced in design while hanging out in jazz clubs and befriending Miles Davis and Andy Warhol. In 1957, he co-founded the design company Brownjohn, Chermayeff & Geismar, which specialised in book jackets, album covers and corporate work. In 1960, Brownjohn moved himself and his family to London where he worked for advertising agency J. Walter Thompson and McCann Erickson.

In 1963, Bond production company, EON, approached Brownjohn to design the main title sequence for *From Russia with Love*. A year later, EON again approached him to design the title sequence and poster campaign for *Goldfinger*. His poster design featured a large image of the Golden Girl onto which he superimposed the figures of James Bond and Pussy Galore. A full-length body shot was also used in campaigns around the world, usually with a modesty-saving, strategically placed Bond.

This version of the poster was created for use in the front of British buses. It is one of my favourite Bond posters. The striking graphic is all the more powerful for being free of text – in 1964, Bond was already such an established institution that no words were necessary. And the same remains true today.

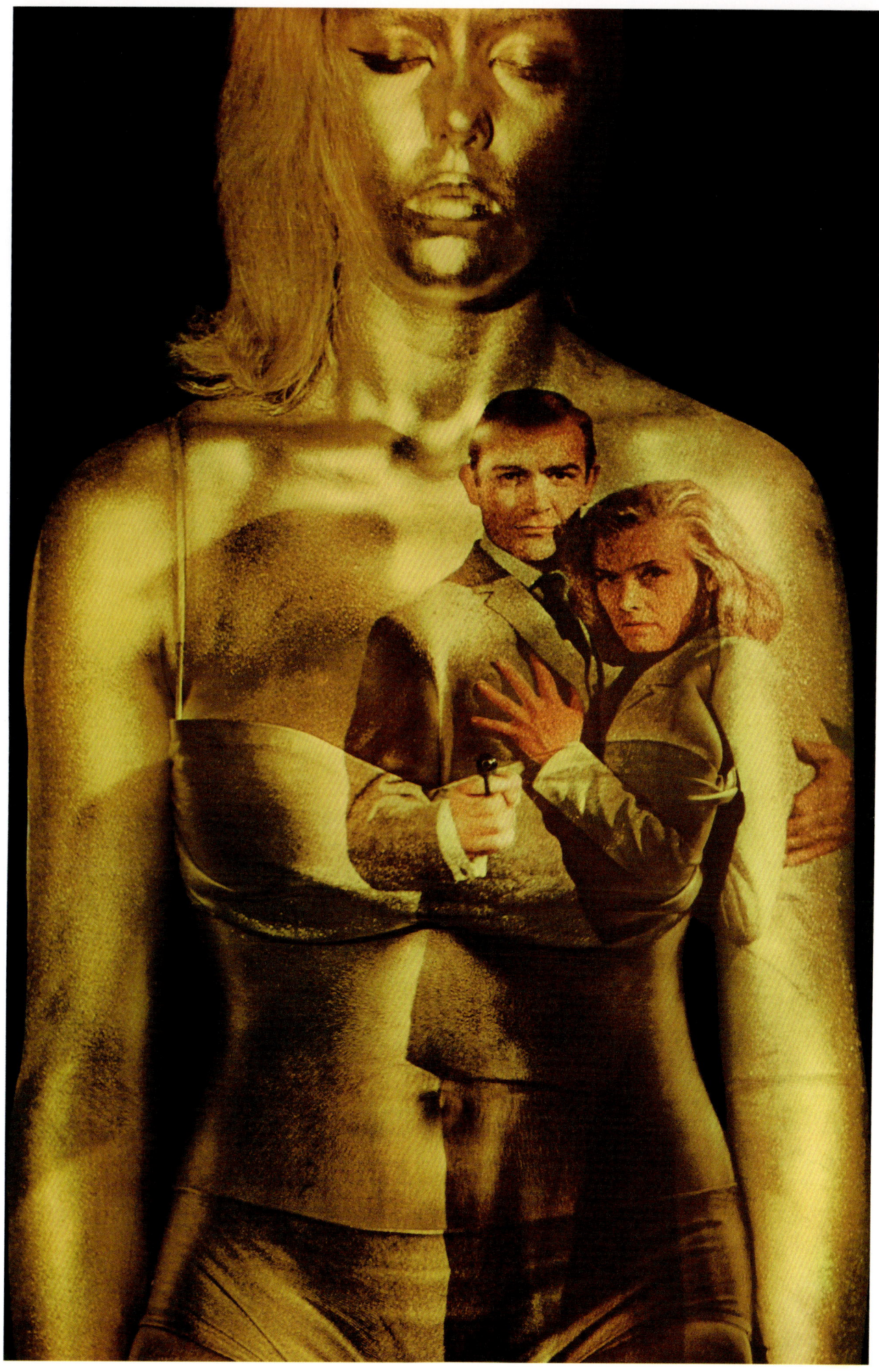

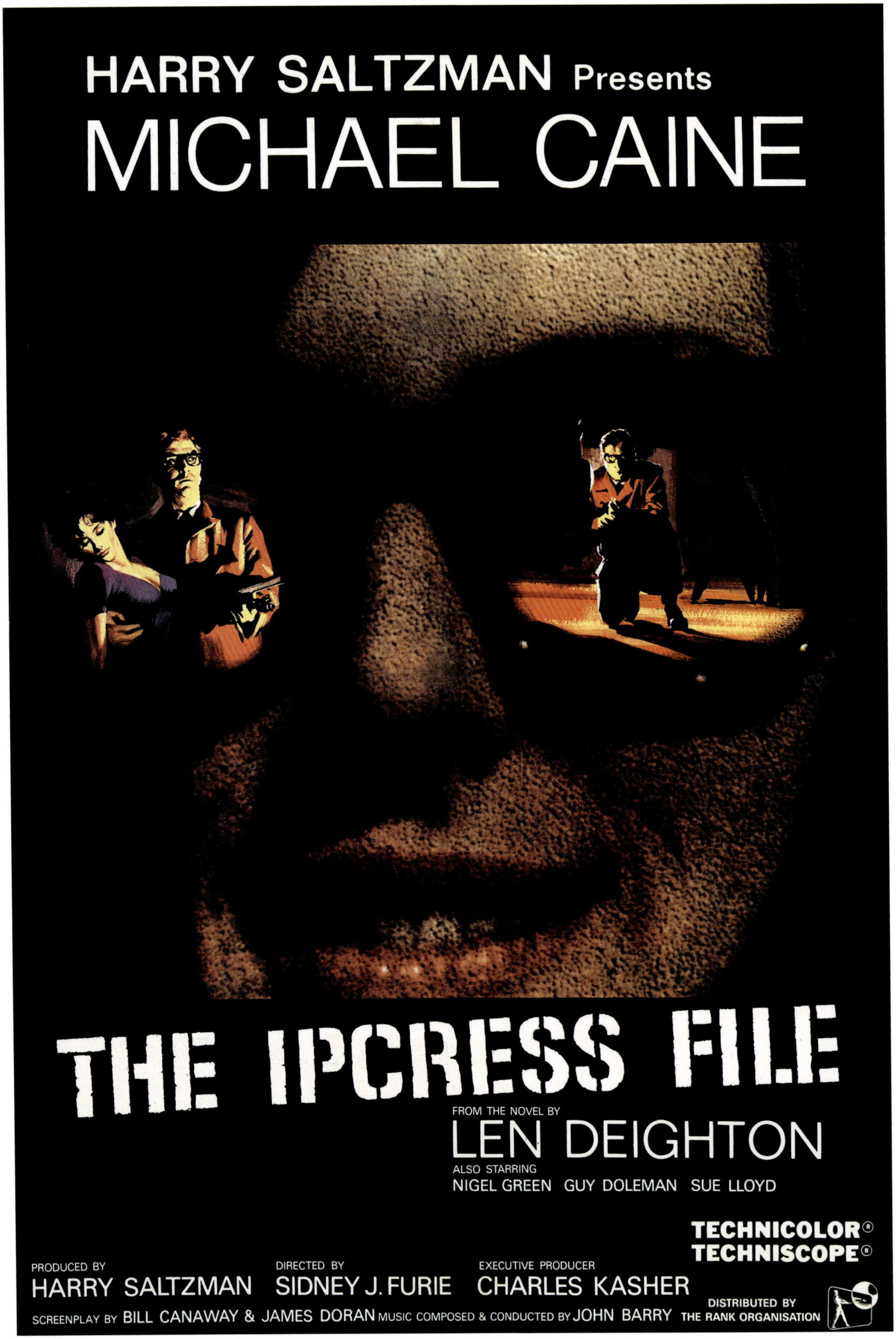

THE IPCRESS FILE 1965
BRITISH POSTER, ART BY ANGELO CESSELON

This is the best poster on *The Ipcress File*. It features artwork by Angelo Cesselon and was designed as a British 'one sheet' to be used for cinematic releases in British colonies. It is one of the rarest posters of the 1960s.

Angelo Cesselon (1922-1992) was one of the most influential of the new wave of poster artists to emerge in Italy after the Second World War. He worked for all the major studios and was an immense talent. In 1955, he received the Italian Spiga Cambelloti prize as best cinematographic painter of the year. His design for *The Ipcress File* is indicative of his style, which favoured one large dominating portrait in place of more traditional scene-based imagery. Cesselon also had an instinctive ability to capture the spirit or theme of a movie in a single image, as is demonstrated by his overriding use of the glasses image, reflecting the blurry and confused ability of Harry Palmer to see clearly.

CHELSEA GIRLS 1966
BRITISH POSTER, ART BY ALAN ALDRIDGE

The award-winning Alan Aldridge (b.1937) is a graphic designer and illustrator. His wildly creative vision saw him become one of the defining artists of London in the Swinging Sixties and his distinctive style reflected the psychedelic and experimental spirit of the age. In 1963 he was hired by Penguin books, where he revolutionised the publisher's image by abandoning its traditional typographical cover designs in favour of bold, boundary-pushing graphics. In 1968 he set-up his own design agency, INK, and was much-sought after by bands like The Rolling Stones and The Beatles (John Lennon hired him as the band's official design consultant.) Aldridge was also approached by friend Andy Warhol, who asked him to design the poster for the London premiere of his new film, *Chelsea Girls*. The resulting design has become one of Aldridge's most celebrated works, with Warhol famously remarking that he wished the film was as good as the poster. Aldridge had originally proposed the advent calendar concept for the Beatles' *White Album*. The final *Chelsea Girls* poster featured British actress Clare Shenstone as the 'calendar girl' with photography by Donald Silverstein. The image won Aldridge a Silver Award from the Design and Art Directors Club. The censors, however, remained unimpressed and the fly-posting of the poster across London briefly led to Aldridge's arrest warrant.

Warhol's film had a very limited release and the small number of posters that were printed were pasted onto walls and underground stations, with the result that very few original copies of this poster exist. Most of the copies that have surfaced on the market in recent years are from a 1970 reprint of the poster by Motif Editions, which is only distinguished from the real thing by a tiny line of text running up the model's left leg.

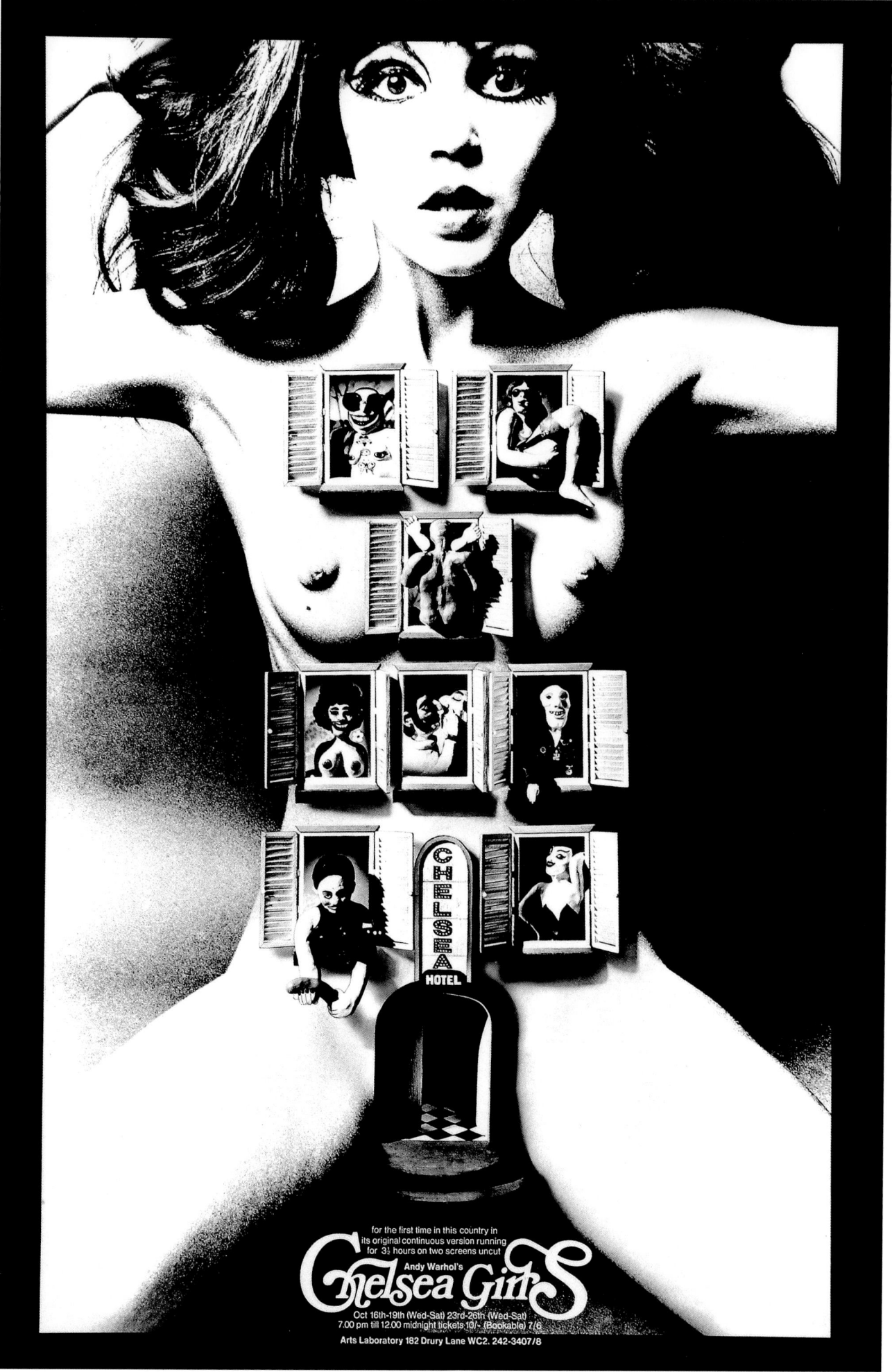

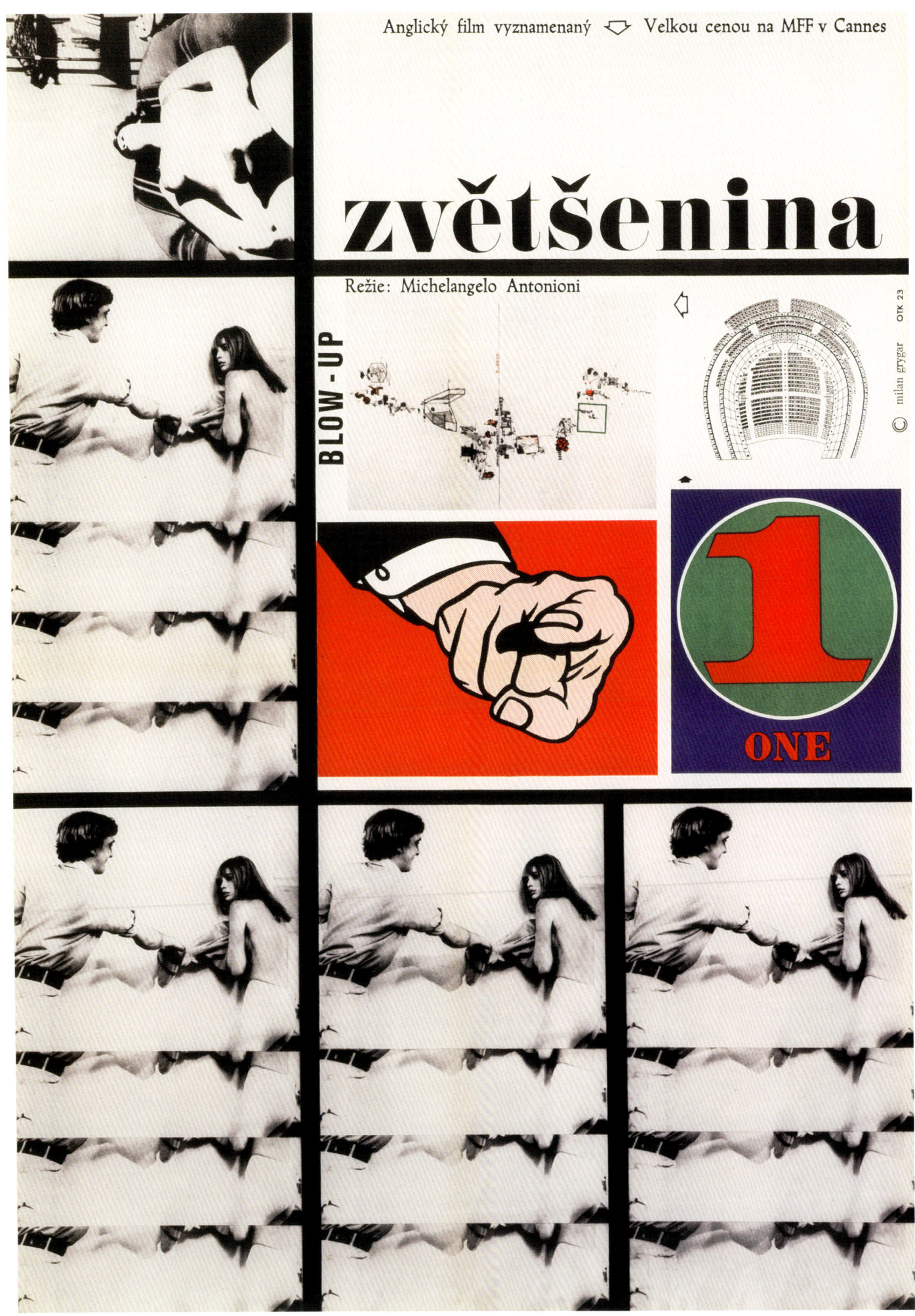

BLOW-UP 1966
CZECHOSLOVAKIAN POSTER, ART BY MILAN GRYGAR

Milan Grygar (b.1926) is an important Czechoslovakian artist, famous for his unique audiovisual explorations of the connection between drawing and sound, and for his many movie posters. His work has been exhibited in museums and galleries around the world.

Grygar's poster for the Czechoslovakian release of *Blow-Up* is the most graphically interesting piece on the film, incorporating famous works by other artists – such as Lichtenstein's finger-pointing, Bill Brandt's distorted nudes and Robert Indiana's numbers – into the design. In choosing to include such contemporary artworks, Grygar managed to capture the pop art aesthetic and mood of Antonioni's landmark film about photography and London in the 1960s.

PLAYTIME 1967
POLISH POSTER, ART BY JERZY FLISAK

Jacques Tati's *Playtime* saw the consummate director return to one of his most successful comedic characters, Monsieur Hulot – the bumbling star of his previous hits, *Les vacances de Monsieur Hulot* and *Mon Oncle*. In *Playtime*, Hulot's whirling confusion wandering around Paris is reflected to glorious effect on artist Jerzy Flisak's Polish poster for the film. Flisak's bold, almost deliberately clumsy, approach also captured the charm and appeal of Tati's ageing clown.

Jerzy Flisak (1930-2008) was a respected Polish graphic artist, renowned for his satirical cartoons, movie posters, children's books and animated films. Flisak studied architecture at the Warsaw University of Technology. While there, he became the graphic editor of the weekly satirical magazine, and after graduating in 1953, continued to publish satirical illustrations in magazines across Poland. He began working in the field of movie posters in 1955. As with his poster for *Playtime*, Flisak's work was often characterised by strong colours and simple bold designs infused with humour.

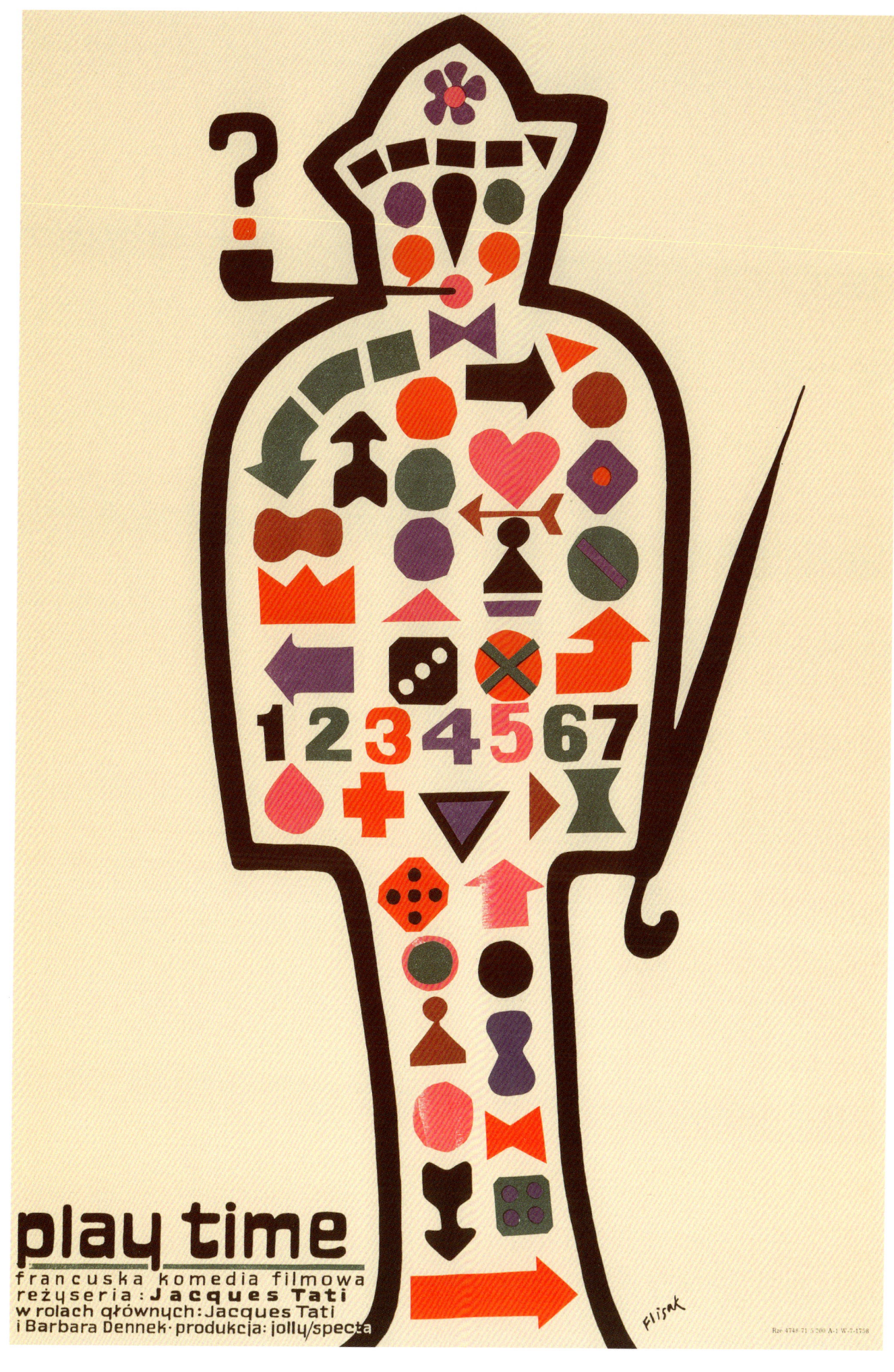

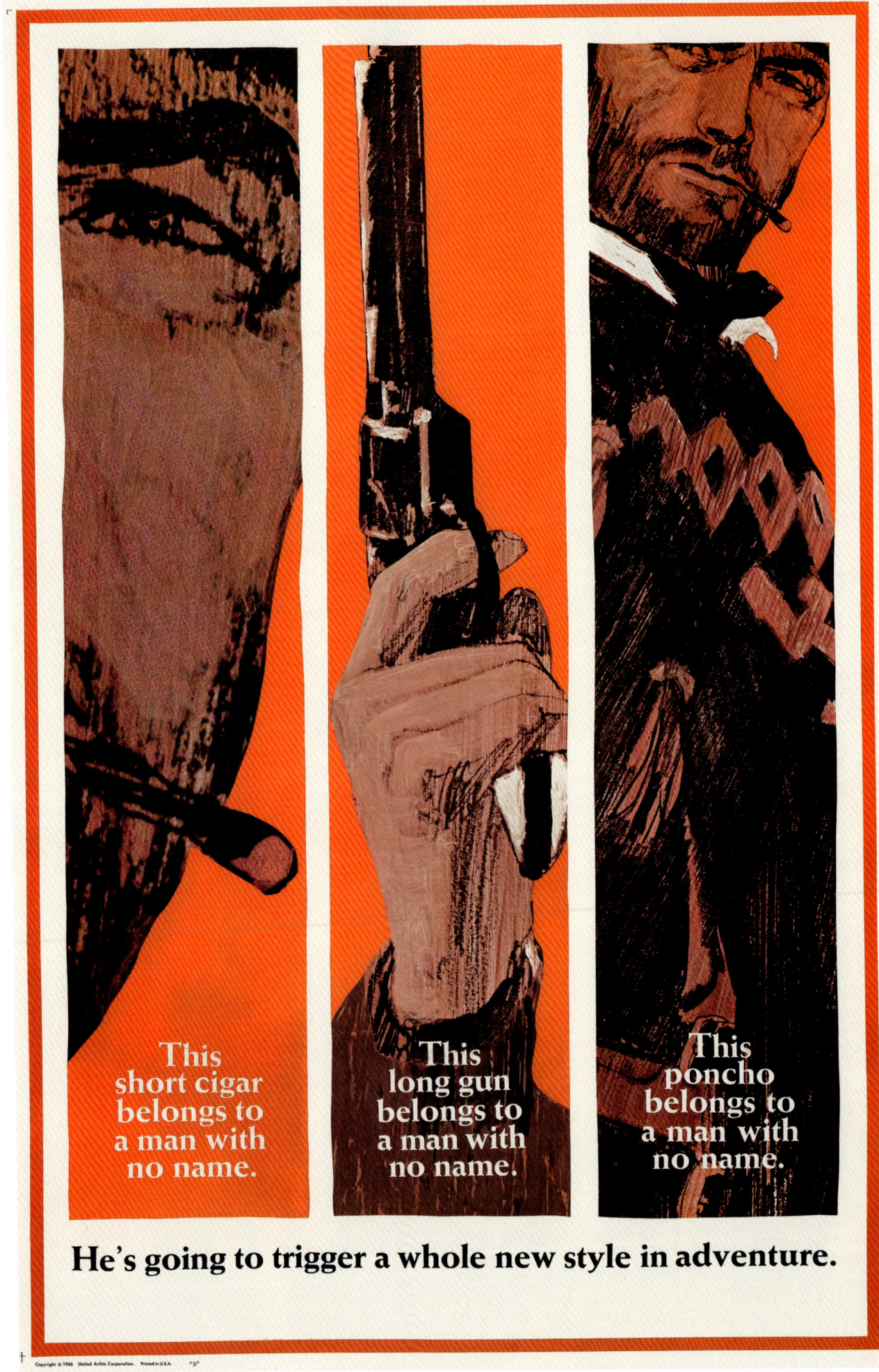

A Fistful of Dollars 1964
American poster, art by Fred Otnes

Artist Fred Otnes' artwork for the advance poster for *A Fistful of Dollars* introduced Clint Eastwood's most famous alter ego to audiences for the first time. The teasing advance campaign did not even give away the film's title and, instead, simply presented Eastwood's character as 'the man with no name' – a moniker synonymous with the Leone trilogy to this day. (In a blink-and-you'll-miss-it moment, he is actually hailed in the film by the name of 'Joe'.)

Fred Otnes (b.1930) is a celebrated collage artist. He trained at the Art Institute of Chicago and by the mid-1950s, while still in his early twenties, had already established himself as a successful commercial artist in advertising and magazine illustration. In the mid-1960s, he developed a bold new style using a pioneering and unique collage technique. He often used this medium to depict prescient social issues, such as the Civil Rights movement and the Vietnam War. Much in demand, Otnes has received over 200 awards for his work. Since the mid-1980s, he has focussed on gallery work.

LA CHINOISE 1967

JAPANESE POSTER, ART BY KIYOSHI AWAZU

Kiyoshi Awazu's design for Jean-Luc Godard's *La Chinoise* is one of my favourite Japanese film posters. I was privileged enough to meet the designer in person in 2001 and he was everything I had pictured – cool, hip and warmly friendly. Awazu's work was often influenced by pop culture and was usually painted or illustrated. *La Chinoise* is one of his few wholly photographic posters. It remains recognisably Awazu by the clean design and his typical pallet of vibrant colours.

Kiyoshi Awazu (1929-2009) was one of Japan's leading graphic designers of the twentieth century. A self-taught artist, Awazu first came to attention for his award-winning poster for *Give Back Our Sea* at the Japan Advertising Exhibition in 1955 – beginning a lifelong association with social causes. In 1958 he won first prize at the World Film Poster Competition in France and, a year later, he opened the Awazu Design Institute (today the Awazu Design Room). In 1970 he won a Silver Medal and special mention at the Warsaw International Poster Biennale. Although primarily known for his poster designs, Awazu was also a respected writer and filmmaker, winning an award for his art direction of the 1969 film, *Shinjû: Ten no amijima* (*Double Suicide*). In 1990 Awazu was awarded a Medal with Purple Ribbon by the Japanese government as a person of outstanding artistic merit. His works are held in the permanent collections of the Museum of Modern Art in New York, the Museum of Modern Art in Toyama and at the Stedelijk Museum in Amsterdam.

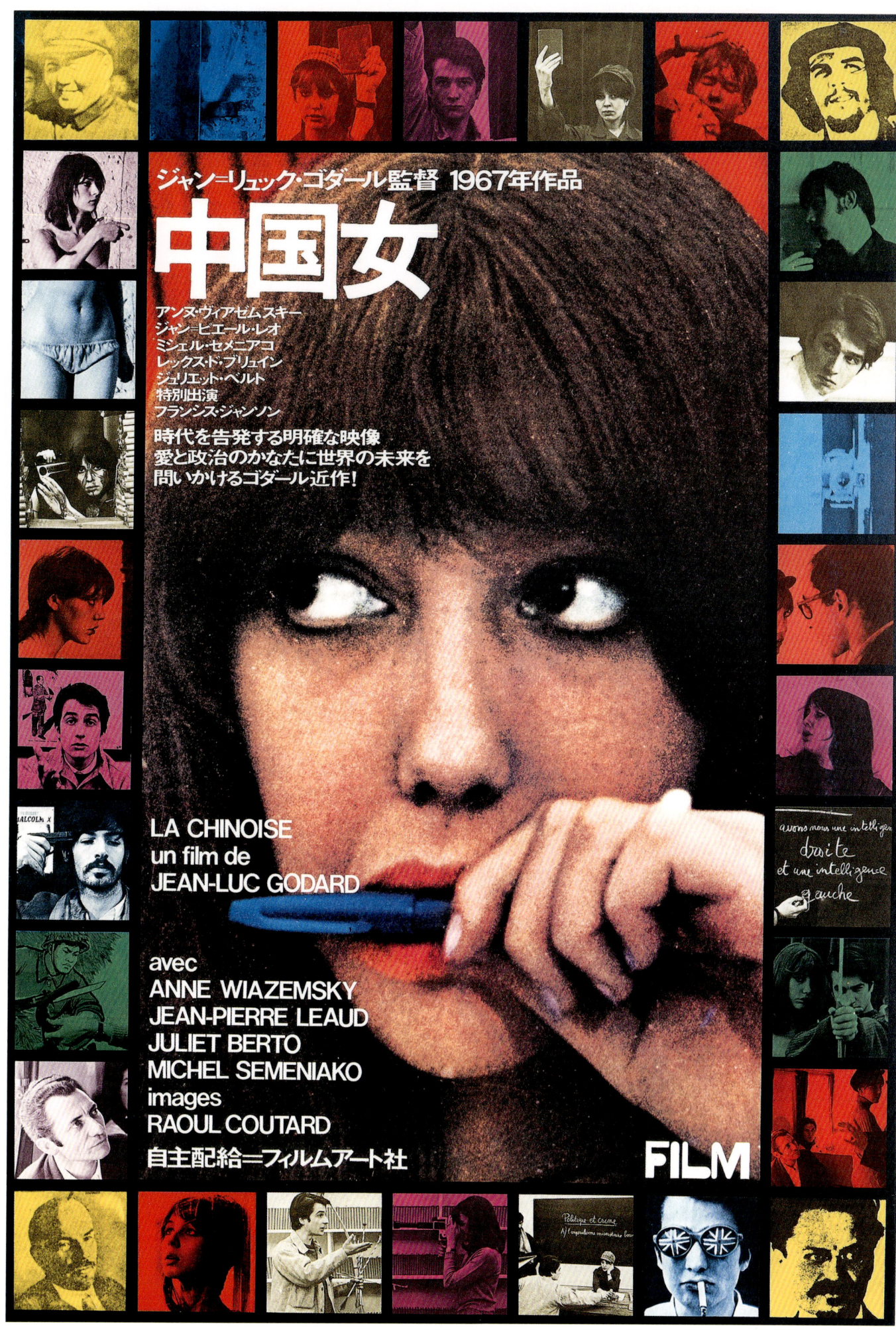

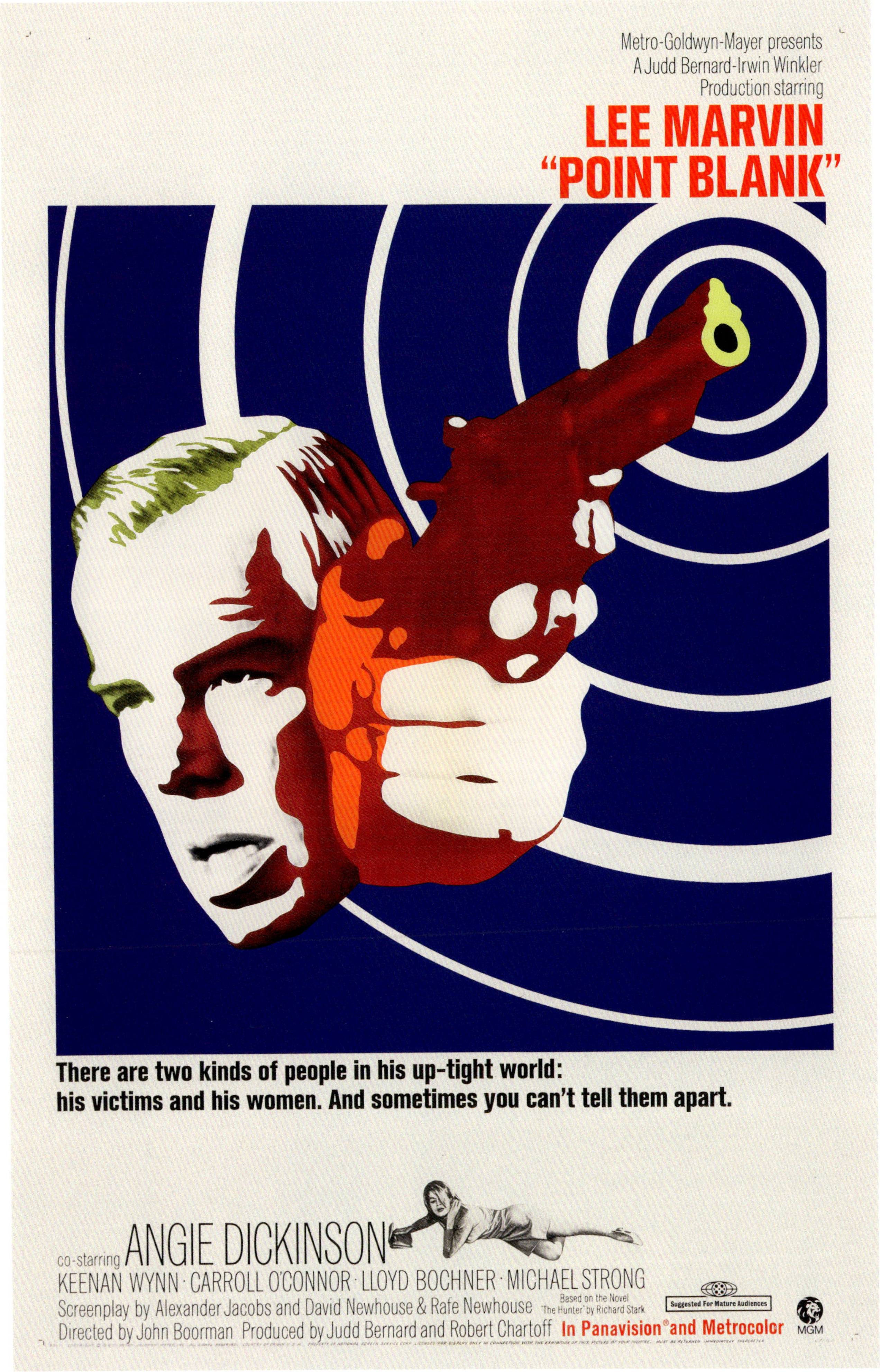

Metro-Goldwyn-Mayer presents
A Judd Bernard-Irwin Winkler
Production starring

LEE MARVIN
"POINT BLANK"

**There are two kinds of people in his up-tight world:
his victims and his women. And sometimes you can't tell them apart.**

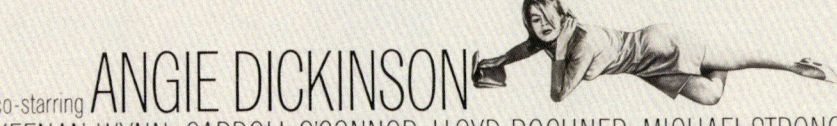

co-starring ANGIE DICKINSON
KEENAN WYNN · CARROLL O'CONNOR · LLOYD BOCHNER · MICHAEL STRONG
Screenplay by Alexander Jacobs and David Newhouse & Rafe Newhouse Based on the Novel "The Hunter" by Richard Stark
Directed by John Boorman Produced by Judd Bernard and Robert Chartoff In Panavision® and Metrocolor

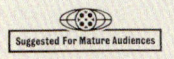

POINT BLANK 1967

AMERICAN POSTER, DESIGN BY NELSON LYON, ART BY SERRANO

This poster for the American release of *Point Blank* is a great piece of design – pop-art in feel, it also emphasised the loner aspect of Lee Marvin's central character, Walker. It was designed by Nelson Lyon, who worked as a creative director for MGM at the time. He used an in-house illustrator for the artwork – a young hippy everyone in the office simply referred to as 'Serrano'.

Nelson Lyon (1939-2012) was a designer, photographer, writer and filmmaker. He was part of the counterculture of the 1960s and 1970s, close friends with Andy Warhol and William Burroughs. He was a successful writer on *Saturday Night Live* and made a celebrated satirical X-rated movie, *The Telephone Book*, with friend Merv Bloch in 1971. He was also an avid movie poster collector. Lyon was at the height of his career when he embarked on a three-day drug binge with John Belushi in 1982 that resulted in the comedian's death. Although legally acquitted of blame, Lyon never escaped the stain on his reputation and it effectively ended his career.

ROSEMARY'S BABY 1968
AMERICAN POSTER, DESIGN BY STEVE FRANKFURT, ART BY PHILIP GIPS

Something of a real-life Don Draper, Steve Frankfurt (1931-2012) was an original Mad Man – one of the top creative directors on Madison Avenue in the 1960s. He joined leading firm, Young & Rubicam, in 1957 as an art director and became their youngest ever president in 1968 (Young & Rubicam are name-checked in the *Mad Men* series as a rival firm). According to *Bloomberg*, Frankfurt was responsible for some of the 'most distinctive advertising campaigns in US business history'.

In a pre media-savvy age, Hollywood sometimes had to turn to Madison Avenue for effective marketing campaigns. Robert Evans, the producer of *Rosemary's Baby*, approached Frankfurt after Paramount had failed to come up with any kind of suitable campaign that would both satisfy the censors and not reveal the film's plot. Even then, Paramount were not convinced giving the job to an ad man was the right choice so (in a trick Don Draper would be proud of) Frankfurt promised the studio that if they did not like what he presented, then he would not charge for the work.

Frankfurt's approach for the *Rosemary's Baby* campaign centred around his 'less is more' philosophy. As he told *The New York Times*, 'The idea was not to show the baby ... not to show anything ... we bought ads in the birth announcements section of newspapers saying, "Pray for Rosemary's baby".' The *Pray for Rosemary's Baby* tagline was everywhere – in newspapers, stencilled on sidewalks, pasted on walls, stamped on matchbooks. Frankfurt designed the accompanying movie poster with fellow creative, Philip Gips, a childhood friend and internationally recognised Yale designer. A baby carriage on a rock in Central Park, set against Mia Farrow's supine profile in cloying green, was a masterclass in key art and one of the most effective movie posters of the decade.

Frankfurt eventually worked on over 50 films. The taglines that he created have become almost as famous as the films themselves. It was Frankfurt who reminded us that 'Every father's daughter is a virgin' (*Goodbye Columbus*, 1969), proclaimed that 'X was never like this' (*Emmanuelle*, 1974) and cautioned that 'In space, no one can hear you scream' (*Alien*, 1979). He revolutionised the way in which movies were marketed.

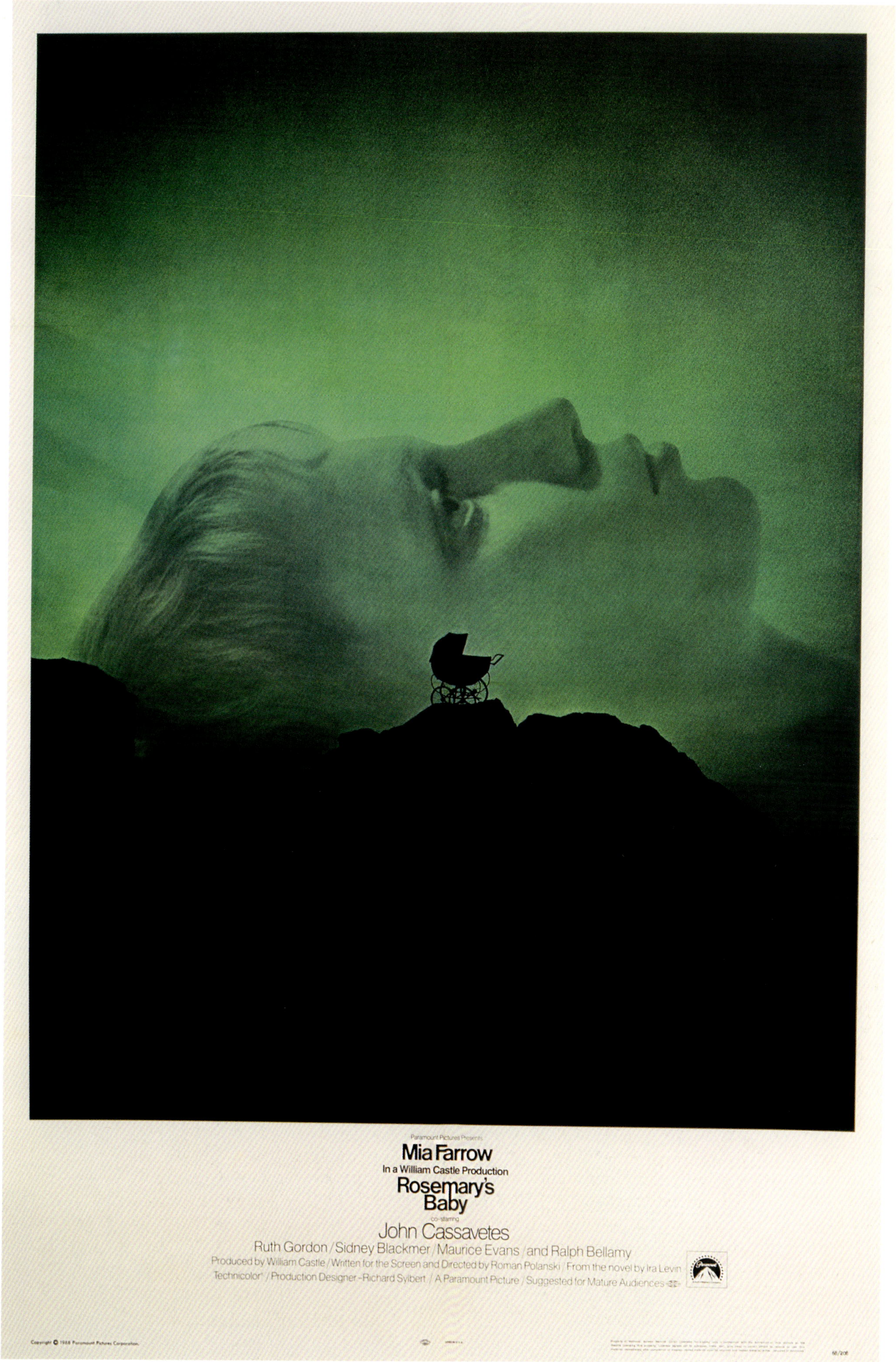

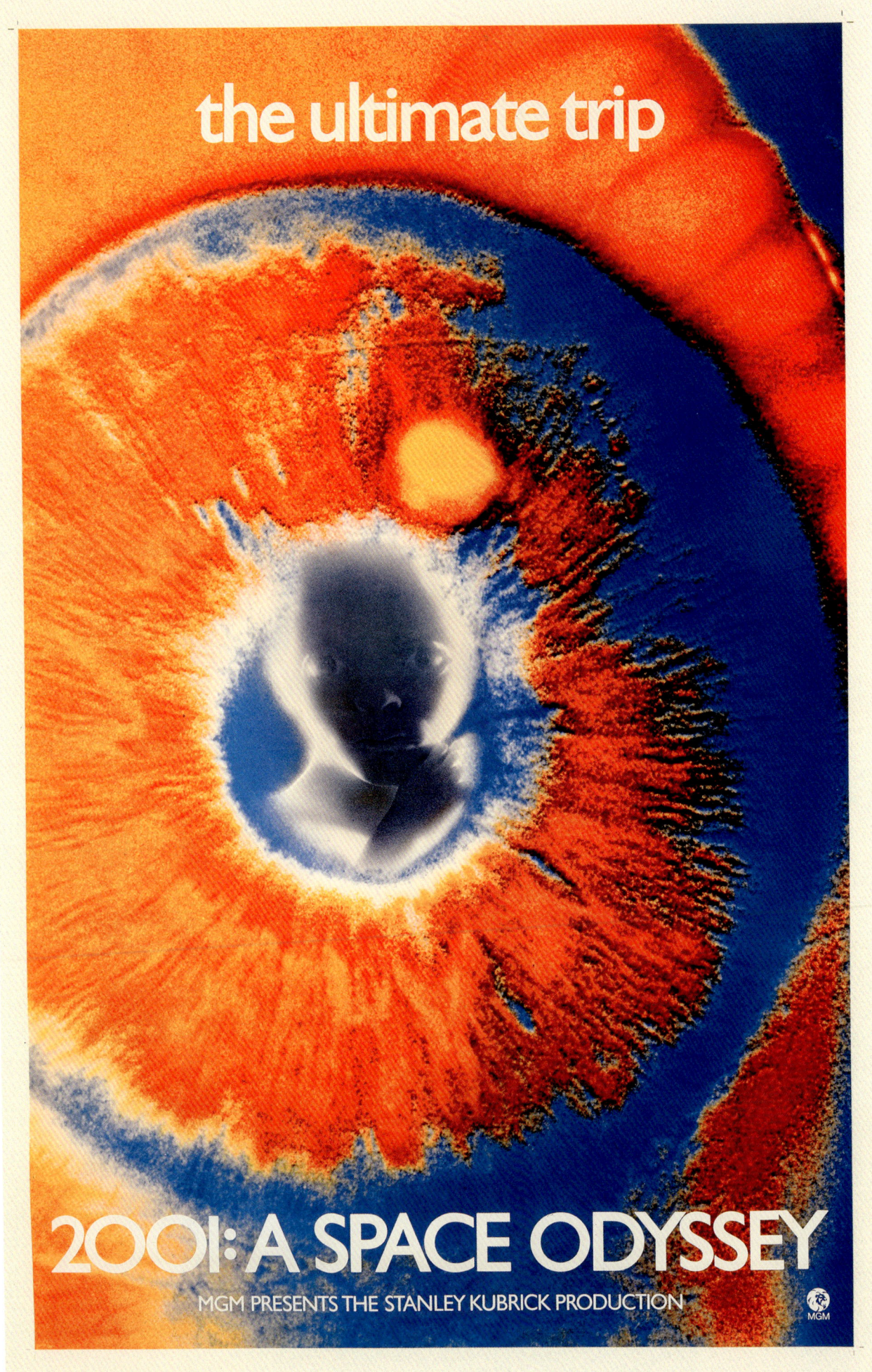

2001: A Space Odyssey 1968
American poster, Design by Mike Kaplan

Designer Mike Kaplan has worn various hats in the film world: producer, director, actor, distributor, marketer and avid movie poster collector – the latter the source of our friendship. Mike is an enormous talent and is the designer responsible for some of the most exciting movie posters of the 1960s onwards, including *A Clockwork Orange* with illustrator Philip Castle in 1971, and his award-winning campaigns for *Welcome to L.A.* (1976) and *Marlene* (1984). His film posters often incorporate the work of leading contemporary artists, such as David Hockney for *A Bigger Splash* (1974), Allen Jones for *Maîtresse* (1976) and ceramic artist Karen Donleavy for *A Wedding* (1978).

The first movie poster campaign Kaplan ever worked on was for Stanley Kubrick's *2001: A Space Odyssey* and the 'Style D' poster remains my favourite of all of his film poster designs. This exceptionally rare poster is one of the most evocative posters of the 1960s. The *Ultimate Trip* tagline, above the image of the Star Child embryo floating in an iris, captured the experimental mood of the time. If ever a tagline has captured the zeitgeist, this is it. In a forerunner of today's guerrilla marketing techniques, this poster was not part of the main studio campaign and was instead used for 'wild' pastings on New York City walls and subway stations.

When Kubrick's visionary opus was initially premiered, the film did not receive the glowing praise that had been expected and, instead, critics and audiences were left bewildered and confused. It was MGM's most expensive film to date and this, combined with poor advance sales, made the studio very nervous. Kubrick was forced to do an immediate re-edit, cutting 19 minutes from the running time before the film's mainstream release five days later. However, within just a few days of the premiere's bemused reception, the tide began to noticeably shift, fuelled by two influential reviews: first from the *Christian Science Monitor*, which called the film 'revolutionary'; and second from Joseph Gelmis, a critic at the widely read *Newsday*, who took the unheard of step of retracting his initial negative review. He concluding on second viewing:

*After seeing **2001: A Space Odyssey** a second time, I'm convinced it is a masterwork. Take it from one who mistrusts superlatives and who suspects that most critics who second-guess themselves are grandstanding: this awesome film is light-years ahead of any science fiction you have ever seen and owes more to the mystical visions of Jung and William Blake than to H.G. Wells or Jules Verne.*

Kaplan cannily recognised that the marketing campaign for the film had to be relaunched – at a young (potentially high) audience, who would flock to multiple viewings of the film. The *Ultimate Trip* campaign embodied this approach. In addition to the 'iris' wild pastings version, a full embryo close-up was also used for the film's official 70mm relaunch at New York's Ziegfeld Theatre in 1970 and for subsequent re-releases throughout the 1970s.

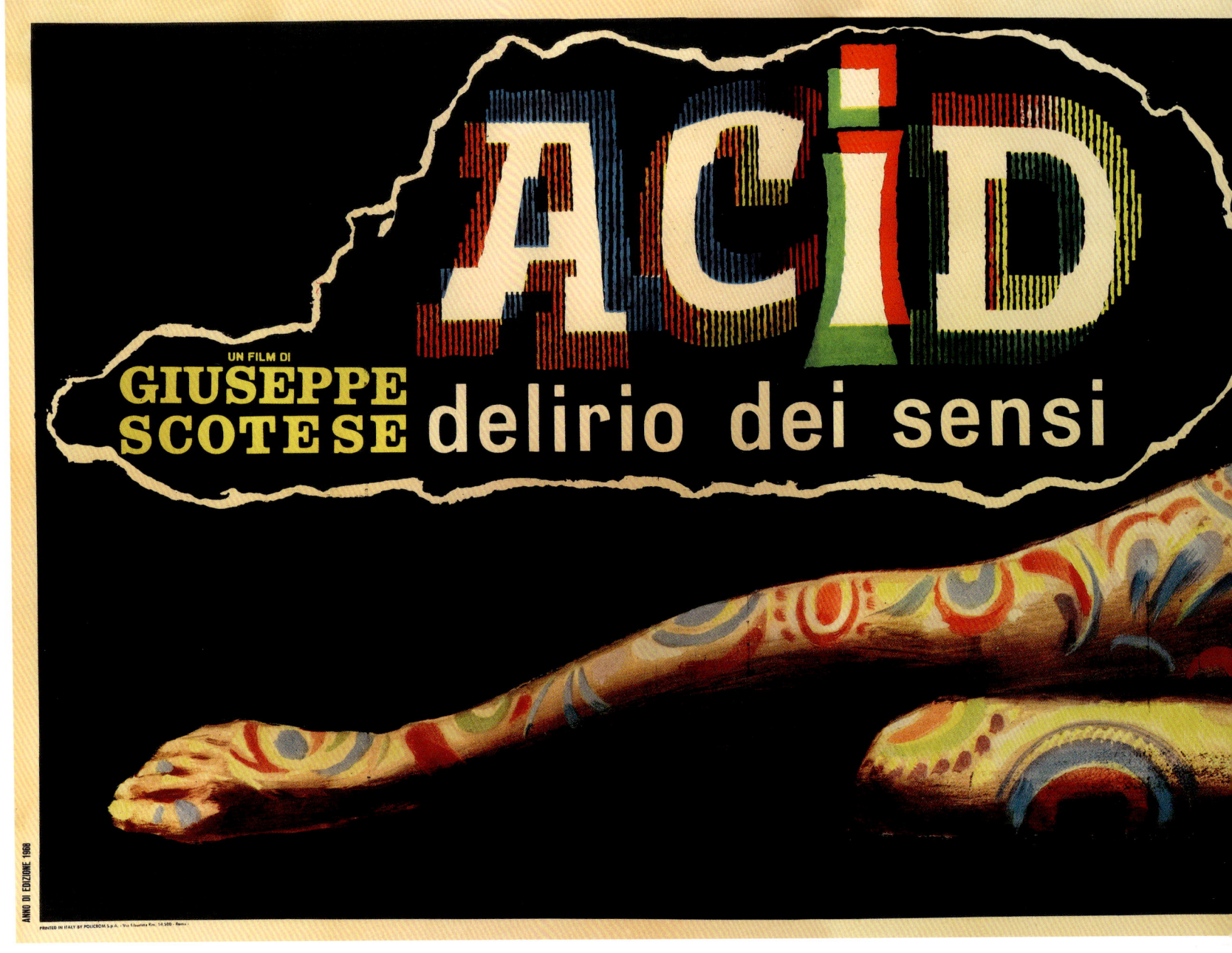

ACID – DELIRIO DEI SENSI 1968
ITALIAN POSTER, ARTIST UNKNOWN

During the 1960s, shrewd, low-budget producers fed a demand for free-spirited films featuring the wonders of recreational drugs. They churned out low-budget, poor quality movies that targeted a young and apparently insatiable audience. *Acid – delirio dei sensi* was one such offering from Italy. The film was less than brilliant. Its promotional art, on the other hand, was phenomenal. This banner poster is a particularly striking example of Italian design: a perfectly crafted, sensual illustration of a naked woman painted, tattoo-like, from head to toe, surmounted by typography evocative of the drug's effects. This image has become iconic, although the film itself has been long forgotten. Only five copies of this poster have ever surfaced. They were discovered together in Rome in the mid-1990s in the drawer of a movie poster dealer who did not know he had them or where they had come from.

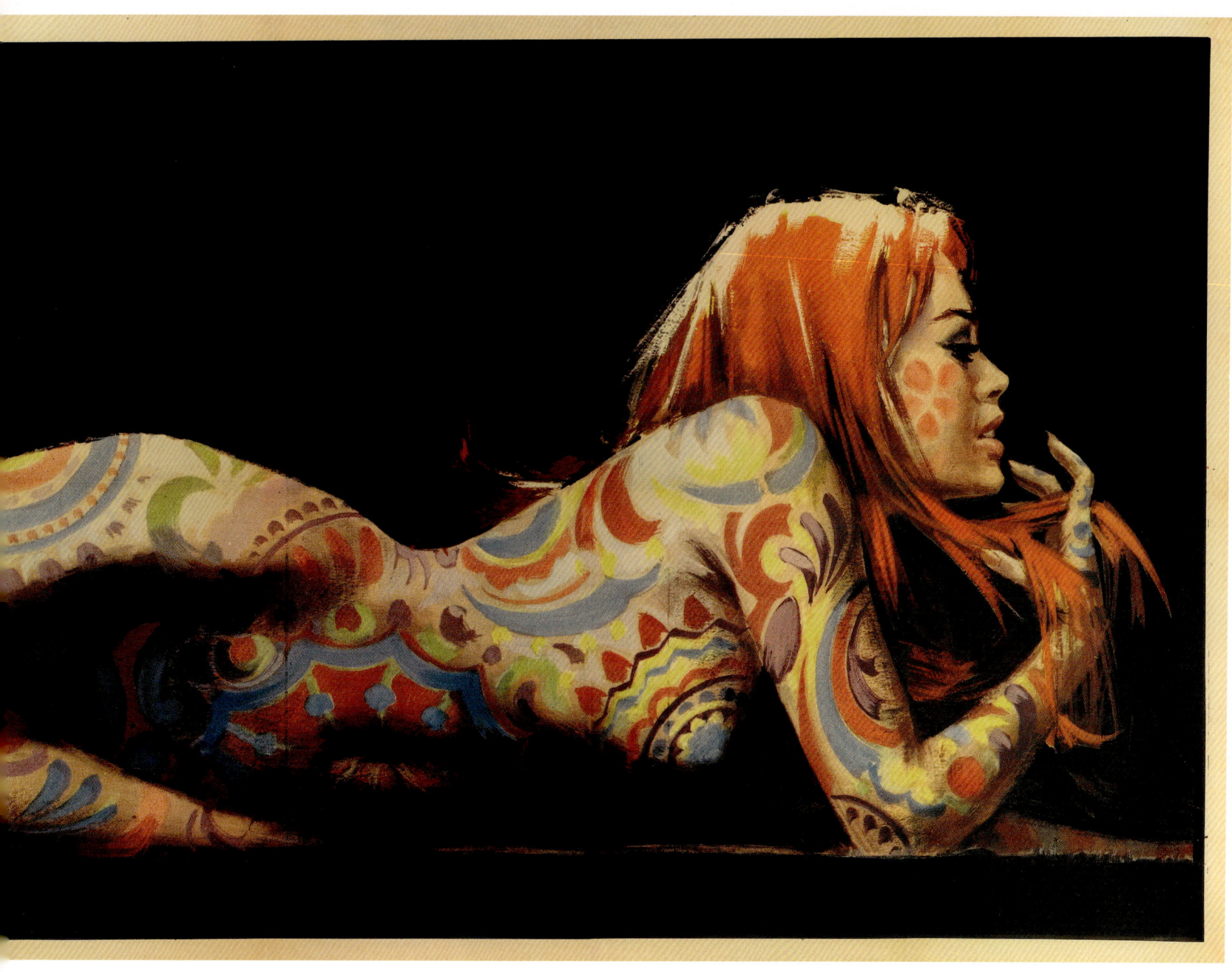

THE FRENCH CONNECTION 1971
AMERICAN POSTER, ARTIST UNKNOWN

Director William Friedkin's *The French Connection*, starring Gene Hackman, is one of the greatest cop films of all time and winner of five Academy Awards, including Best Picture, Best Director and Best Actor. It featured superb performances from Hackman and his supporting cast, a gritty documentary-style of filming by Friedkin on the streets of New York and one of the most exciting car chase scenes in cinema history.

Despite its now iconic status, when the idea for *The French Connection* was originally conceived, the industry could not have been less enthusiastic. In the late 1960s, Friedkin was not yet an established name in Hollywood and was known, if at all, for his award-winning television documentaries. He was approached by producer Phil D'Antoni, who had just purchased the rights to a book by Robin Moore about the real-life experiences of a couple of New York narcotics detectives. Friedkin and D'Antoni spent over two years trying to get studio interest in the project, with Friedkin recalling that, 'Every studio in town had passed on it. Most of them passed on it twice.' After reworking the script for a third time, Fox studio boss, Darryl F. Zanuck, finally gave them the go-ahead, but only if they could bring it in under $1.5 million, telling them, 'If you guys can make the film for that, go ahead. But I won't be here when you finish it.' (Zanuck was fired from the studio just days after giving the project the green light.) With such a low budget, Friedkin failed to get any of the actors he had hoped to secure for the lead role – apparently being rejected by Paul Newman, James Caan and Robert Mitchum. He was initially strongly opposed to hiring Gene Hackman, who was an almost unknown face and not a big star. The film ultimately proved to be the making of both of their careers.

This 'style B' American poster was one of the first to be designed for the film and, without a known actor or director, it was marketed purely on its subject matter – a rare approach for the time. The tagline and photograph – suggesting speed, thrills and crime – were very effective. Perhaps realising what a crucial part of the film's success the car chase would be, the main 'style A' poster depicted the climax of the chase, when Hackman shoots his fleeing suspect (also shown in the vertical photo strip on this design). Although an effective poster in itself, my favourite has always been this alternative style – interesting, unusual and embodying the realism of the film.

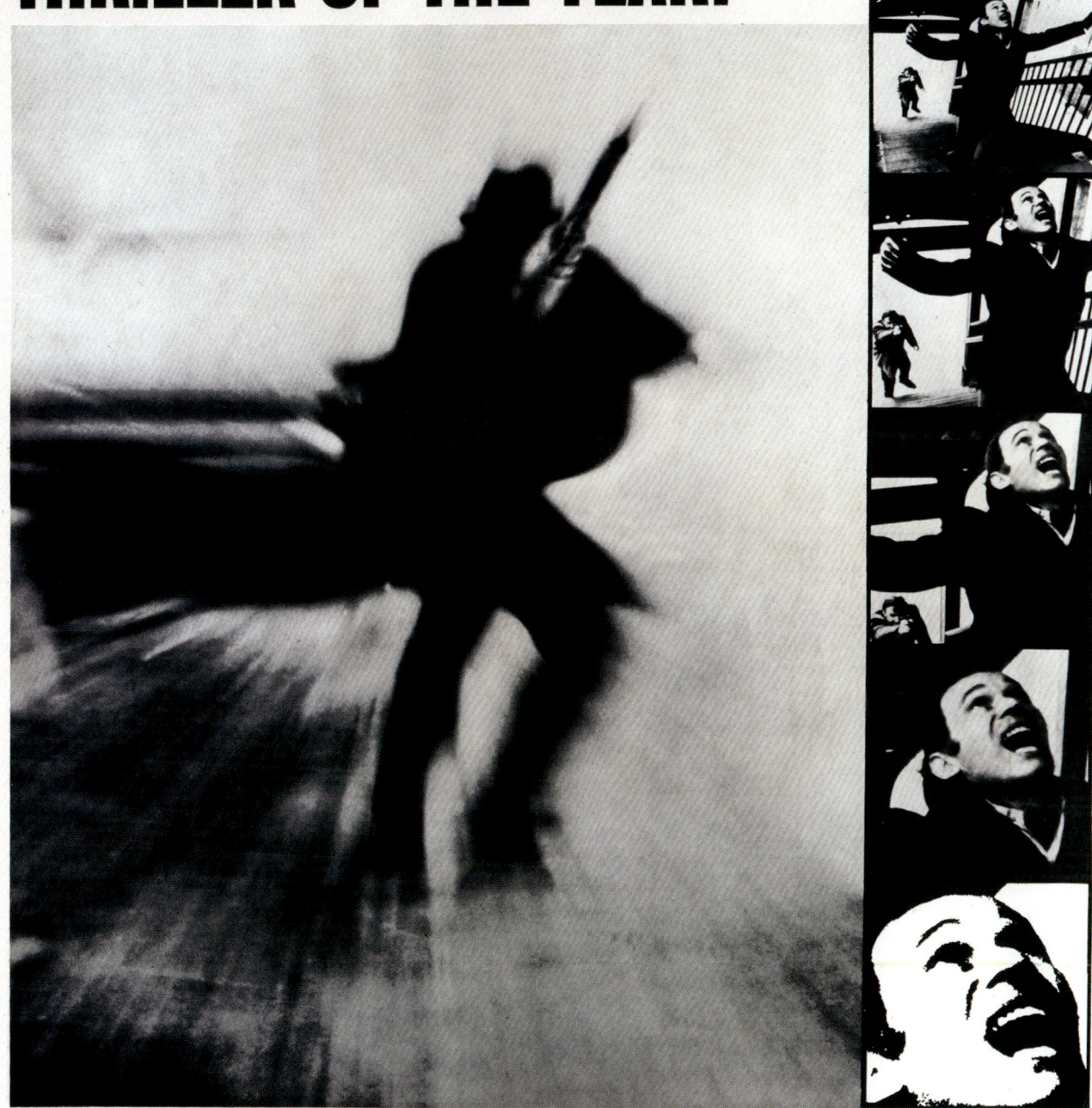

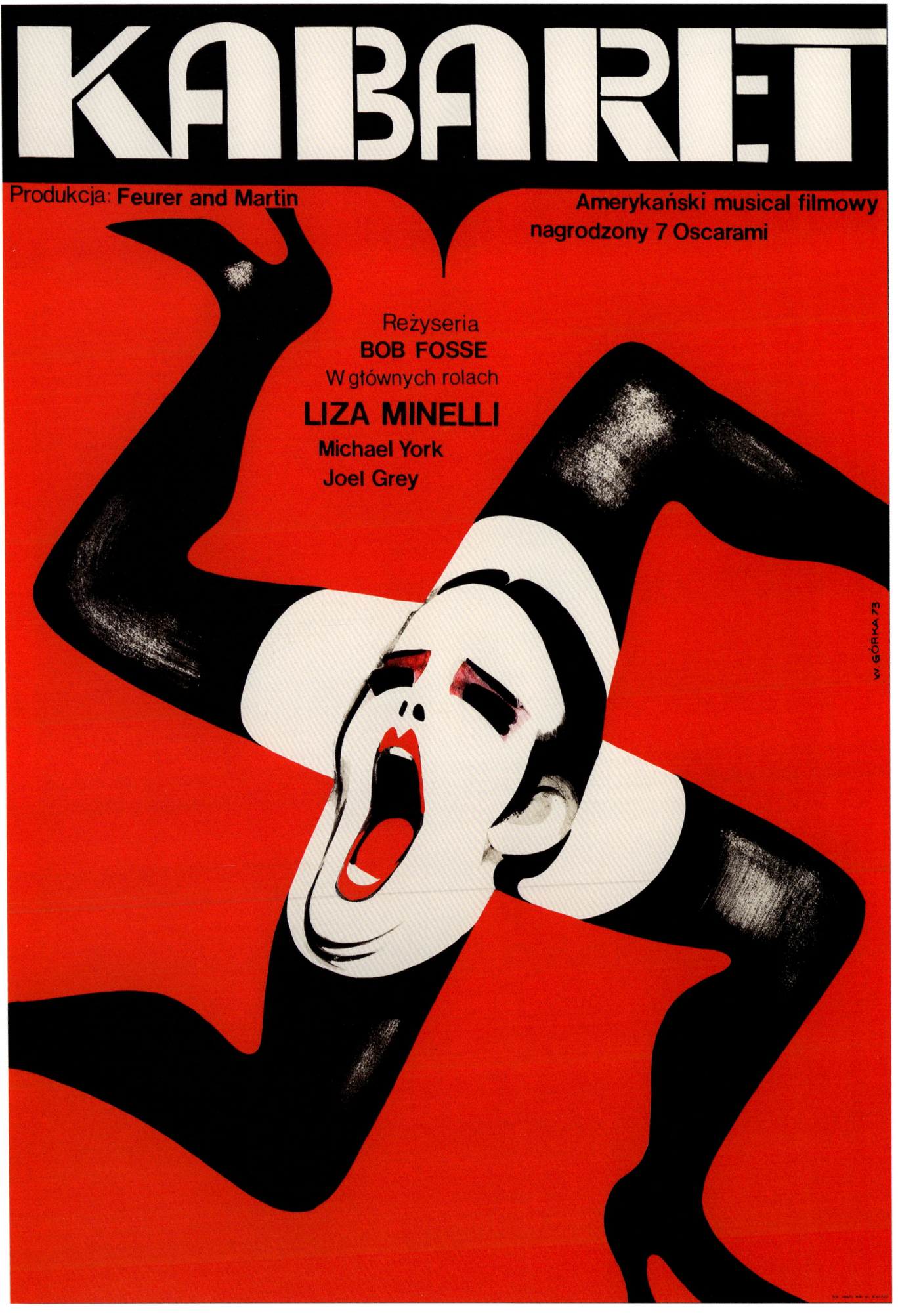

Cabaret 1972

Polish poster, Art by Wiktor Gorka

Polish artist Wiktor Gorka created this poster for director Bob Fosse's *Cabaret*. With its shocking use of the swastika and Minelli's singing face, almost distorted into a scream of torture, it remains one of the most famous and sought-after Polish film posters of the twentieth century.

Wiktor Gorka (1922-2004) studied at the Academy of Fine Arts in Krakow and won several awards for his poster designs over the course of his lifetime. He taught art as a visiting professor at several leading academies in Mexico from 1971 to 1991. In addition to *Cabaret*, he is also famous for his posters for *Spartacus* (1960) and *2001: A Space Odyssey* (1968).

MAGNUM FORCE 1973
AMERICAN POSTER, DESIGN BY BILL GOLD, PHOTO BY PHILIPPE HALSMAN

This American poster for *Magnum Force* is one of the best posters of the 1970s. It jumps out at you as a punchy, clean design. For several years, I never knew who was responsible until I finally met designer Bill Gold a few years ago. Our conversations about the extraordinary body of work he created over a lifetime eventually became the huge collector's opus, *Bill Gold: PosterWorks* (Reel Art Press, 2010). In addition to being a ferociously talented designer, Bill has always had an incredible ability to find the most appropriate artist to work on a particular project. For *Magnum Force*, he brought on board one of the greats of twentieth century photography, Philippe Halsman. In *PosterWorks*, Bill discusses the genesis of their collaboration and the development of the final poster design:

*I wanted to use a named photographer, and I'd studied with Philippe Halsman ... So when I was approached for **Magnum Force**, I said: 'Halsman's the guy I'll get for that.' And I took him to a screening, and when I told him what the movie was going to be about, he said: 'I hate guns; I can't stand guns.' Which wasn't a good start. Then the picture opened and all of a sudden you see a huge .44 Magnum pointing right at you and Harry pulling the trigger. To have a gun pointed at you in that kind of way is not very pleasant if you've got any imagination. And the sound was loud, so Halsman jumped a little bit. After the screening was over, I said, 'I'm sorry I exposed you to that kind of experience,' and he said he understood and after seeing the whole movie he felt a bit differently about it. Then we went off to the studio ... and the two of us met Clint, and Clint started calling Halsman 'the maestro'. They kidded around together, very relaxed. We knew we wanted it to be a 'dominant gun' kind of shoot – with the gun six feet tall in some shots! – and we used a very wide-angle lens, a 28 or something like that. The session took only a couple of hours. And Clint was totally excited about working with Philippe Halsman. Halsman knew by then exactly what he was after, and all he did was ask Clint to get into position, and of course Clint did anything he wanted. I added the out of perspective target, behind Clint.*

Philippe Halsman (1906-1979) was one of the defining photographers of his generation and a true great of twentieth century photography. Originally born in Latvia, Halsman set up his own photographic studio in Paris in 1932 and established himself as France's leading portrait photographer. After Hitler's rise to power, he moved to New York and within two years had his first photograph published in *Life* magazine. It was the start of a lifelong collaboration and his photographs appeared on the cover of the magazine more than any other artist – a total of 101 times. His work also appeared in *Look*, *Esquire*, *Paris Match* and *Saturday Evening Post*.

Halsman's photographs often favoured surrealism. He had a close friendship with Salvador Dalí and in 1948 Halsman shot one of his most famous and groundbreaking images, *Dalí Atomicus* – a photographic homage to Dalí's own painting, *Leda Atomica*. Halsman's shot captured Dalí, his cats, his furniture, paintings and water, all suspended in mid-air.

Halsman was also renowned for taking shots of his subjects jumping, believing that through the action of leaping, part of a person's mask fell away and their true nature was revealed. Some of the many people who jumped for Halsman include Marilyn Monroe, Richard Nixon and the Duke and Duchess of Windsor.

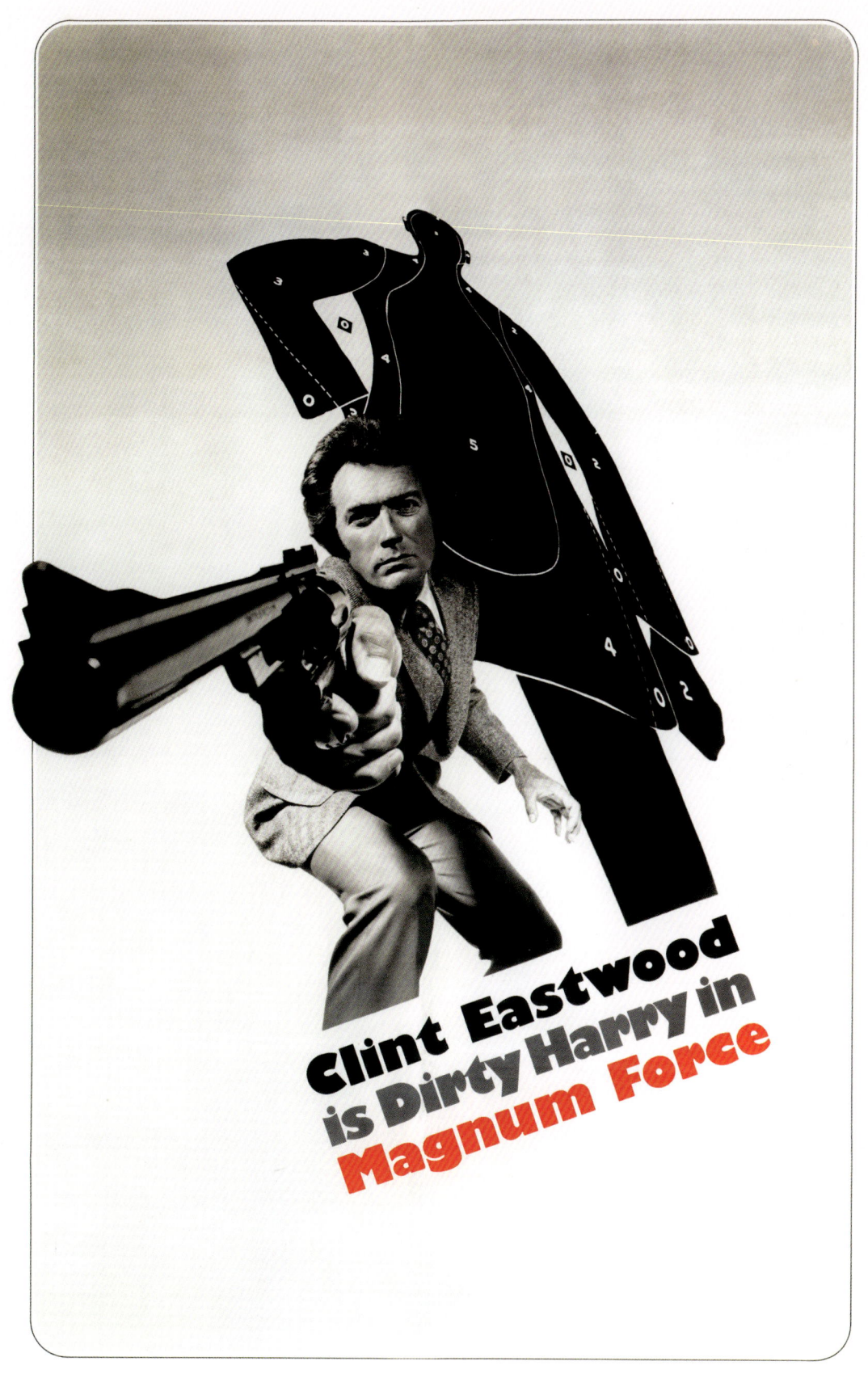

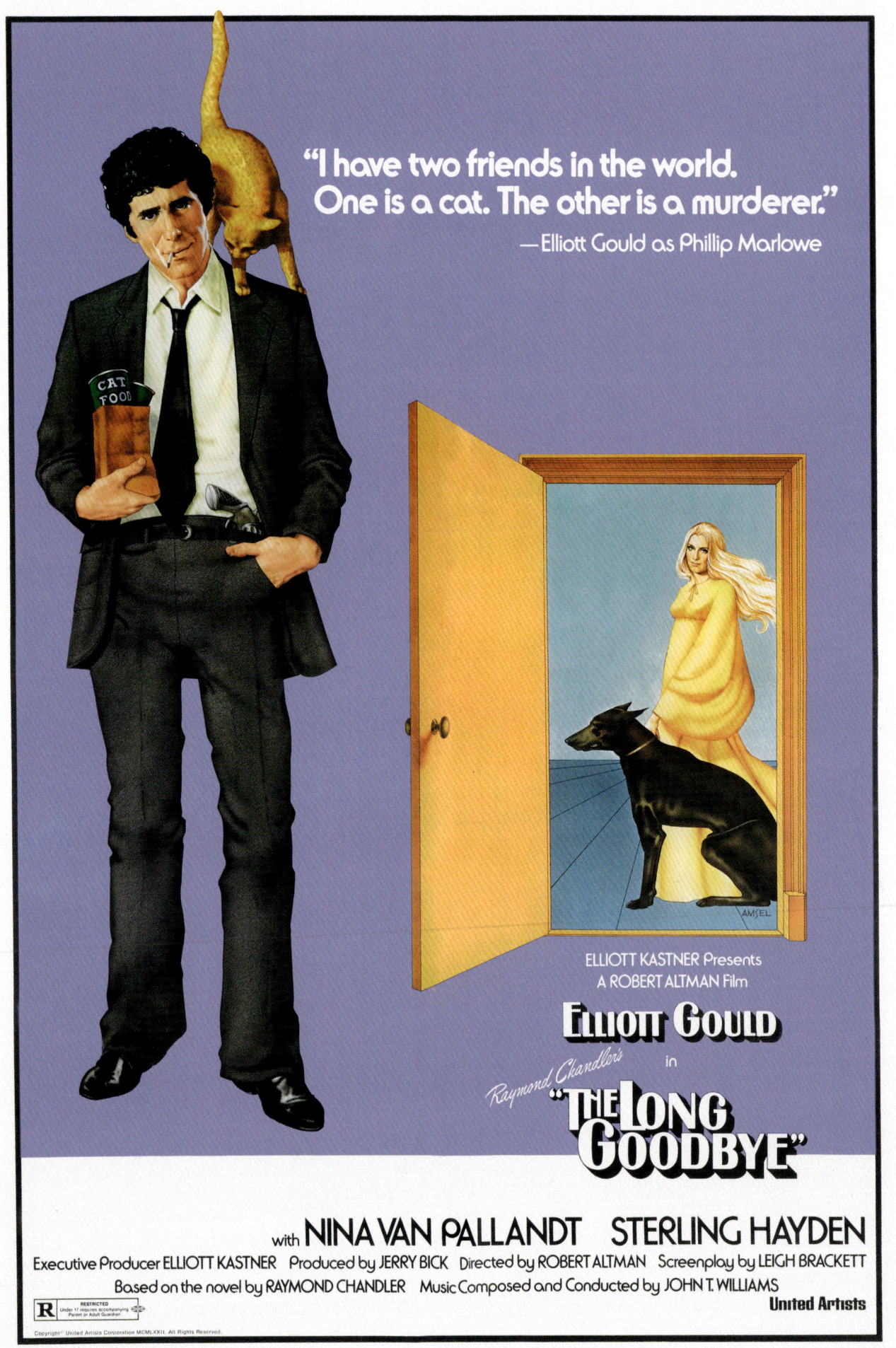

THE LONG GOODBYE 1973

AMERICAN POSTER, ART BY RICHARD AMSEL

The prodigious talent of Richard Amsel (1947-1985) exploded onto the professional art world in 1969 when, at the age of 22, he won a nationwide competition to create the poster art for the film *Hello, Dolly!* Amsel's innovative style combined a modern, idiosyncratic approach with a nostalgic nod towards the past. He became the leading pop illustrator of the 1970s, painting star portraits for the cover of *Time* magazine, including Ingrid Bergman, Clark Gable and Elvis Presley. Until his untimely death at the age of 37, Amsel designed an impressive number of film posters, including *The Sting* (1973), *Chinatown* (1974, see p.15) and *Raiders of the Lost Ark* (1981). He won numerous awards, including the New York and Los Angeles Society of Illustrators Awards.

The Long Goodbye is my favourite Robert Altman film and Amsel's design is also my favourite poster on the title. Done in the Surrealist style of Magritte, the design was befitting of the film – looking back at the noir genre from the viewpoint of the 1970s. After an initially lukewarm public response to the film, Amsel's campaign was pulled in favour of a different approach that emphasised the more madcap elements of the plot and which was illustrated by artist Jack Davis. Amsel's original posters are now much sought-after by collectors.

THE BIG SLEEP 1946
SWEDISH RE-RELEASE POSTER, DESIGN BY OLLE FRANKZÉN

Although I have already included an original 1946 French poster for *The Big Sleep* in this 'essentials' list (see p.101), I also had to include this much later 1974 re-release Swedish poster. I love the Lichtenstein approach – turning Bogie into the hero of his own comic book – and the humour of the tagline, *Such a lot of guns around town and so few brains*.

The design was by Swedish artist Olle Frankzén (b.1944). Frankzén graduated from Beckman's College of Design in Stockholm in the 1960s with a degree in advertising, which didn't excite him that much at the time, 'I was never that hooked on advertising, to draw and paint attracted me more. I did, however, find my training in typography of great use.'

By the 1970s, Frankzén had established himself as a designer of note. He had a design company, 'Design 2001 AB', with the architect Lennart Clemens and theatrical set designer Nisse Skoog, which focussed on the film industry. They were instrumental in designing and establishing the renowned 'Filmstaden' – a complex of cinemas across Sweden. The first thing that greeted visitors as they arrived to watch a film was a fluttering flag with the Filmstaden logo designed by Frankzén. He also worked on the posters and adverts for the cinemas' releases – everything from imported foreign films like *The Big Sleep* to home-grown Swedish films by Ingmar Bergman. In the mid-1970s, a publisher plagiarised the poster for *The Big Sleep* in one of their advertising campaigns. As compensation, they offered Frankzén the opportunity to work for them on their design campaigns. Thus began a new period of his life working with the publishing industry – becoming particularly known for his Stephen King cover art. He also illustrated for the daily news press and journals. An exhibition of Frankzén's film posters was held at the National Museum in Stockholm in 1983.

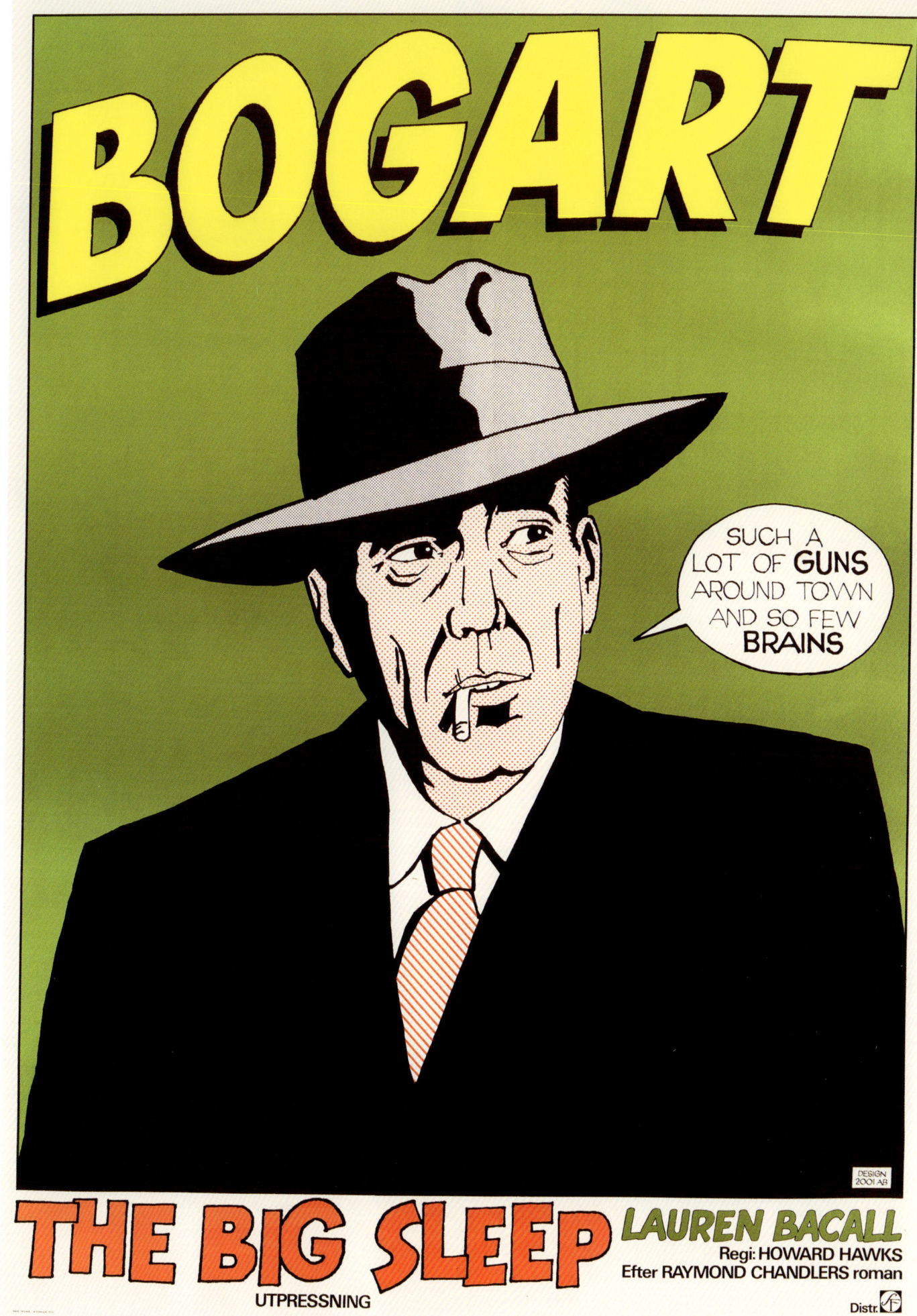

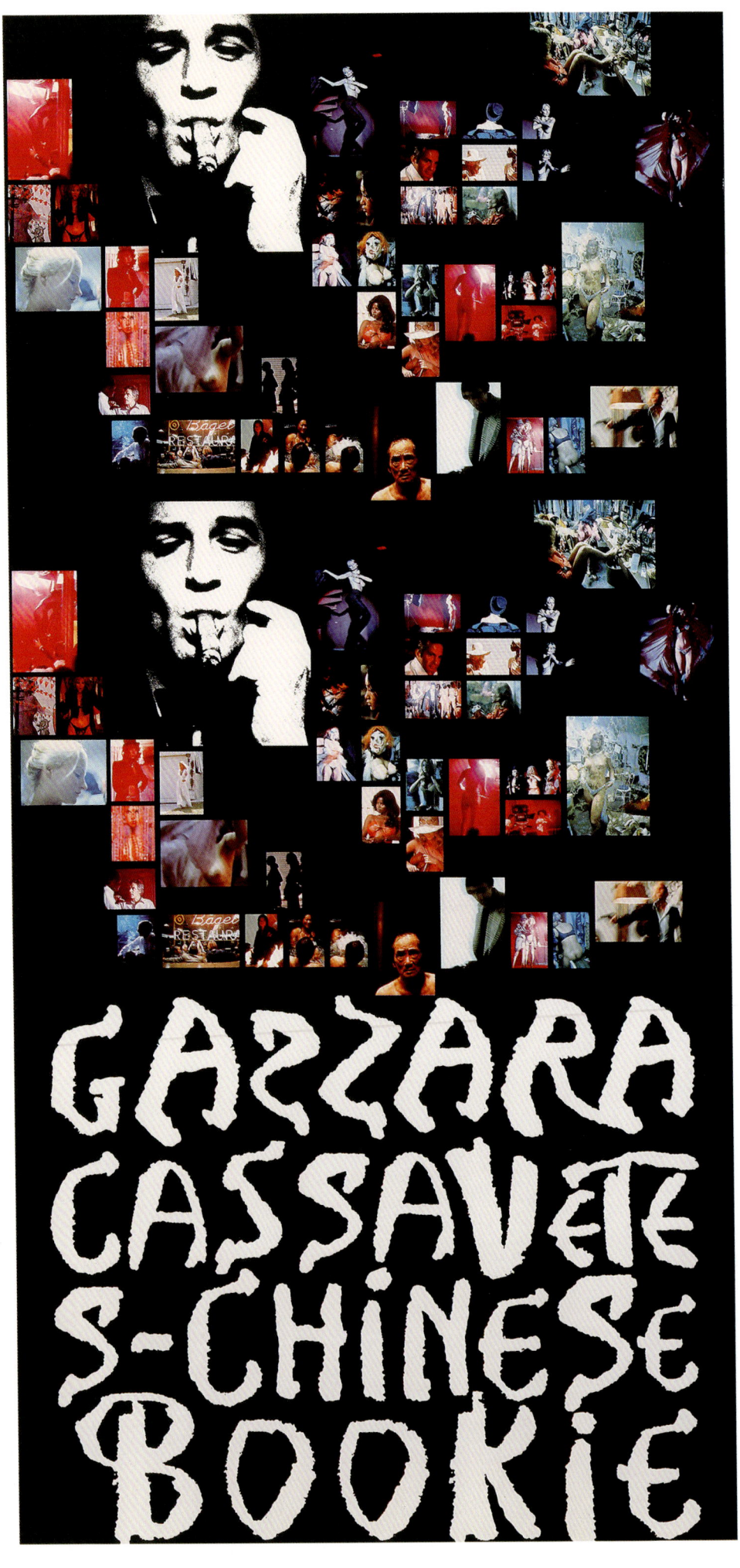

THE KILLING OF A CHINESE BOOKIE 1976
AMERICAN POSTER, DESIGN AND PHOTOS BY SAM SHAW

I love John Cassavetes. As a film student in London in the mid-1980s, I discovered his work for the first time and have unashamedly been a huge fan ever since. Often called the first American independent, Cassavetes' body of work paved the way for a more vibrant American cinema. From his first film *Shadows*, in 1959, through *Faces* (1968) and *A Woman Under the Influence* (1974), his work was fresh and ruthlessly innovative. *The Killing of a Chinese Bookie* is one of my favourites – a character study starring Cassavetes' constant, Ben Gazarra, as the perennially hopeful owner of a sleazy strip joint who has to kill the boss of a Chinese crime syndicate to clear a debt and save his business. An exploration of identity, the film was also an examination of the American dream and the price it demanded.

The producer on the film was fellow New Yorker, Sam Shaw (1912-1999), a close friend of Cassavetes who had been working with him since *Shadows*. Shaw was also a celebrated Hollywood photographer and had shot everyone from Humphrey Bogart and Marlon Brando to Elizabeth Taylor and Audrey Hepburn. (He took the most iconic 'flying skirt' shot of Marilyn Monroe on the set of *The Seven Year Itch*.) In addition to producing *Chinese Bookie*, Shaw was also the special photographer on set and was responsible for the advertising campaign for the film's release. Shaw created the posters in-house and the resulting designs featured his own photography and were innovative and experimental – an apt reflection of the film.

ANNIE HALL 1977

AMERICAN POSTER, ARTIST UNKNOWN

The American poster for *Annie Hall* is very effective and is one of the simplest but most iconic posters of the 1970s. The choice of photo was clever. Of the hundreds of hours of footage that was shot for the film, the heart of the movie can be distilled down to this one key image. Keaton and Allen are facing each other in an open posture that reflects the crux of their chemistry – both on and off screen. The still is taken from the pivotal moment in their on-screen relationship, where Allen's Alvy declares his 'luff with two ffs' for Annie. This was also the first movie where Allen moved away from straight-up comedy and a seriousness came into his work – again reflected in the choice of photograph, which doesn't instantly scream 'comedy' but rather is suggestive of a greater emotional depth on offer. The photograph also succeeds as a showcase for the film's celebrated fashion – Keaton's quirky, mannish Ralph Lauren ensemble and Allen's laid-back Ivy cool.

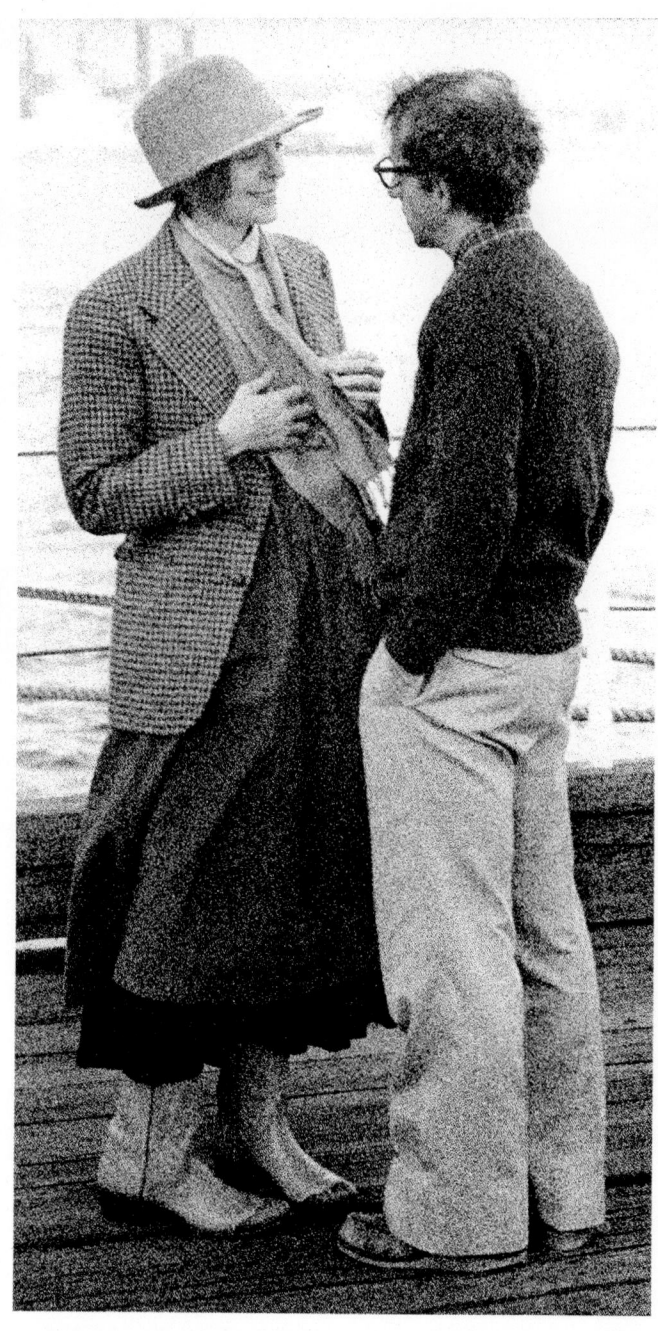

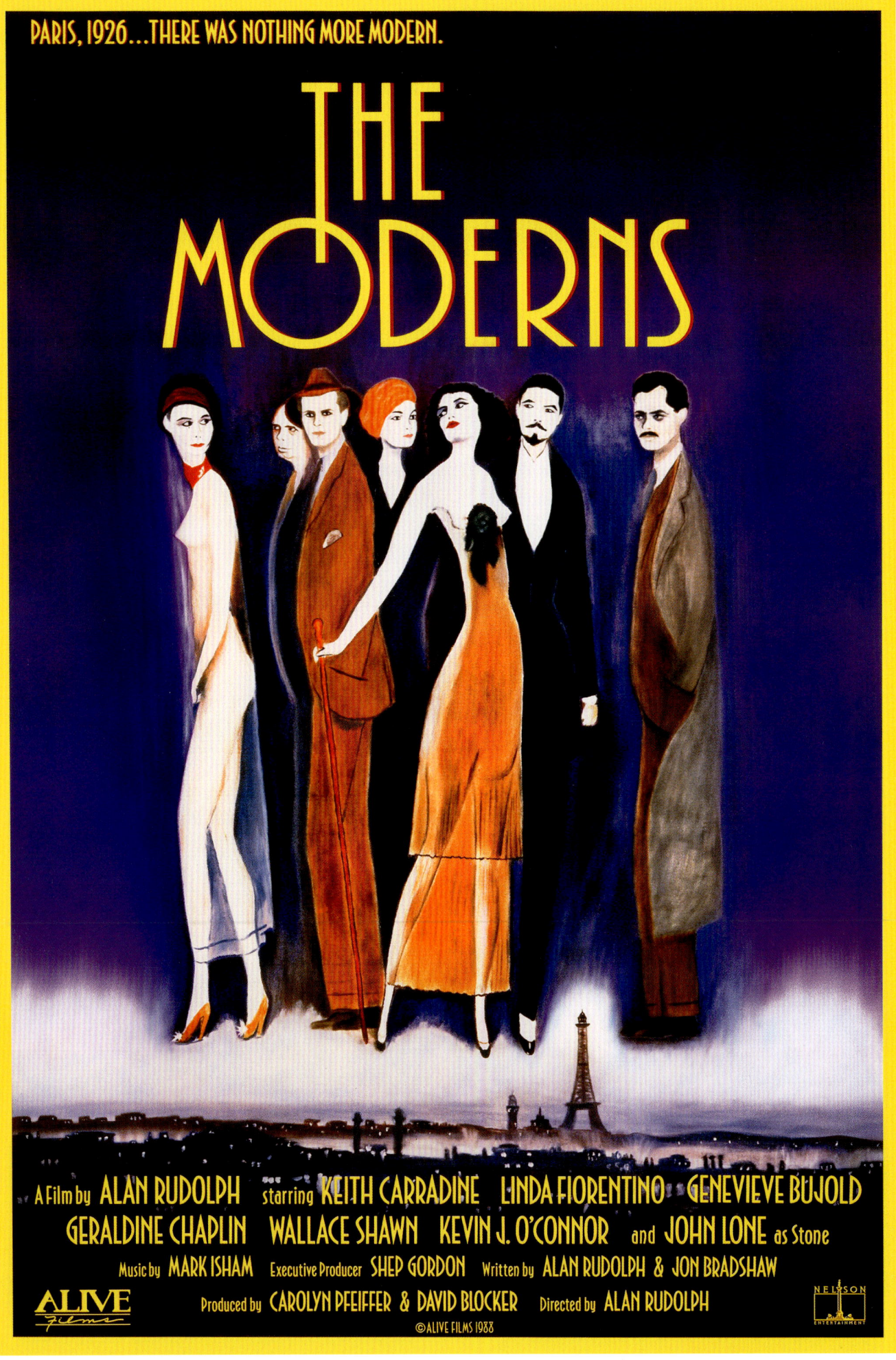

The Moderns 1988
American poster, Art by Keith Carradine

Keith Carradine and Alan Rudolph first met when they worked together on Robert Altman's *Nashville* (Carradine as actor, Rudolph as assistant director). They became close friends and over the following years made four excellent films together – *Welcome to L.A.*, *Choose Me*, *Trouble in Mind* and *The Moderns*.

    The Moderns is a wry ensemble piece set in the bohemian Paris of the 1920s – populated by Gertrude Stein, Ernest Hemingway and Alice B. Toklas. Carradine plays an American artist caught up in a reluctant agreement to forge three paintings – by Cézanne, Modigliani and Matisse. The canvases, and several more featured in the film, were actually painted by Carradine himself. He commented in an interview at the time, 'I'd done some painting when I was younger and I wanted it to feel right in the film, so I asked David Blocker (the film's co-producer) to send an easel and paints and canvases to my hotel room. After work I'd go back to the hotel and order room service and paint.' The poster for the film's release was also painted by Carradine. Its elegance is a fitting reflection of Rudolph's stylish approach, and the equal weight given to all of the characters also mirrors the ensemble nature of the film.

UNFORGIVEN 1992
AMERICAN POSTER, DESIGN BY BILL GOLD, PHOTO BY EDDIE ADAMS

In 1942, a young man at Warner Bros art department created a poster for *Casablanca*. Over the next 63 years, posters for *A Streetcar Named Desire*, *Dial M for Murder*, *Bonnie and Clyde*, *Bullitt*, *My Fair Lady*, *Get Carter*, *Dirty Harry*, *The Untouchables* and *Unforgiven* became coveted items, cherished by movie-goers all over the world. The same artist was responsible for them all. Bill Gold's life's work spans six decades and over 2000 films. He is the man behind campaigns for the greatest movies the world has ever seen.

Gold's 'teaser' poster for *Unforgiven* was designed towards the end of his career (he officially retired in 2003). In a decade that saw a general decline in the quality of movie posters as an art form, Gold's poster was a stunning rebuke to this trend and demonstrated the power that a single image could still have. In *Bill Gold: PosterWorks*, author Christopher Frayling discusses the success of this design:

*Bill Gold's finest achievement of the 1990s – one which has justly been called 'the single most compelling image in all of the Eastwood poster art' – was the 'teaser' poster for **Unforgiven** showing Clint Eastwood in a long coat with his back to the viewer, his head bowed, his hands clasped behind his back, holding a pistol. We can just about see his profile. This image .... brilliantly encapsulates the character of William Munny in the movie.*

Bill used Pulitzer Prize-winning photographer Eddie Adams to shoot the image of Eastwood. Eddie Adams (1933-2004) was one of the most published and honoured American photographers of the twentieth century. He won over 500 awards for his work, including accolades from World Press, New York Press and Overseas Press Club.

Adams covered 13 wars as a photojournalist. His 1968 Pulitzer-winning photograph of the exact moment a Viet Cong lieutenant is executed in the street in Saigon became one of the most publicised images of the Vietnam War and a key symbol for the growing anti-war movement at home. It remains one of the most powerful and enduring photographs of the twentieth century.

In addition to his commanding war work, Adams also photographed six US presidents and hundreds of celebrities over the course of his career, either in a freelance capacity, as a 'special correspondent' for Associated Press (the first and only photographer to hold the title), or as special correspondent for *Parade* magazine (where he worked from the early 1980s until his death in 2004). He also worked on commercial projects in advertising and film, including the campaigns for *Bird* and *Unforgiven* with Bill Gold.

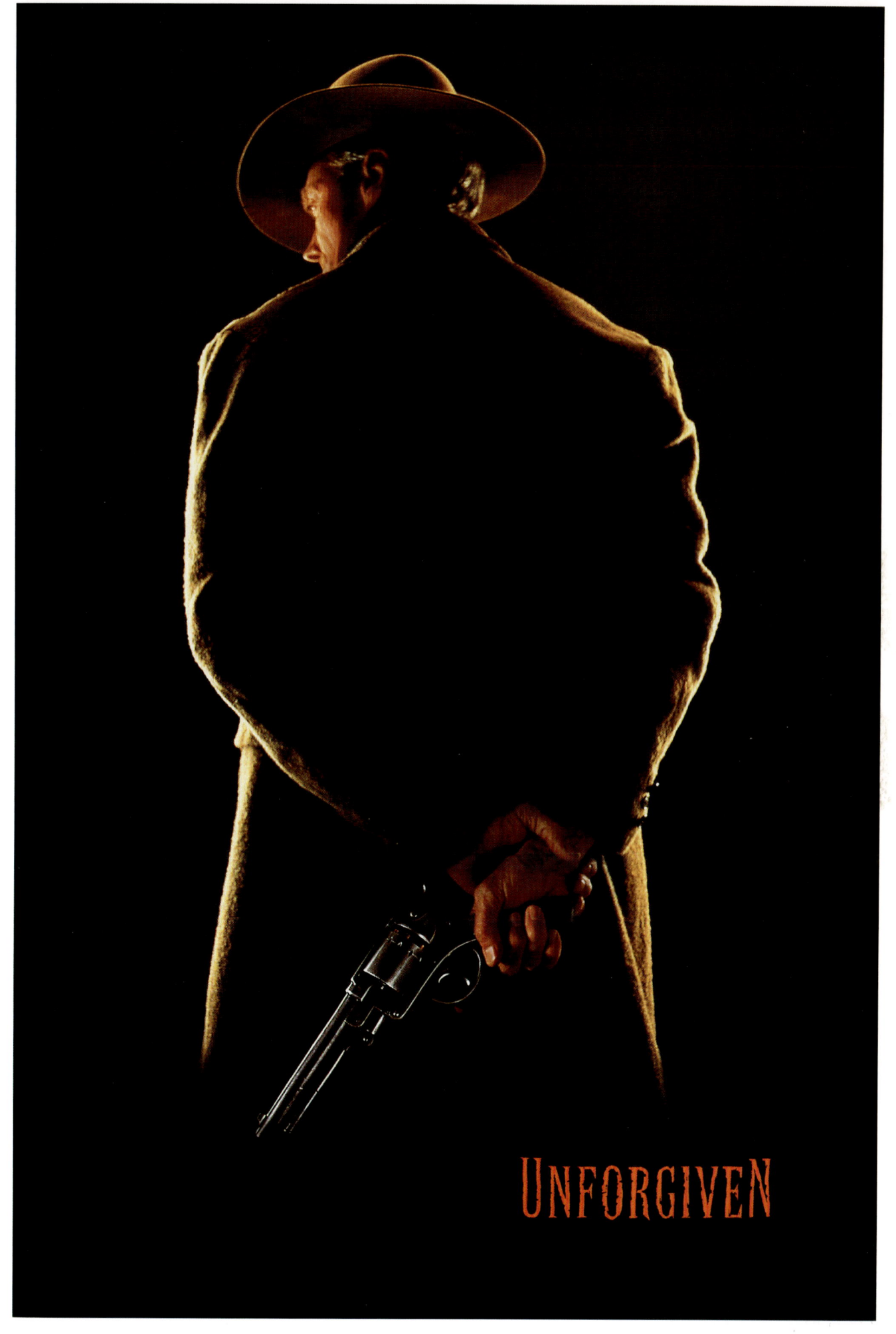

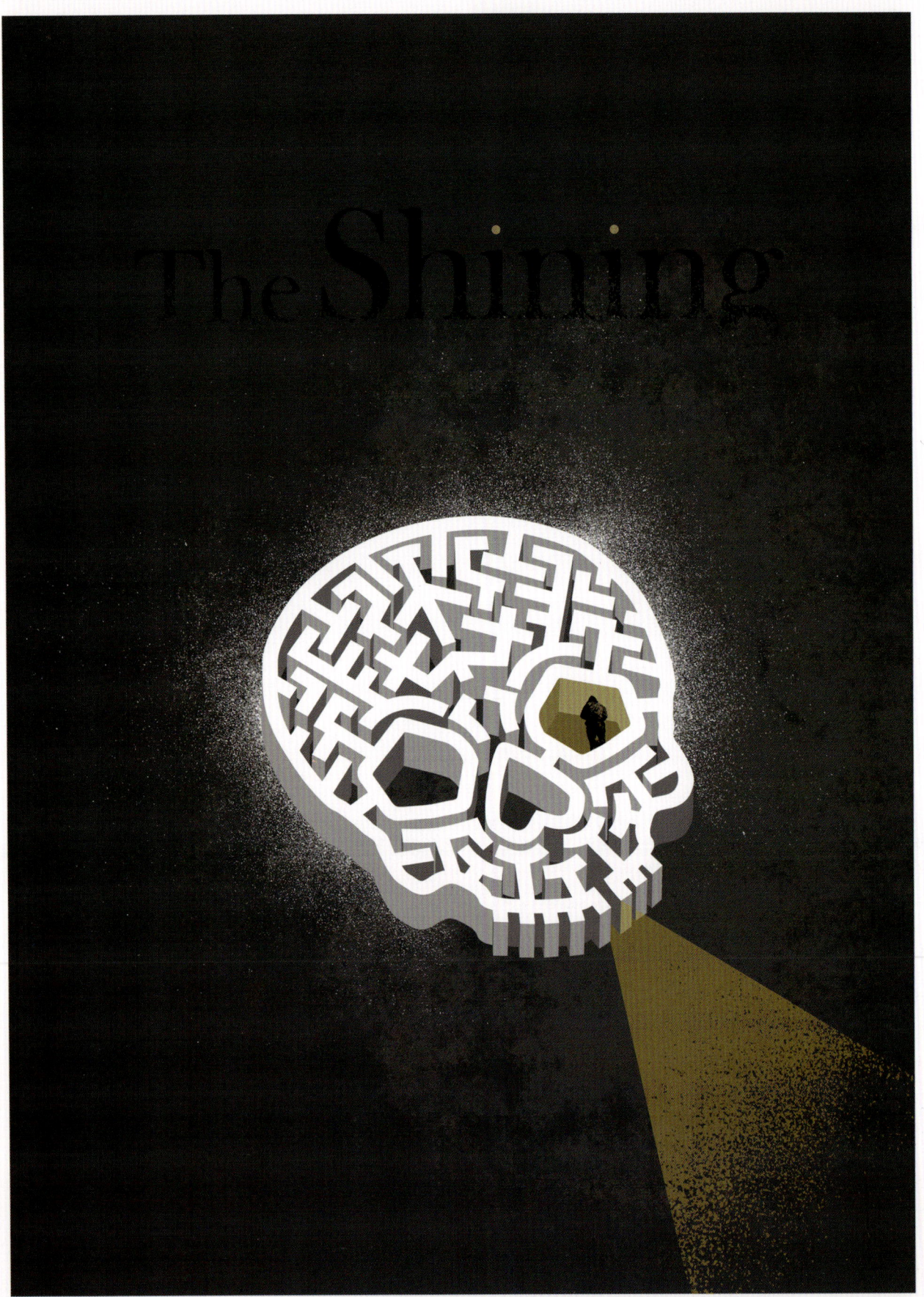

The Shining 1980
American re-release poster, Design by Jeff Kleinsmith

Modern movie poster design is rarely something to get excited about and standard issue posters for today's Hollywood blockbusters seldom deviate from the 'large photographic head shots' formula. One company bucking the trend is the Alamo Drafthouse cinema in Austin, Texas. Since around 2003, the Alamo, working with their art boutique, Mondo, have been producing their own limited edition silkscreen posters. They employ leading contemporary graphic artists and the results are some of the most innovative and exciting movie posters ever designed. Not to be confused with 'fan' posters, the Alamo posters are all produced for specific cinematic releases, from classic movies to new releases. Over the past ten years, these stunning limited edition prints – hand-signed and numbered – have become highly prized and collected. Their importance in the history of movie poster design has recently been recognised by the Academy of Motion Picture Arts and Sciences' Margaret Herrick Library, which has partnered with the Alamo to archive their original posters.

This poster for the Alamo's 2008 'Rolling Roadshow' screening of *The Shining* is one of my favourite examples in recent years. It was designed by Jeff Kleinsmith, who comments on his creative process:

I felt that the last part of the movie where he is chasing his son through the maze was a key moment in the film. To me it was an analogy for what he was dealing with in his own mind, that was building throughout the story. The skull was the appropriate and obvious image to use as the maze shape, given the carnage shown previously in the film. And, rather than show him chasing the boy, I chose to trap him forever in the eye since, even if he finds his way out, he is still trapped forever in his own mind.

Jeff Kleinsmith (b.1967) is the co-owner of Patent Pending Design and New Rage Records in Seattle; former art director at *The Rocket* magazine and he has been art director at Sub Pop Records for over 18 years. Throughout this time, he has produced countless posters and album covers for as many bands. Kleinsmith's work has appeared in numerous design books and magazines, and in various gallery shows, and his work is in the permanent collection at Experience Music Project and The Rock and Roll Hall of Fame. Kleinsmith teaches advanced design at Seattle's School of Visual Concepts and he has a client list that includes, amongst others, DreamWorks, Columbia Records, Elektra Records, *Wired* magazine, and Nike. Jeff was recently named one of the 40 most influential designers by *i-D* magazine and one of the 25 most important people in Seattle. A monograph of his work is currently in production, with an official release date yet to be announced.

APPENDIX

PAGE: 4
ALFRED HITCHCOCK POSES NEXT TO A POSTER OF HIMSELF FOR HIS FILM PSYCHO AT THE PREMIERE IN PARIS (1960).
PHOTO © BETTMANN/CORBIS

PAGE: 7
JACQUES TATI HEADING TOWARDS THE HOTEL CARLTON WITH HIS 'NEPHEW' ALAIN BERCOURT. HIS NEW FILM MON ONCLE WAS BEING PREMIERED AT THE 11TH CANNES FILM FESTIVEL IN MAY 1958.
PHOTO © HENRI CARTIER-BRESSON/MAGNUM PHOTOS

PAGE: 8
METROPOLIS POSTER DETAIL (SEE P.34)

PAGE: 11
MON ONCLE POSTER DETAIL (SEE P.152)

PAGE: 12
JEAN-PIERRE LÉAUD AND PATRICK AUFFAY STEAL A MOVIE STILL FROM THE CINEMA IN A SCENE FROM LES QUATRES CENTS COUPS (1959)
COURTESY OF THE FRENCH NEW WAVE COLLECTION

PAGE: 15
CHINATOWN (1973)
ORIGINAL ARTWORK BY RICHARD AMSEL
PRIVATE COLLECTION

PAGE: 16
THE MALTESE FALCON (1942/1992)
LIMITED EDITION OF 20 PRINTS. ARTIST'S PROOF
IN-HOUSE DESIGN FOR WARNER BROS EXECUTIVES FOR THE FIFTIETH ANNIVERSARY.
ARTWORK BY PIETRO PSAIER
PRIVATE COLLECTION

PAGE: 18
FEDERICO FELLINI AND MARCELLO MASTROIANNI HOLD UP A POSTER FOR THEIR FILM LA DOLCE VITA, C.1960.
PHOTO © DAVID LEES/CORBIS

PAGE: 21
LE AVVENTURE STRAORDINARISSIME DI SATURNINO FARANDOLA (1913)
ORIGINAL ITALIAN 79 x 55 IN. (201 x 140 CM)
ART BY ALBERT ROBIDA (1848-1926)
COURTESY OF THE HASTINGS COLLECTION

PAGE: 22
LES VAMPIRES (1916)
ORIGINAL FRENCH 94 x 63 IN. (240 x 160 CM)
ART BY ACHILLE LUCIEN MAUZAN (1873-1925)
PRIVATE COLLECTION

PAGE: 25
BLIND HUSBANDS (1919)
ORIGINAL US 22 x 14 IN. (56 x 36 CM)
ARTIST UNKNOWN
COURTESY OF THE IRA M. RESNICK COLLECTION

PAGE: 26
OPIUM (1919)
ORIGINAL AUSTRIAN 74 x 50 IN. (188 x 127 CM)
ART BY THEO MATEJKO (1893-1946)
PRIVATE COLLECTION

PAGE: 29
HOLLYWOOD (1923)
ORIGINAL US 41 x 27 IN. (104 x 69 CM)
ART DIRECTION ATTRIBUTED TO VINCENT TROTTA (1886-1970)
PRIVATE COLLECTION

PAGE: 30
L'INHUMAINE (1924)
ORIGINAL FRENCH 63 x 47 IN. (160 x 119 CM)
ART BY GEORGES 'DJO' BOURGEOIS (1898-1937)
PRIVATE COLLECTION

PAGE: 33
BERLIN: DIE SINFONIE DER GROSSTADT (1927)
ORIGINAL FRENCH 63 x 47 IN. (160 x 119 CM)
ART BY VENABERT (DATES UNKNOWN)
PRIVATE COLLECTION

PAGE: 34
METROPOLIS (1927)
ORIGINAL GERMAN 82 x 38 IN. (208 x 97 CM)
ART BY HEINZ SCHULZ-NEUDAMM (1899-1969)
REEL POSTER ARCHIVE

PAGE: 36-37
METROPOLIS (1927)
ORIGINAL FRENCH 94 x 126 IN. (240 x 360 CM)
BORIS BILINSKY (1900-1948)
COURTESY OF THE BERLIN FILM MUSEUM

PAGE: 39
GRASS: A NATION'S BATTLE FOR LIFE (1925)
ORIGINAL US 41 x 27 IN. (104 x 69 CM)
ARTIST UNKNOWN
PRIVATE COLLECTION

PAGE: 40
UNDERWORLD (1927)
ORIGINAL US 41 x 27 IN. (104 x 69 CM)
STYLE B
ARTIST UNKNOWN
COURTESY OF THE JQL COLLECTION

PAGE: 43
THE CANARY MURDER CASE (1929)
ORIGINAL US 41 x 27 IN. (104 x 69 CM)
BASED ON PHOTO BY EUGENE ROBERT RICHEE (1896-1972)
PRIVATE COLLECTION

PAGE: 44
INGAGI (1930)
ORIGINAL US 81 x 41 IN. (206 x 104 CM)
ARTIST UNKNOWN
REEL POSTER ARCHIVE

PAGE: 47
M (1931)
ORIGINAL FRENCH 63 x 47 IN. (160 x 119 CM)
ART BY CECCHETTO (DATES UNKNOWN)
COURTESY OF THE CHRIS DARK COLLECTION

PAGE: 48
FRANKENSTEIN (1931)
ORIGINAL US 41 x 27 IN. (104 x 69 CM)
ADVANCE (TEASER) POSTER
ART BY KAROLY GROSZ (DATES UNKNOWN)
PRIVATE COLLECTION

PAGE: 50
SCARFACE (1932)
ORIGINAL US 36 x 14 IN. (91 x 36 CM)
ARTIST UNKNOWN
COURTESY OF THE RON MOORE COLLECTION

PAGE: 53
WHAT PRICE HOLLYWOOD? (1932)
ORIGINAL US 41 x 27 IN. (104 x 69 CM)
ARTIST UNKNOWN
COURTESY OF THE IRA M. RESNICK COLLECTION

PAGE: 55
EXTASE (1933)
ORIGINAL FRENCH 63 x 47 IN. (160 x 119 CM)
ART BY CARLO MARIANI (DATES UNKNOWN)
COURTESY OF THE CHRIS DARK COLLECTION

PAGE: 57
KING KONG (1933)
ORIGINAL US 81 x 41 IN. (206 x 104 CM)
STYLE B
ART DIRECTION BY DAVID L. STRUMF (DATES UNKNOWN)
ART BY S. BARRETT MCCORMICK (DATES UNKNOWN) AND BOB SISK (DATES UNKNOWN)
REEL POSTER ARCHIVE

PAGE: 58
SUPERNATURAL (1933)
ORIGINAL US 41 x 27 IN. (104 x 69 CM)
ART DIRECTION BY VINCENT TROTTA (1886-1970) AND MAURICE KALLIS (1903-1988)
PRIVATE COLLECTION

PAGE: 61
LADIES THEY TALK ABOUT (1933)
ORIGINAL US 41 x 27 IN. (104 x 69 CM)
ART BY ALBERTO VARGAS (1896-1982)
PRIVATE COLLECTION

PAGE: 63
LE SEXE FAIBLE (1933)
ORIGINAL FRENCH 63 x 47 IN. (160 x 119 CM)
ART BY PAUL COLIN (1892-1985)
PRIVATE COLLECTION

PAGE: 64
NARCOTIC (1933)
ORIGINAL US 81 x 41 IN. (206 x 104 CM)
ARTIST UNKNOWN
COURTESY OF THE CHRIS DARK COLLECTION

PAGE: 67
HORSE FEATHERS (1932)
ORIGINAL US 41 X 27 IN. (104 X 69 CM)
RE-RELEASE 1937
ART BY CONSTANTIN ALAJÁLOV (1900-1987)
PRIVATE COLLECTION

PAGE: 68
THE LAST GANGSTER (1937)
ORIGINAL FRENCH 63 X 47 IN. (160 X 119 CM)
STYLE B
ART BY JEAN JACQUELIN (1905-1989)
COURTESY OF THE BOYNETT COLLECTION

PAGE: 71
BRINGING UP BABY (1938)
ORIGINAL FRENCH 63 X 47 IN. (160 X 119 CM)
ART BY BERNARD LANCY (1892-1964)
PRIVATE COLLECTION

PAGE: 73
STAGECOACH (1939)
ORIGINAL US 41 X 27 IN. (104 X 69 CM)
ART DIRECTION BY HERBERT JAEDICKER (DATES UNKNOWN)
PRIVATE COLLECTION

PAGE: 74
SULLIVAN'S TRAVELS (1941)
ORIGINAL US 41 X 27 IN. (104 X 69 CM)
STYLE B
ART DIRECTION BY MAURICE KALLIS (1903-1988)
PRIVATE COLLECTION

PAGE: 77
THIS GUN FOR HIRE (1942)
ORIGINAL US 41 X 27 IN. (104 X 69 CM)
ART DIRECTION BY MAURICE KALLIS (1903-1988)
COURTESY OF THE GREG FERLAND COLLECTION

PAGE: 78
THE OUTLAW (1942)
ORIGINAL 81 X 81 IN. (206 X 206 CM)
PREMIERE POSTER
PHOTO BY GEORGE HURRELL (1904-1992)
COURTESY OF THE TAREK ABUZAYYAD COLLECTION

PAGE: 81
THE BIG SHOT (1942)
ORIGINAL FRENCH 63 X 47 IN. (104 X 69 CM)
ART BY BORIS GRINSSON (1907-1999)
COURTESY OF THE JQL COLLECTION

PAGE: 83
CASABLANCA (1942)
ORIGINAL FRENCH 63 X 47 IN. (160 X 119 CM)
ART BY PIERRE PIGEOT (DATES UNKNOWN)
PRIVATE COLLECTION

PAGE: 84
DEVIL'S HARVEST (1942)
ORIGINAL US 41 X 27 IN. (104 X 69 CM)
ARTIST UNKNOWN
PRIVATE COLLECTION

PAGE: 87
CABIN IN THE SKY (1943)
ORIGINAL US 41 X 27 IN. (104 X 69 CM)
STYLE C
ART BY AL HIRSCHFELD (1903-2003)
COURTESY OF THE JQL COLLECTION

PAGE: 89
TEEN AGE (1944)
ORIGINAL US 41 X 27 IN. (104 X 69 CM)
ARTIST UNKNOWN
PRIVATE COLLECTION

PAGE: 91
TO HAVE AND HAVE NOT (1944)
ORIGINAL ITALIAN 39 X 27 IN. (99 X 69 CM)
ART BY LUIGI MARTINATI (1893-1984)
PRIVATE COLLECTION

PAGE: 92
DOUBLE INDEMNITY (1944)
ORIGINAL SPANISH 39 X 27 IN. (99 X 69 CM)
ART BY LOPEZ REIZ (DATES UNKNOWN)
COURTESY OF THE TONI LORENZO COLLECTION

PAGE: 94-95
BRIEF ENCOUNTER (1945)
ORIGINAL BRITISH 30 X 40 IN. (76 X 102 CM)
ARTIST UNKNOWN
PRIVATE COLLECTION

PAGE: 97
THE LOST WEEKEND (1945)
ORIGINAL FRENCH 63 X 47 IN. (160 X 119 CM)
STYLE B
ART BY BORIS GRINSSON (1907-1999)
PRIVATE COLLECTION

PAGE: 98
GILDA (1946)
ORIGINAL US 41 X 27 IN. (104 X 69 CM)
STYLE B
ART DIRECTION BY JACK KERNESS (1911-2010)
PHOTO BY ROBERT COBURN (1900-1990)
PRIVATE COLLECTION

PAGE: 101
THE BIG SLEEP (1946)
ORIGINAL FRENCH 63 X 47 IN. (160 X 119 CM)
ART BY VICENTE CRISTELLYS (D.1970)
PRIVATE COLLECTION

PAGE: 102
NOTORIOUS (1946)
ORIGINAL FRENCH 31 X 24 IN. (79 X 61 CM)
ART BY PIERRE SEGOGNE (DATES UNKNOWN)
PRIVATE COLLECTION

PAGE: 105
OUT OF THE PAST (1947)
ORIGINAL US 41 X 27 IN. (104 X 69 CM)
ART BY WILLIAM ROSE (DATES UNKNOWN)
COURTESY OF THE GREG FERLAND COLLECTION

PAGE: 106
KISS OF DEATH (1947)
ORIGINAL US 41 X 27 IN. (104 X 69 CM)
ART DIRECTION BY JEROME NOVAK (DATES UNKNOWN)
PRIVATE COLLECTION

PAGE: 109
THE LADY FROM SHANGHAI (1947)
ORIGINAL ITALIAN 55 X 39 IN. (140 X 99 CM)
ART BY ANSELMO BALLESTER (1897-1974)
COURTESY OF THE HASTINGS COLLECTION

PAGE: 110
FORCE OF EVIL (1948)
ORIGINAL ITALIAN 79 X 55 IN. (201 X 140 CM)
ART BY AVERARDO CIRIELLO (1918-?D.)
PRIVATE COLLECTION

PAGE: 113
LADRI DI BICICLETTE (1948)
ORIGINAL ITALIAN 79 X 55 IN. (201 X 140 CM)
ART BY ERCOLE BRINI (1913-1989)
PRIVATE COLLECTION

PAGE: 114
THE ASPHALT JUNGLE (1950)
ORIGINAL ITALIAN 79 X 55 IN. (201 X 140 CM)
ART BY C. PREVITERA (DATES UNKNOWN)
PRIVATE COLLECTION

PAGE: 117
NO WAY OUT (1950)
ORIGINAL US 41 X 27 IN. (104 X 69 CM)
ART BY PAUL RAND (1914-1996)
PRIVATE COLLECTION

PAGE: 118
SUNSET BOULEVARD (1950)
ORIGINAL POLISH 33 X 23 IN. (84 X 58 CM)
ART BY WALDEMAR SWIERZY (B.1931)
PRIVATE COLLECTION

PAGE: 121
GUN CRAZY (1950)
ORIGINAL US 41 X 27 IN. (104 X 69 CM)
ARTIST UNKNOWN
COURTESY OF THE GREG FERLAND COLLECTION

PAGE: 122
THE BIG HEAT (1953)
ORIGINAL ITALIAN 79 X 55 IN. (201 X 140 CM)
ART BY ANSELMO BALLESTER (1897-1974)
COURTESY OF THE DAVE KEHR COLLECTION

PAGE: 125
LE SALAIRE DE LA PEUR (1953)
ORIGINAL FRENCH 63 X 47 IN. (160 X 119 CM)
STYLE B
ART BY ROBERT LEVEQUE
COURTESY OF THE BOYNETT COLLECTION

PAGE: 126-127
FROM HERE TO ETERNITY (1953)
ORIGINAL FRENCH 63 x 94 IN. (160 x 239 CM)
ART BY RENÉ PÉRON (1904-1972)
PRIVATE COLLECTION

PAGE: 128
CRIME WAVE (1954)
ORIGINAL ITALIAN 79 x 55 IN. (201 x 140 CM)
ART BY LUIGI MARTINATI (1893-1984)
PRIVATE COLLECTION

PAGE: 131
THE BIG KNIFE (1955)
ORIGINAL ITALIAN 79 x 55 IN. (201 x 140 CM)
ART BY NICOLA SIMBARI (DATES UNKNOWN)
COURTESY OF THE BOYNETT COLLECTION

PAGE: 133
THE BIG KNIFE (1955)
ORIGINAL GERMAN 33 x 23 IN. (84 x 58 CM)
ART BY HANS BRAUN (DATES UNKNOWN)
PRIVATE COLLECTION

PAGE: 134
THE BIG KNIFE (1955)
ORIGINAL US 22 x 28 IN. (56 x 71 CM)
STYLE B
ARTIST UNKNOWN
PRIVATE COLLECTION

PAGE: 136-137
KISS ME DEADLY (1955)
ORIGINAL US 22 x 28 IN. (56 x 71 CM)
STYLE B
ARTIST UNKNOWN
PRIVATE COLLECTION

PAGE: 138
12 ANGRY MEN (1957)
ORIGINAL US 22 x 28 IN. (56 x 71 CM)
STYLE B
ARTIST UNKNOWN
PRIVATE COLLECTION

PAGE: 141
LES DIABOLIQUES (1955)
ORIGINAL FRENCH 31 x 24 IN. (79 x 61 CM)
ART BY RAYMOND GID (1905-2000)
COURTESY OF THE FRENCH NEW WAVE COLLECTION

PAGE: 142
INVASION OF THE BODY SNATCHERS (1955)
ORIGINAL US 41 x 27 IN. (104 x 69 CM)
ARTIST UNKNOWN
COURTESY OF THE BOYNETT COLLECTION

PAGE: 145
THE MAN WITH THE GOLDEN ARM (1955)
ORIGINAL US 41 x 27 IN. (104 x 69 CM)
PREMIERE POSTER
ART BY SAUL BASS (1920-1996)
COURTESY OF THE ADRIAN MURRELL COLLECTION

PAGE: 146
ANATOMY OF A MURDER (1959)
ORIGINAL US 41 x 27 IN. (104 x 69 CM)
ART BY SAUL BASS (1920-1996)
COURTESY OF THE BOYNETT COLLECTION

PAGE: 147
VERTIGO (1958)
ORIGINAL US 40 x 30 IN. (102 x 76 CM)
ART BY SAUL BASS (1920-1996)
PRIVATE COLLECTION

PAGE: 148
UN CONDAMNÉ À MORT S'EST ÉCHAPPÉ OU LE VENT SOUFFLE OÙ IL VEUT (1956)
ORIGINAL FRENCH 63 x 47 IN. (160 x 119 CM)
STYLE B
ART BY PAUL COLIN (1892-1985)
COURTESY OF THE FRENCH NEW WAVE COLLECTION

PAGE: 151
ATTACK OF THE 50 FOOT WOMAN (1958)
ORIGINAL US 41 x 27 IN. (104 x 69 CM)
ART BY REYNOLD BROWN (1917-1991)
PRIVATE COLLECTION

PAGE: 152
MON ONCLE (1958)
ORIGINAL FRENCH 63 x 47 IN. (160 x 119 CM)
ART BY PIERRE ÉTAIX (B.1928)
COURTESY OF THE FRENCH NEW WAVE COLLECTION

PAGE: 155
ASCENSEUR POUR L'ÉCHAFAUD (1958)
ORIGINAL POLISH 33 x 23 IN. (84 x 58 CM)
ART BY JAN LENICA (1928-2001)
COURTESY OF THE FRENCH NEW WAVE COLLECTION

PAGE: 156
À BOUT DE SOUFFLE (1960)
ORIGINAL FRENCH 31 x 24 IN. (79 x 61 CM)
ART BY CLÉMENT HUREL (1927-2008)
COURTESY OF THE FRENCH NEW WAVE COLLECTION

PAGE: 159
PICKPOCKET (1959)
ORIGINAL FRENCH 16 x 12 IN. (41 x 30 CM)
ART BY CHRISTIAN BROUTIN (B.1933)
COURTESY OF THE FRENCH NEW WAVE COLLECTION

PAGE: 160
LA DOLCE VITA (1959)
ORIGINAL ITALIAN 79 x 55 IN. (201 x 140 CM)
STYLE A
ART BY GIORGIO OLIVETTI (1908-?D.)
COURTESY OF THE GREG FERLAND COLLECTION

PAGE: 163
LA DOLCE VITA (1960)
ORIGINAL ITALIAN 79 x 55 IN. (201 x 140 CM)
STYLE B
ART BY SANDRO SIMEONI (1928-2007)
COURTESY OF THE GREG FERLAND COLLECTION

PAGE: 164-165
PSYCHO (1960)
ORIGINAL BRITISH 30 x 40 IN. (76 x 102 CM)
STYLE B
ARTIST UNKNOWN
PRIVATE COLLECTION

PAGE: 166-167
PEEPING TOM (1960)
ORIGINAL BRITISH 30 x 40 IN. (76 x 102 CM)
ARTIST UNKNOWN
PRIVATE COLLECTION

PAGE: 168
BREAKFAST AT TIFFANY'S (1961)
ORIGINAL US 41 x 27 IN. (104 x 69 CM)
PREMIERE POSTER
ART BY ROBERT E. MCGINNIS (B.1926)
PRIVATE COLLECTION

PAGE: 170-171
THE CONNECTION (1962)
ORIGINAL BRITISH 30 x 40 IN. (76 x 102 CM)
ACADEMY CINEMA
ART BY PETER STRAUSFELD (1910-1980)
COURTESY OF THE BOYNETT COLLECTION

PAGE: 173
8½ (1963)
ORIGINAL CZECHOSLOVAKIAN 33 x 23 IN. (84 x 58 CM)
ART BY BEDŘICH DLOUHÝ (B.1932)
COURTESY OF THE BOYNETT COLLECTION

PAGE: 174
THE BIRDS (1963)
ORIGINAL POLISH 33 x 23 IN. (84 x 58 CM)
ART BY BRONISŁAW ZELEK (B.1935)
COURTESY OF THE BOYNETT COLLECTION

PAGE: 177
GOLDFINGER (1964)
ORIGINAL BRITISH 30 x 20 IN. (76 x 51 CM)
ART BY ROBERT BROWNJOHN (1925-1970)
© 1964 DANJAQ LLC AND UNITED ARTISTS CORPORATION
COURTESY OF THE JQL COLLECTION

PAGE: 178
THE IPCRESS FILE (1965)
ORIGINAL BRITISH 41 x 27 IN. (104 x 69 CM)
ART BY ANGELO CESSELON (1922-1992)
COURTESY OF THE BOYNETT COLLECTION

PAGE: 181
CHELSEA GIRLS (1966)
ORIGINAL BRITISH 30 x 20 IN. (76 x 51 CM)
ART BY ALAN ALDRIDGE (B.1937)
COURTESY OF THE BOYNETT COLLECTION

PAGE: 182
BLOW-UP (1966)
ORIGINAL CZECHOSLOVAKIAN 33 x 23 IN. (84 x 58 CM)
ART BY MILAN GRYGAR (B.1926)
PRIVATE COLLECTION

PAGE: 185
PLAYTIME (1967)
ORIGINAL POLISH 33 X 23 IN. (84 X 58 CM)
ART BY JERZY FLISAK (1930-2008)
PRIVATE COLLECTION

PAGE: 186
A FISTFUL OF DOLLARS (1964)
ORIGINAL US 41 X 27 IN. (104 X 69 CM)
ADVANCE POSTER
ART BY FRED OTNES (B.1930)
COURTESY OF THE CHRISTOPHER FRAYLING COLLECTION

PAGE: 189
LA CHINOISE (1967)
ORIGINAL JAPANESE 28 X 20 IN. (72 X 51 CM)
ART BY KIYOSHI AWAZU (1929-2009)
COURTESY OF THE FRENCH NEW WAVE COLLECTION

PAGE: 190
POINT BLANK (1967)
ORIGINAL US 41 X 27 IN. (104 X 69 CM)
DESIGN BY NELSON LYON (1939-2012)
ART BY SERRANO (DATES UNKNOWN)
PRIVATE COLLECTION

PAGE: 193
ROSEMARY'S BABY (1968)
ORIGINAL US 41 X 27 IN. (104 X 69 CM)
DESIGN BY STEVE FRANKFURT (1931-2012)
ART BY PHILIP GIPS (DATES UNKNOWN)
PRIVATE COLLECTION

PAGE: 194
2001: A SPACE ODYSSEY (1968)
ORIGINAL US 41 X 27 IN. (104 X 69 CM)
STYLE D
DESIGN BY MIKE KAPLAN
COURTESY OF THE BOYNETT COLLECTION

PAGE: 196-197
ACID – DELIRIO DEI SENSI (1968)
ORIGINAL ITALIAN 39 X 108 IN. (99 X 274 CM)
ARTIST UNKNOWN
PRIVATE COLLECTION

PAGE: 199
THE FRENCH CONNECTION (1971)
ORIGINAL US 41 X 27 IN. (104 X 69 CM)
STYLE B
ARTIST UNKNOWN
COURTESY OF THE BOYNETT COLLECTION

PAGE: 200
CABARET (1972)
ORIGINAL POLISH 33 X 23 IN. (84 X 58 CM)
ART BY WIKTOR GORKA (1922-2004)
REEL POSTER ARCHIVE

PAGE: 203
MAGNUM FORCE (1973)
ORIGINAL US 41 X 27 IN. (104 X 69 CM)
DESIGN BY BILL GOLD (B.1921)
PHOTO BY PHILIPPE HALSMAN (1906-1979)
PRIVATE COLLECTION

PAGE: 204
THE LONG GOODBYE (1973)
ORIGINAL US 41 X 27 IN. (104 X 69 CM)
ART BY RICHARD AMSEL (1947-1985)
PRIVATE COLLECTION

PAGE: 207
THE BIG SLEEP (1946)
ORIGINAL SWEDISH 39 X 27 IN. (99 X 69 CM)
RE-RELEASE 1974
ART BY OLLE FRANKZÉN (B.1944)
COURTESY OF THE BOYNETT COLLECTION

PAGE: 208
THE KILLING OF A CHINESE BOOKIE (1976)
ORIGINAL US 38 X 18 IN. (97 X 46 CM)
DESIGN AND PHOTOS BY SAM SHAW (1912-1999)
PRIVATE COLLECTION

PAGE: 211
ANNIE HALL (1977)
ORIGINAL US 41 X 27 IN. (104 X 69 CM)
ARTIST UNKNOWN
REEL POSTER ARCHIVE

PAGE: 212
THE MODERNS (1988)
ORIGINAL US 41 X 27 IN. (104 X 69 CM)
ART BY KEITH CARRADINE (B.1949)
PRIVATE COLLECTION

PAGE: 215
UNFORGIVEN (1992)
ORIGINAL US 41 X 27 IN. (104 X 69 CM)
FIRST ADVANCE
DESIGN BY BILL GOLD (B.1921)
PHOTO BY EDDIE ADAMS (1933-2004)
PRIVATE COLLECTION

PAGE: 216
THE SHINING (1980)
ORIGINAL US 36 X 24 IN. (91 X 61 CM)
2008 ALAMO DRAFTHOUSE 'ROLLING ROADSHOW' RELEASE
LIMITED, HAND NUMBERED AND SIGNED EDITION OF 250.
ART BY JEFF KLEINSMITH (B.1967)
COURTESY OF JEFF KLEINSMITH

Title index

12 Angry Men, 138
2001: A Space Odyssey, 194
400 Blows, The, 12
8½, 173

Acid – delirio dei sensi, 196-7
Anatomy of a Murder, 146
Annie Hall, 211
Ascenseur pour l'échafaud, 155
Asphalt Jungle, The, 115
Attack of the 50 Foot Woman, 151
Avventure straordinarissime di Saturnino Farandola, Le, 21

Berlin: Die Sinfonie der Grosstadt, 33
Bicycle Thieves, 113
Big Heat, The, 122
Big Knife, The, 131, 133, 134
Big Shot, The, 81
Big Sleep, The, 101, 207
Birds, The, 174
Blind Husbands, 25
Blow-Up, 182
Bout de souffle, À, 156
Breakfast at Tiffany's, 168
Breathless, 156
Brief Encounter, 94-5
Bringing Up Baby, 71

Cabaret, 200
Cabin in the Sky, 87
Canary Murder Case, The, 43
Casablanca, 83
Chelsea Girls, 181
Chinatown, 15
Chinoise, La, 189
Condamné à mort s'est échappé, Un, 148
Connection, The, 170-1
Crime Wave, 128

Deadly is the Female, 121
Devil's Harvest, 84
Diaboliques, Les, 141
Dolce Vita, La, 18, 160, 163

Double Indemnity, 92

Elevator to the Gallows, 155
Extase, 55

Fistful of Dollars, A, 186
Force of Evil, 110
Frankenstein, 48
French Connection, The, 199
From Here to Eternity, 126-7

Gilda, 98
Goldfinger, 177
Grass: A Nation's Battle for Life, 39
Gun Crazy, 121

Hollywood, 29
Horse Feathers, 67

Ingagi, 44
Inhumaine, L', 30
Invasion of the Body Snatchers, 142
Ipcress File, The, 178

Killing of a Chinese Bookie, The, 208
King Kong, 57
Kiss Me Deadly, 136-7
Kiss of Death, 106

Ladies They Talk About, 61
Ladri di biciclette, 113
Lady from Shanghai, The, 109
Last Gangster, The, 68
Lift to the Scaffold, 155
Long Goodbye, The, 204
Lost Weekend, The, 97

M, 47
Magnum Force, 203
Maltese Falcon, The, 16
Man Escaped, A, 148
Man with the Golden Arm, The, 145
Metropolis, 8, 34, 36-7

Moderns, The, 212
Mon Oncle, 7, 11, 152

Narcotic, 64
No Way Out, 117
Notorious, 102

Opium, 26
Out of the Past, 105
Outlaw, The, 78

Peeping Tom, 166-7
Pickpocket, 159
Playtime, 185
Point Blank, 190
Psycho, 4, 164-5

Quatre Cents Coups, Les, 12

Rosemary's Baby, 193

Salaire de la peur, Le, 125
Scarface, 50
Sexe faible, Le, 63
Shining, The, 216
Stagecoach, 73
Sullivan's Travels, 74
Sunset Boulevard, 118
Supernatural, 58

Teen Age, 89
This Gun For Hire, 77
To Have and Have Not, 91

Underworld, 40
Unforgiven, 215

Vampires, Les, 22
Vertigo, 147

Wages of Fear, The, 125
Weaker Sex, The, 63
What Price Hollywood?, 53

Artist index

Adams, Eddie, 215
Alajálov, Constantin, 67
Aldridge, Alan, 181
Amsel, Richard, 15, 204
Awazu, Kiyoshi, 189

Ballester, Anselmo, 109, 122
Bass, Saul, 145, 146, 147
Bilinsky, Boris, 36-7
Bourgeois, George 'Djo', 30
Braun, Hans, 133
Brini, Ercole, 113
Broutin, Christian, 159
Brown, Reynold, 151
Brownjohn, Robert, 177

Carradine, Keith, 212
Cecchetto, 47
Cesselon, Angelo, 178
Ciriello, Averardo, 110
Coburn, Robert, 98
Colin, Paul, 63, 148
Cristellys, Vicente, 101

Dlouhý, Bedřich, 173

Étaix, Pierre, 7, 11, 152

Flisak, Jerzy, 185
Frankfurt, Steve, 193
Frankzén, Olle, 207

Gid, Raymond, 141

Gips, Philip, 193
Gold, Bill, 203, 215
Gorka, Wiktor, 200
Grinsson, Boris, 81, 97
Grosz, Karoly, 48
Grygar, Milan, 182

Halsman, Philippe, 203
Hirschfeld, Al, 87
Hurel, Clément, 156
Hurrell, George, 78

Jacquelin, Jean, 68
Jaedicker, Herbert 73

Kallis, Maurice, 58, 74, 77
Kaplan, Mike, 194
Kerness, Jack, 98
Kleinsmith, Jeff, 216

Lancy, Bernard, 71
Leveque, Robert, 125
Lyon, Nelson, 190

McCormick, Barrett, 57
McGinnis, Robert E., 168
Mariani, Carlo, 55
Martinati, Luigi, 91, 128
Matejko, Theo, 26
Mauzan, Achille Lucien, 22

Novak, Jerome, 106

Olivetti, Giorgio, 160
Otnes, Fred, 186

Péron, René, 126-7
Pigeot, Pierre, 83
Previtera, C., 115
Psaier, Pietro, 16

Rand, Paul, 117
Reiz, Lopez, 92
Richee, Eugene Robert, 43
Robida, Albert, 21
Rose, William, 105

Schulz-Neudamm, Heinz, 8, 34
Segogne, Pierre, 102
Serrano, 190
Shaw, Sam, 208
Simbari, Nicola, 131
Simeoni, Sandro, 18, 163
Sisk, Bob, 57
Strausfeld, Peter, 170-1
Strumf, David L., 57
Swierzy, Waldemar, 118

Trotta, Vincent, 29, 58

Vargas, Alberto, 61
Venabert, 33

Zelek, Bronisław, 174

Acknowledgements

Apart from my 'team' directly involved in producing this book which I owe a huge thank you to, I would like to thank the following friends and colleagues for their continual help and support:

Tarek AbuZayyad; Farhad Amir Ahmadi; Richard Allen; Lisa Baker; Richard Barclay; Paul Barthaud; Dominique Besson; Merv Bloch; Daniel Bouteiller; Luisa Brassi, Glyn Callingham; Jean-Louis Capitaine; Anne Coco; Chris Dark; Priya Elan; Greg Ferland; Olle Frankzén; Leslie Gardner; Richard Garvey; Dan Gennoe; Jim Gipe; Marc Glanville; Kim Goddard; Bill Gold; Armando Giuffrida; Trevor Gray; Roxanna Hajiani; Helmut Hamm; Richard Harris; Ross Hastings; Bruce Hershenson; Sarah Hodgson; Andy Howick; Katuya Ishida; Beth Jacques; Maria Johnson; Mike Kaplan; Dave Kehr; Jeff Kleinsmith; Billie Kisch; Peter Langs; Sara Lindström; John Longhurst; Toni Lorenzo; June Marsh; Phoebe Martel; Ed Mason; Kirby McDaniel; Ron Moore; Adrian Murrell; Regina Nepsha; Bill Ndini; Samira Kafala Noakes and Jake Noakes; Bruno Nouril and Ksenia Yachmetz Nouril; Hamid and Doris Nourmand; Sammy and Shaeda Nourmand; Gabriele Pantucci; Luigi Paratella; Fari Peyman; Eric Rachlis; Stephen Rebello; Ira M. Resnick; Walter Reuben; Steve Rose; Matt Severson; Ken Schacter; Philip Shalam; Jonathan Stone; Dan Strebin; Parisa Taghizadeh; Claudia Teachman; Caroline Theakstone; Channing Thomson; Carey Wallace; Offer Waterman; Katherine Williams; Fred Zentner and Serge and Florence Zreik.

Special thanks to Andy Johnson for always being there when I have needed him and photographing all the material that I have ever used in any of the books and catalogues which I produced; Eric Jean-Baptiste (my favorite restorer) for always doing a top notch job on the posters that I've handled; John Kisch for always being on my side; Joseph Baldassare for helping me every step of the way in setting R|A|P up and getting it on the road and my friend Joe Burtis for being Joe Burtis.

Bibliography

Specific quotes: p.31: Loos, Adolf, quote taken from L'Herbier, Marcel, *La tête qui tourne* (Belfond, 1979); p.35, Lang, Fritz, quote taken from Bogdanovich, Peter, *Who the Devil Made It?* (Arrow Books, 1998); p.52, Selznick, David O., quote taken from Selznick, David O., *Memo From David O. Selznick* (Viking Press, 1972); p.60, Vargas, Alberto, quote taken from Holstead, Carol E., 'Vargas, Alberto', *American National Biography Online* (<http://www.anb.org/articles/17/17-01424.html>, accessed 8 March 2013); p.79, Russell, Jane, quote taken from Thornton, Michael, 'The Siren with the Two Greatest Assests in Tinseltwon', *The Daily Mail* (<http://www.dailymail.co.uk/femail/article-1362040>, accessed 2 March 2013); p.111: Polonsky, Abraham, quote taken from Pechter, W., 'Abraham Polonsky and 'Force of Evil'', *Film Quarterly*, vol. 15, nr. 3 – Spring 1962; p.116: Moholy-Nagy, László, quote taken from Heller, Steven, 'Thoughts on Rand', *Print*, May/June 1997, Vol. 51, Issue 3; p.123, Ballester, Anselmo, quote taken from Dell'anno, M. and Soccio M., *Cinema di carta: cinquant'anni di manifesti cinematografici* (Foggia, 1984); p.144, Scorsese, Martin, quote taken from p.vi of Bass, Jennifer and Kirkham, Pat, *Saul Bass: A Life in Film & Design* (Laurence King, 2011); p.192: Frankfurt, Steve, quote taken from Elliott, Stuart, 'A TV Salute to the Designer of Some Memorable Movie Promotions', *The New York Times* (28 April 2005); p.198, Friedkin, William, quote taken from King, Susan, 'Friedkin Restores His 'Connection'', *LA Times* (27 September 2001); p.202: Gold, Bill, quote taken from Frayling, Christopher and Nourmand, Tony, *Bill Gold: PosterWorks* (Reel Art Press, 2010); p.213: Carradine, Keith, quote taken from Champin, Charles, 'Keith Carradine Paints His Way into 'The Moderns' corner', *LA Times* (22 March 1988); p.214: Frayling, Christopher, quote taken from Frayling, Christopher and Nourmand, Tony, *Bill Gold: PosterWorks* (Reel Art Press, 2010); p.217, Kleinsmith, Jeff, quote taken from correspondence directly with Reel Art Press, February 2013.

General bibliography: Bass, Jennifer and Kirkham, Pat, *Saul Bass: A Life in Film & Design* (Laurence King, 2011); 'Blind Husbands', *The New York Times* (8 December 1919); 'Blind Husbands', *Variety* (12 December 1919); Bogdanovich, Peter, *Who the Devil Made It?* (Arrow Books, 1998); Curry, Adrian, '"Jules et Jim" and an Interview with Designer Christian Broutin' *Notebook Digital Magazine* (<http://mubi.com/notebook>, accessed 26 Feb 2013); Dell'anno, M. and Soccio M., *Cinema di carta: cinquant'anni di manifesti cinematografici* (Foggia, 1984); Elliott, Stuart, 'A TV Salute to the Designer of Some Memorable Movie Promotions', *The New York Times* (28 April 2005); Gelmis, Joseph, 'Another Look at Space Odyssey', *Newsday* (20 April 1968); Godfrey, Jason, *Bibliographic: 100 Classic Graphic Design Books* (Laurence King, 2009); Frayling, Christopher and Nourmand, Tony, *Bill Gold: PosterWorks* (Reel Art Press, 2010); Fuller, Graham, 'Film: An Undervalued American Classic', *The New York Times* (18 June 2000); Hall, Mordaunt, 'Scarface', *The New York Times* (20 May 1932); Heller, Steven, *Paul Rand* (Phaidon Press, 1999); Heller, Steven, 'Thoughts on Rand', *Print*, May/June 1997, Vol. 51, Issue 3; L'Herbier, Marcel, *La tête qui tourne* (Belfond, 1979); Holstead, Carol E., 'Vargas, Alberto', *American National Biography Online* (<http://www.anb.org/articles/17/17-01424.html>, accessed 8 March 2013); Kanner, Bernice, 'On Madison Avenue: FGB Covers the Bases', *New York Magazine* (11 Mar 1991); King, Susan, 'Friedkin Restores His 'Connection'', *LA Times* (27 September 2001); Life Editors, 'Speaking of Pictures ... A Frenchman Foresaw Mechanized War in 1883, *Life* (15 June 1942); Pechter, W., 'Abraham Polonsky and 'Force of Evil'', *Film Quarterly*, vol. 15, nr. 3 – Spring 1962; Rebello, Steve and Allen, Richard, *Reel Art: Great Posters from the Golden Age of the Silver Screen* (Abbeville Press, 1988); Resnick, Ira, *Starstruck: Vintage Movie Posters from Classic Hollywood* (Abbeville Press, 2010); Scorsese, Martin and Wilson, Michael Henry, *A Personal Journey With Martin Scorsese Through American Movies* (Hyperion Books, 1997); Selznick, David O., *Memo From David O. Selznick* (Viking Press, 1972); Thornton, Michael, 'The Siren with the Two Greatest Assests in Tinseltwon', *The Daily Mail* (<http://www.dailymail.co.uk/femail/article-1362040>, accessed 2 March 2013); Weiler, A.H., '12 Angry Men', *The New York Times* (15 April 1957); Wells, H.G., 'Metropolis', *The New York Times* (17 April 1927); Winsten, Archer, 'The Asphalt Jungle', *New York Post* (June 1950); Champin, Charles, 'Keith Carradine Paints His Way into 'The Moderns' corner', *LA Times* (22 March 1988).

Published 2013 by Reel Art Press, an imprint of Rare Art Press Ltd., London, UK.
www.reelartpress.com

First edition
10 9 8 7 6 5 4 3 2 1

ISBN: 978-0-9572610-8-2

Copyright © Rare Art Press Ltd., 2013.
All rights reserved.

Copyright © introduction text: Christopher Frayling
Copyright © all text in format: Rare Art Press Ltd, 2013.

No part of this publication may be reproduced, stored in a retrieval system, or transmitted in any form or by any means, electronic, mechanical, photocopying, recording or otherwise, without written permission of the publisher. Any person who does any unauthorized act in relation to this publication may be liable to criminal prosecution and civil claims for damages. Every effort has been made to seek permission to reproduce those images whose copyright does not reside with Rare Art Press Ltd., and we are grateful to the individuals and institutions who have assisted in this task. Any omissions are entirely unintentional, and the details should be addressed to Rare Art Press Ltd.

Printed in China